The Betrayal of the Body

BOOKS BY ALEXANDER LOWEN, M.D.

Fear of Life
The Language of the Body
Love and Orgasm
Pleasure

The Betrayal of
the Body

Alexander Lowen, M.D.

COLLIER BOOKS

Macmillan Publishing Company

NEW YORK

COLLIER MACMILLAN PUBLISHERS

LONDON

LIBRARY OF CONGRESS CATALOG CARD NUMBER: 67-12796

ISBN 0-02-077300-5

First Collier Books Edition 1969

20   19

Macmillan Publishing Company
866 Third Avenue, New York, N.Y. 10022
Collier Macmillan Canada, Inc.

Macmillan Books are available at special discounts for bulk purchases for sales promotions, premiums, fund-raising, or educational use. Special editions or book excerpts can also be created to specification. For details, contact:

Special Sales Director
Macmillan Publishing Company
866 Third Avenue
New York, New York 10022

Printed in the United States of America

TO MY PATIENTS

*Whose courage to confront
their terror and despair
inspires these pages*

ACKNOWLEDGMENTS

Mrs. Adele Lewis, Executive Secretary of The Institute for Bio-Energetic Analysis, gave generously of her time and energy to the preparation of this book—editing, offering criticism, and making suggestions. For her indefatigable effort I am deeply grateful. Dr. John C. Pierrakos listened patiently to many readings and offered comments. Mr. Walter Skalecki prepared the drawings and diagrams. Mr. Carl Morse, senior editor of the Macmillan Company, helped greatly with his support and advice. To these people and others who have shown a sincere interest in my ideas and work, I wish to express my gratitude.

Contents

1. **THE PROBLEM OF IDENTITY**   1
   The Image versus Reality   3
   Reality and the Body   5
   The Ego and the Body   7

2. **THE SCHIZOID DISTURBANCE**   19
   Varieties of Schizoid Personality and Behavior   22
   Approaches to the Schizoid Problem   29

3. **THE DEFENSE AGAINST TERROR**   36
   Fear and Terror   36
   The Dynamics of the Schizoid Defense   40
   The Schizoid Barricade   43
   The Schizoid Retreat   47
   Breakdown and Schizophrenia   49

4. **THE FORSAKEN BODY**   53
   Self-possession   53
   The Schizoid Mask   55
   Bodily Rigidity, Fragmentation, and Collapse   62

5. **THE BODY IMAGE**   71
   The Mask of the Clown   73
   The Doll   77
   Depersonalization   82
   Seduction and Rejection   86

6. **THE PSYCHOLOGY OF DESPERATION**   91
   Self-destructive Behavior   91
   The Technique of Survival   95

7.   ILLUSION AND REALITY   109
     Desperation and Illusion   109
     Despair and Dissociation   114
     Parental Unreality   120
     The Reigning Illusions   123

8.   DEMONS AND MONSTERS   128

9.   THE PHYSIOLOGY OF PANIC   145
     Respiration   146
     Energy Metabolism   157
     Motility   160

10. EATING AND SLEEPING   165
     Compulsion and Illusion   165
     Eating and Sexuality   167
     Paranoid Behavior and Overeating   170
     Sleeping   182

11. ORIGIN AND CAUSES   189
     Constitutional Factors   190
     Psychological Factors   197
     The Trauma of Identification   200
     Sex and Paranoia   206

12. RECLAIMING THE BODY   209
     The Therapy of a Schizoid Person   225

13. THE ACHIEVEMENT OF IDENTITY   232
     Unmasking the Role   234
     Self-assertion   241
     Transference, Resistance, and
         Countertransference   248

14. THE EGO AND THE BODY   252
     Bewitchment   252
     Community versus Causality   255
     The Conceptual Emotions   260
     Knowledge and Understanding   265

     NOTES   271

The Betrayal of the Body

1

The Problem
of Identity

NORMALLY, people don't ask themselves, Who am I? One's identity is taken for granted. Each person carries in his wallet papers that serve to identify him. Consciously, he knows who he is. However, below the surface a problem of identity exists. On the border of consciousness he is disturbed by dissatisfactions, uneasy about decisions, and tormented by the feeling of "missing out" on life. He is in conflict with himself, unsure of his feelings, and his insecurity reflects his problem of identity. When dissatisfaction becomes despair and insecurity verges on panic an individual may ask himself, Who am I? This question indicates that the façade through which a person seeks identity is crumbling. The use of a façade or the adoption of a role as a means to achieve identity denotes a split between the ego and the body. I define this split as the schizoid disturbance which underlies every problem of identity.

For example, a famous artist walked into my office and said, "I am confused and desperate. I don't know who I am. I walk down the street and ask myself, Who are you?"

It would have been meaningless to reply, "You are the well-known painter whose work hangs in many museums." He knew that. What he complained of was a loss of the feeling of self, the loss of contact with some vital aspect of existence that gives meaning to life. This missing element was an identification with the body, the foundation upon which a personal life is erected. My artist patient became actively aware of this missing element in a dramatic experience. He told me:

1

The other day I looked in the mirror, and I became frightened when I realized it was me. I thought, This is what people see when they look at me.

The image was a stranger. My face and my body didn't seem to belong to me. . . . I felt very unreal.

This experience, in which there is a loss of feeling of the body, with accompanying sensations of strangeness and unreality, is known as a depersonalization. It denotes a break with reality and occurs in the first stages of a psychotic episode. If it continues, the person loses not only the feeling of identity but also his conscious awareness of identity. Fortunately, this episode was short-lived in my patient. He was able to reestablish some contact with his body, so that the feeling of unreality disappeared. However, his identification with his body remained tenuous, and the problem of his identity persisted.

The feeling of identity stems from a feeling of contact with the body. To know who one is, an individual must be aware of what he feels. He should know the expression on his face, how he holds himself, and the way he moves. Without this awareness of bodily feeling and attitude, a person becomes split into a disembodied spirit and a disenchanted body. I will return again to the case of the artist.

As he sat opposite me, I saw his drawn face, his empty eyes, his tightly set jaw, and his frozen body. In his immobility and shallow breathing, I could sense his fear and panic. He, however, was not aware of the gauntness of his face, the blankness of his eyes, the tension in his jaw, or the tightness of his body. He did not feel his fear and panic. Being out of touch with his body, he only sensed his confusion and desperation.

The complete loss of body contact characterizes the schizophrenic state. Broadly speaking, the schizophrenic doesn't know who he is, and is so much out of touch with reality that he cannot even phrase the question. On the other hand, the schizoid individual knows he has a body and is, therefore, oriented in time and space. But since his ego is not identified with his body and does not perceive it in an alive way, he feels unrelated to the world and to people. Similarly, his conscious sense of identity is unrelated to the way he feels about himself. This conflict does not exist in a healthy person whose ego is identified with his body and in whom the knowledge of his identity stems from the feeling of the body.

A confusion of identity typifies most persons in our culture. Many people struggle with a diffused sense of unreality about themselves and their lives. They become desperate when the ego image they have created proves empty and meaningless. They feel threatened and become angry when the role they have adopted in life is challenged. Sooner or later, an identity based on images and roles fails to provide satisfaction. Depressed and discouraged, they consult a psychiatrist. Their problem is, as Rollo May points out, the schizoid disturbance.

> Many psychotherapists have pointed out that more and more patients exhibit schizoid features and the "typical" kind of psychic problem in our day is not hysteria, as it was in Freud's time, but the schizoid type—that is to say, the problem of persons who are detached, unrelated, lacking in affect, tending towards depersonalization, and covering up their problems by means of intellectualizations and technical formulations. . . .
>
> There is also plenty of evidence that the sense of isolation, the alienation of one's self from the world is suffered not only by people in pathological conditions, but by countless "normal" persons as well in our day.[1]

The alienation of people in the modern world—the estrangement of man from his work, his fellow man, and himself—has been described by many authors and is the central theme of Erich Fromm's writings. The alienated individual's love is romanticized, his sex is compulsive, his work is mechanical, and his achievements are egotistic. In an alienated society, these activities lose their personal meaning. This loss is replaced by an image.

THE IMAGE VERSUS REALITY

The schizoid disturbance creates a dissociation of the image from reality. The term "image" refers to symbols and mental creations as opposed to the reality of physical experience. This is not to say that images are unreal, but they have a different order of reality than bodily phenomena. An image derives its reality from its association with feeling or sensation. When this association is disrupted, the image becomes abstract. The discrepancy between image and reality is most clearly seen in delusional schizophrenics. The classic example is the demented person who imagines he is Jesus Christ or Napoleon. On the other hand, "mental health" refers to the condition where image and reality coincide. A healthy person has an image of himself that agrees with the way his body looks and feels.

In the social realm the image has its positive as well as its negative aspects. The alleviation of suffering and misfortune on a large scale would not be possible without the use of an image to mobilize a mass response. Every humanitarian effort has achieved its goal through the use of an appealing image. But an image can be used negatively to incite hatred and to bring destruction upon others. When a policeman is pictured as a symbol of suppressive authority he becomes an object of distrust and hatred. When the Red Chinese portray the American as a devilish exploiter of people he becomes a monster to be destroyed. The image blots out the personal humanity of an individual. It reduces him to an abstraction. It becomes easy to kill a human being if one sees him only as an image.

If the image is dangerous on a social level, where its function is openly admitted, its effects are disastrous in personal relationships, where its action is insidious. One sees this in the family where a man tries to fulfill his image of fatherhood in opposition to the needs of his children. Just as he sees himself in terms of his image, so he views his child as an image rather than as a person with feelings and desires of his own. In this situation, upbringing takes the form of trying to fit the child to an image that is frequently a projection of the father's unconscious self-image. The child who is forced to conform to a parent's unconscious image loses his sense of self, his feeling of identity, and his contact with reality.

The loss of the feeling of identity has its roots in the family situation. Brought up according to images of success, popularity, sex appeal, intellectual and cultural snobbery, status, self-sacrifice, and so forth, the individual sees others as images instead of looking at them as people. Surrounded by images, he feels isolated. Reacting to images, he feels unrelated. In attempting to fulfill his own image, he feels frustrated and cheated of emotional satisfaction. The image is an abstraction, an ideal, and an idol which demands the sacrifice of personal feeling. The image is a mental conception which, superimposed on the physical being, reduces bodily existence to a subsidiary role. The body becomes an instrument of the will in the service of the image. The individual is alienated from the reality of his body. Alienated individuals create an alienated society.

REALITY AND THE BODY

A person experiences the reality of the world only through his body. The external environment impresses him because it impinges upon his body and affects his senses. In turn, he responds to this stimulation by acting upon the environment. If the body is relatively unalive, a person's impressions and responses are diminished. The more alive the body is, the more vividly does he perceive reality and the more actively does he respond to it. We have all experienced the fact that when we feel particularly good and alive, we perceive the world more sharply. In states of depression the world appears colorless.

The aliveness of the body denotes its capacity for feeling. In the absence of feeling the body goes "dead" insofar as its ability to be impressed by or respond to situations is concerned. The emotionally dead person is turned inward: thoughts and fantasies replace feeling and action; images compensate for the loss of reality. His exaggerated mental activity substitutes for contact with the real world and can create a false impression of aliveness. Despite this mental activity, his emotional deadness is manifested physically. We shall find that his body looks "dead" or unalive.

An overemphasis upon the role of the image blinds us to the reality of the life of the body and its feelings. It is the body that melts with love, freezes with fear, trembles in anger, and reaches for warmth and contact. Apart from the body these words are poetic images. Experienced in the body, they have a reality that gives meaning to existence. Based on the reality of bodily feeling, an identity has substance and structure. Abstracted from this reality, identity is a social artifact, a skeleton without flesh.

A number of experiments have shown that when this interaction between the body and the environment is greatly reduced, a person loses his perception of reality.[2] If an individual is deprived of sensory stimulation for a length of time he will begin to hallucinate. The same thing happens when his motor activity is severely curtailed. In both situations the decrease of body sensation caused by the absence of external stimulation or internal motor activity reduces the person's feeling of his body. When a person loses touch with his body, reality fades out.

The aliveness of a body is a function of its metabolism and motility. Metabolism provides the energy that results in movement. Obviously, when metabolism is reduced, motility is decreased. But this relationship works in reverse too. Any decrease in the body's motility affects its metabolism. This is because motility has a direct effect upon respiration. As a general rule, the more one moves, the more one breathes. When motility is reduced, oxygen intake is diminished, and the metabolic fires burn lower. An active body is characterized by its spontaneity and its full and easy respiration. It will be shown in a subsequent chapter that breathing and motility are severely restricted in the schizoid body. As a result, its energy production tends to be low.

The intimate connection between breathing, moving, and feeling is known to the child but is generally ignored by the adult. Children learn that holding the breath cuts off unpleasant sensations and feelings. They suck in their bellies and immobilize their diaphragms to reduce anxiety. They lie very still to avoid feeling afraid. They "deaden" their bodies in order not to feel pain. In other words, when reality becomes unbearable, the child withdraws into a world of *images*, where his ego compensates for the loss of body feeling by a more active fantasy life. The adult, however, whose behavior is governed by the image, has repressed the memory of the experiences which forced him to "deaden" his body and abandon reality.

Normally, the image is a reflection of reality, a mental

construction which enables the person to orient his movements for more effective action. In other words, the image mirrors the body. When, however, the body is inactive, the image becomes a substitute for the body, and its dimensions expand as body awareness recedes. "The Secret Life of Walter Mitty" is one vivid portrayal in fiction of how images may compensate for the passivity of the individual.

Image formation is a function of the ego. The ego, as Sigmund Freud said, is first and foremost a body ego. As it develops, however, it becomes antithetical to the body— that is, it sets up values in seeming opposition to those of the body. On the body level an individual is an animal, self-centered and oriented toward pleasure and the satisfaction of needs. On the ego level the human being is a rational and creative being, a social creature whose activities are geared to the acquisition of power and the transformation of the environment. Normally, the ego and the body form a close working partnership. In a healthy person the ego functions to further the pleasure principle of the body. In the emotionally disturbed person the ego dominates the body and asserts that its values are superior to those of the body. The effect is to split the unity of the organism, to change a working partnership into an open conflict.

THE EGO AND THE BODY

The conflict between the ego and the body may be slight or severe: the neurotic ego dominates the body, the schizoid ego denies it, while the schizophrenic ego dissociates from it. The neurotic ego, afraid of the nonrational nature of the body, attempts merely to subdue it. But when the fear of the body amounts to panic, the ego will deny the body in the interest of survival. And when the fear of the body reaches the proportion of terror the ego dissociates from the body, completely splitting the personality and producing the schizophrenic condition. These distinctions are clearly illustrated in the way these different personalities respond to the sexual urge. To the healthy ego sex is an expression of love. The neurotic ego sees sex as a means of conquest or ego glorification. For the schizoid ego sex is an opportunity to obtain the physical closeness and warmth upon which survival depends. The schizophrenic ego, divorced from the body, finds no meaning in the sexual act.

The conflict between the ego and the body produces a split in the personality which affects all aspects of an individual's existence and behavior. In this chapter, we will study the divided and contradictory identities of the schizoid and neurotic personalities. In the following chapters other manifestations of this split will be examined. As part of this study we will want to find out how the split develops, what factors produce it, and what techniques are available to treat it. It should be evident at this point that the split cannot be resolved without improving the condition of the body. Breathing must be deepened, motility increased, and feelings evoked if the body is to become more alive and its reality is to govern the ego image.

In the split personality two identities arise which contradict each other. One is based upon the ego image; the other upon the body. Several methods are available to elucidate these identities. The history of the patient and the meaning of his activities tell us something about his ego identity. An examination of the appearance and movement of his body tells us about his body identity. Figure drawings and other projective techniques supply important information about who the person is. Finally, every patient will reveal in his thoughts and feelings his opposing views of himself.

I shall present two case histories to illustrate the ideas set forth above. The first case is that of a young woman who stated that her problem was one of *anomie*. She had picked up this term from reading an article in *Esquire* and from reading Betty Friedan's book *The Feminine Mystique*. Friedan defines *anomie* as "that bored, diffuse feeling of purposelessness, non-existence, non-involvement with the world that can be called *anomie*, or loss of identity, or merely felt as the problem that has no name."[8] *Anomie* is a sociological term which means *normlessness* or, as I prefer, *formlessness*. My patient, whom I will call Barbara, described her condition as:

> . . . a feeling of disorientation and emptiness, essentially a blankness. I saw no reason to do anything. I

had no motivation to move. I wasn't actually aware of it until lately. It struck me strongly when I returned from my summer vacation. During the summer I was responsible for my children and the home, but afterward, the maid took over. I felt that the things I do at home were like nervous tics—you know, unnecessary actions.

Barbara was thirty-five years old, married, and the mother of four children. Her activities at home could hardly be described as unnecessary. Even with a maid, she was busy all day with important tasks. One of her immediate difficulties stemmed from her relation to the maid. She wanted to discharge the maid, who was inefficient, but she couldn't bring herself to do it. All her life she suffered from an inability to say No to other people, and it made her feel inadequate as a person. When a conflict became too intense, as in the situation with the maid, she collapsed and gave up. The result was the loss of the sense of self and a feeling of emptiness. Barbara knew this from a previous analysis. She even knew the origin of her difficulty in her childhood relations with her parents. What Barbara didn't know was that she also collapsed physically whenever the stress increased. This physical collapse made her feel helpless.

What caused this physical collapse? She was a woman of average height, with a small head and dainty, regular features. Her eyes were soft, their expression, apprehensive. Her voice came out hesitantly, with frequent pauses between phrases. Her neck was thin and constricted, which partly accounted for her difficulty in speaking. Her shoulders were pulled up in a frightened attitude. Her body was toneless: her superficial muscles were extremely flabby. However, the deep muscles along the backbone, around the shoulder girdle, in the neck and thorax were tightly contracted. Her breathing was very shallow, which added to her difficulty in speaking and accounted also for her poor skin color. Any attempt on her part to breathe more deeply lasted a minute; then her effort collapsed as the upper half of her body sagged downward and she folded up in the middle. Many of her physical functions were depressed: her appetite was poor, her sexual drive

was reduced, and she had trouble sleeping. It was easy to
see why she felt so unalive, so empty.

Barbara couldn't see any connection between her physical state and her psychological attitude. When I pointed
out this connection, she would answer, "If you say so."
She explained that she had no choice but to accept my
analysis of her problem. She didn't like her body and unconsciously she denied it. On some other level, she sensed
the connection, for during the physical therapy, she made
an effort to breathe more fully and to mobilize her muscles
through movement. When the effort became painful, she
would cry for a short time, despite her reluctance to do so.
She remarked that she had suffered too much pain in her
life and she saw no need to experience more. But she also
realized that she was ashamed to show her feelings, and
consequently fought them. She became aware that the crying made her feel better since it made her feel more alive,
and gradually, she gave in more and more to body sensation and feeling. She even tried to express her negation
vocally by saying out loud, "No, I won't!"

Slowly, Barbara improved. She could maintain an activity longer and breathe more easily. The tendency to
collapse diminished. She discharged her maid. Her eyes
brightened perceptibly and she smiled at me. She no longer
complained of *anomie*. She understood that she had to
restore feeling in her body to recover her sense of self and
identity. This improvement in Barbara's condition
stemmed partly from her feeling that she had found someone who could help her, someone who seemed to understand her difficulty. Such an improvement, however,
should be regarded as temporary. The conflicts which en-
gendered her disturbance were alluded to but had not yet
been resolved. Some idea of these conflicts can be obtained
from figure drawings which Barbara made and from her
comments about them.

Figures 1 and 2 are two successive drawings of the
female. Of Figure 1, Barbara said, "She looks silly. Her
shoulders are too broad. She looks Mephistophelian. She
looks demure in a diabolic way." Figure 2 struck Barbara
as "unalive, a mannequin whose face is a death mask."
Figure 3, that of a male, strikes one as having a demonic
or diabolic quality. We see certain similarities between

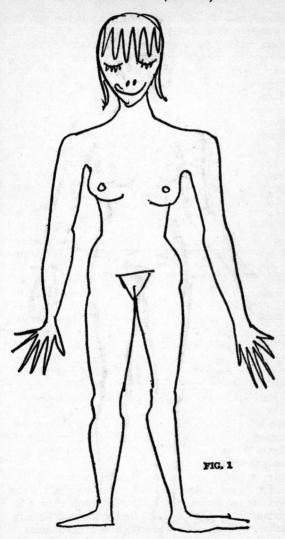

FIG. 1

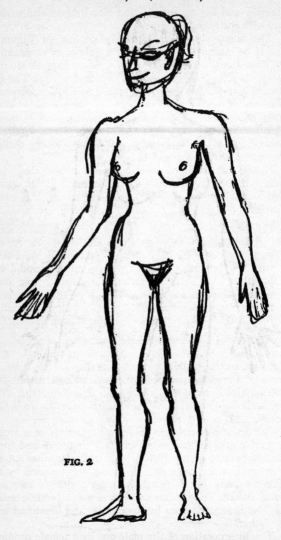

FIG. 2

Figure 1 and Figure 3 which indicate Barbara's identification with the male.

The accentuation of the body outline in Figure 2 should be interpreted as revealing a deficiency or weakness in the perception of her body's periphery. It is an attempt to impose a form upon what is felt to be formless. The loss of muscular tone in Barbara's body gave it an amorphous quality, for which she compensated by drawing heavy body lines.

Who was Barbara? Was she the corpse of Figure 2, portrayed as a wax figure, or was she the diabolic, demure maiden shown in Figure 1?

Looking at Barbara one would have considerable difficulty detecting a perverse side to her nature. Her expression was demure, shy, and apprehensive. But she recognized the demonic aspect of her personality and admitted it.

> I felt most alive when I felt most perverse. At college, sleeping with boys had a perverse quality. I slept with a boy friend of one of my girl friends, and I was proud of it. I bragged about it because I had done something perverse. Another time, I slept with a man, fat and ugly, who paid me for it. I was very proud. I felt I had the ability to do something different.

In terms of her body, toneless and amorphous, Barbara saw herself as an object (unalive, a mannequin) to be sacrificed to the demonic sexual demands of the male. In terms of her ego, expressed by the head and hands, Barbara identified with the demon who demanded this sacrifice and she derived some strange satisfaction from her debasement.

Barbara's mother had also regarded herself as a victim or martyr and her body was similarly shapeless and formless. Barbara obviously identified with her mother on the body level, while on the ego level she was repelled by her mother's body and humiliated by her mother's role as a sexual object. To give her own life a more positive meaning, she dissociated from her femininity and identified with her father.

The incorporation of the male ego by a female produces a witch. The witch upholds the view of the male ego that

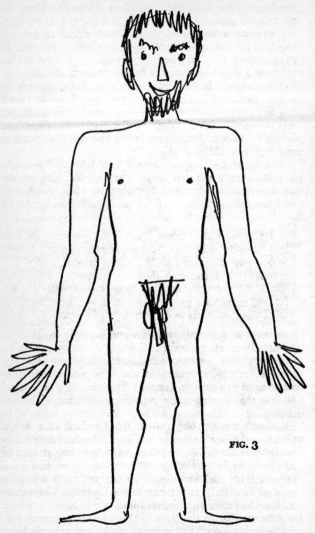

FIG. 3

the female body is an object to be used sexually. Thus, the witch turns against her own body and gloats over its sacrifice because it represents the debased aspect of her personality. At the same time, she compensates for this debasement by elevating her ego image to that of the superior nonconformist who has rejected the old morality.

The demonic drive of the witch also aims to destroy the male ego. By turning against her own femininity, the witch negates the role of love in sex and mocks the male who seeks her. Barbara's sexual submission reflects her contempt for the man. She is, in effect, saying, "I am nothing and you are a fool to want me."

The man who takes possession of a debased object wins a Pyrrhic victory. He is degraded in the eyes of the woman. Thus, Barbara took revenge upon her father, who had participated in the humiliation of the female.

In making her unconscious childhood adjustments to her life situation, she could not have foreseen that the witch's revenge against the male would rob her of *all* feeling, or that by dissociating from her femininity she would be stuck with a "deadened" body and unable to respond to love. Barbara was left without a self because her body belonged to her mother and her ego to her father. As an adult, she came to realize that she was cheated, but she could not renounce the witch as long as she unconsciously accepted the value of her ego image and rejected her body.

Barbara was both the witch and the victim, both the demonic ego who demanded the sacrifice of the female body and the submissive body terrified of the sacrifice. Such a split produces two conflicting identities. The split in Barbara's personality could be expressed in terms of life and death. To save her ego she had no choice but to give up her body. Submitting to her parents' values meant turning against her body, but by this maneuver she assured her survival as well as her sanity. As a child she had to incorporate her father's image of the female (to which her mother assented) and to fantasize that this life-negative attitude had some sublime meaning.

The sacrifice of the body in the schizoid personality is a symbolic act—not that many of these unfortunate beings do not make the literal sacrifice of suicide. Barbara's sacrifice consisted of the rejection of her body, the withdrawal of feeling from it, the denial of its significance as an expression of her being. But her conflict remained alive because her body remained alive and acceded to the symbolic sacrifice only under protest. In this struggle the body has an ally in the rational part of the mind, which, while helpless to overcome the demonic force, is nevertheless strong enough to bring the patient to therapy.

The next case illustrates the split of identity in an individual whose personality was more intact than Barbara's. Henry was a highly successful man in his fifties who consulted me because of a lack of pleasure and satisfaction in his life. He had worked hard and had "made it," but something was missing. "Money is no object," he said in discussing the fee, but money couldn't help him. His success had brought on feelings of depression, the beginning of a stomach ulcer, and a strong desire to "get away from it all." He thought only of the time when he would retire from business, but he had a presentiment that this would be no solution. He was constantly faced with problems which, he said, he could handle if they came one at a time, but all together they were too much.

Describing his youth, Henry said that he had been regarded as the black sheep of the family who would not amount to much. Then one day he resolved to prove that he could succeed. He did, but success brought new challenges and further responsibilities. It wasn't easy to quit. What does one do after one quits? Much as Henry complained about his problems, he was excited by the opportunities they presented. Having committed himself to success, Henry had to go on being successful. This is quite a burden to carry, since success permits no letdown or release except through failure.

Henry's decision to undergo analytic therapy lightened his burden. Some of the burden was shifted to the therapist, and Henry felt better and freer. When I pointed out to him how much he had neglected his body, he was impressed. He made up his mind to devote more attention to his body, and this helped him temporarily. Henry had both the will and the strength to make a significant effort to change his pattern of behavior, but he could not sustain this effort. Actually he regarded therapy as another challenge, to which he responded with his characteristic determination. Thus, therapy itself became another burden.

One day as Henry sat in my office discussing his problems, he let himself go more than usual. His head dropped to one side, his face sagged, he looked very tired, and his eyes had a defeated expression. He looked as if he had been beaten, but didn't know it.

Henry had an ego image of himself as invincible, which denied the inner reality of his feelings. It was not that Henry believed that he would always win. He was simply determined that he would never lose or be beaten down. Yet, physically he was a defeated man who refused to accept defeat. He was defeated in his attempt to find a personal meaning in financial success. He was in despair over his inability to find any pleasure in life. He had come to therapy to avoid the *feeling* of defeat and despair, but he had to accept these feelings to find himself.

Henry's body was more alive than Barbara's. His musculature was better developed, and his skin had warmth and color. He had severe muscular tensions, which produced a bowing of the back, so that he was hunched forward and had to make an effort to straighten up. His neck muscles were very tense, and his neck was shortened. He had great difficulty in breathing under stress, and he showed his respiratory difficulty in the tendency to blow the air out in expiration. He was also a heavy smoker. The tension in his body musculature was so severe that it bound him as if by chains. He was struggling against inner restraints of which he was unconscious, but committing all his energies to success in the outer world. Thus, he was split between the ego image and the reality of his body, between the outer aspects of success and achievement and the inner feeling of defeat and frustration.

Henry's problem could be superficially understood in terms of his neurotic drive for success. In his unconscious mind, his body was a beast of burden to be harnessed to the demands of his ego. The body experienced these demands as a yoke which deprived it of freedom and denied it pleasure and satisfaction. Henry's body, unlike Barbara's, fought back. However, to the degree that he was out of contact with his body and unaware of its feelings, Henry showed schizoid tendencies. The sacrifice of his freedom was not made for financial success, as Henry believed, but for the image of success he had formed in his youth. To mobilize the body for the satisfaction of a real need (hunger, sex, pleasure, etc.) is to use it, while to subvert it for the fulfillment of an ego goal is to misuse or abuse it.

Henry's problem was not as severe as Barbara's. He grasped and accepted the relation between the self and the body. Barbara could only concede a possibility, "If you say so!" Henry recognized that he had to release the muscular tensions in his body and he attacked this problem with an intensity that increased his tension. Barbara sensed the immobility of her body, but felt helpless to do anything about it. Barbara experienced her body as alien to her personality; she even expressed the wish not to have a body, which she viewed as a source of torment. She had been willing to sacrifice her body to satisfy the witch in her. Henry, on the other hand, accepted his body, but misused it. He subjected his body to his egotistic demand for success, hoping thereby to gain his freedom; but when success failed to produce freedom Henry realized he needed help.

The schizoid conflict is a struggle between life and death and can be expressed as "to be or not to be." By contrast, the neurotic conflict stems from guilt and anxiety about pleasure. This is not to say that the schizoid is free from such guilt and anxiety, but in his personality they are subordinated to the imperative need to survive. The schizoid personality pays a price for his existence: that price is the surrender of his right to make overt demands on life. The surrender of this right leads necessarily to some form of sacrifice, such as was seen in Barbara's case, and to an existence which finds its only satisfaction in negation. The negation of life in any form is a manifestation of a schizoid tendency, and in this sense, every emotional problem has a schizoid core.

2

The Schizoid
Disturbance

THE TERM "schizoid" has two meanings. It denotes (1) a tendency of the individual to withdraw from reality and (2) a split in the unity of the personality. Each aspect is a reflection of the other. These two variables are a measure of the emotional health or illness of the individual.

In emotional health the personality is unified and in full contact with reality. In schizophrenia the personality is divided and withdrawn from reality. Between the two lies the broad range of the schizoid states in which the withdrawal from reality is manifested by some degree of emotional detachment and the unity of the personality is maintained by the power of rational thought. Figure 4 illustrates these relationships.

Emotional Health   Emotional Illness

←――――――――――――――――――――――――――――→

Normal   (Neuroses)   Schizoid   Schizophrenic

FIG. 4 Contact with Reality
Unity of the Personality

This schema also includes the psychic disorders known as the neuroses. The neuroses, A. P. Moyes writes, are a "relatively benign group of personality disturbances," in

19

which the "personality remains socially organized."⁴ This is not to say that the neurotic individual has a well-integrated personality. Every neurotic problem stems from a conflict in the personality which splits its unity to some extent and reduces its contact with reality. In both the neuroses and the psychoses there is an evasion of reality; the difference, as Freud points out, is that the neurotic ignores reality while the psychotic denies it. However, every withdrawal or evasion of reality is an expression of the schizoid disturbance.

Against the background of a seemingly adjusted personality, neurotic symptoms have a dramatic quality which dominates the clinical picture. A neurotic phobia, obsession, or compulsion is often so striking that it focuses the attention to the exclusion of the underlying schizoid split. In this situation, treatment tends to be directed to the symptom rather than to the more deep-seated personality problem. Such an approach is necessarily less effective than one which sees the symptoms as a manifestation of the basic conflict between the ego and the body and directs the therapeutic effort to the healing of this split. In Figure 4, I have placed the neuroses in parentheses to indicate that they are included in the schizoid phenomenon.

One reason for the increasing recognition of the schizoid problem is the shift of psychiatric interest from the symptom to the personality. Psychotherapists are growing increasingly aware of the lack of feeling, the emotional detachment, and the depersonalization of their patients. It is now generally recognized that the schizoid condition with its deep-seated anxieties is directly responsible for symptom formation. Important as the symptom is to the disturbed individual, it occupies a secondary role in current psychological thinking. If symptoms are alleviated in psychotherapy without regard to the underlying schizoid disturbance, the treatment is regarded as supportive and the results are considered to be only temporary. To the degree, however, that the schizoid split can be overcome, the improvement in the patient occurs on all levels of his personality.

While psychotherapists are conscious of the widespread incidence of schizoid tendencies in the population, the general public is ignorant of this disorder. The average person still thinks in terms of neurotic symptoms and assumes that in the absence of an alarming symptom, everything is all right. The consequences of this attitude may be disastrous, as in the case of a young person who commits suicide without warning or suffers a so-called nervous breakdown. But even if no tragedy occurs, the effects of the schizoid disturbance are so serious that we cannot overlook its presence in neurotic behavior or wait until a crisis occurs.

Late adolescence is a critical period for the schizoid individual. The strong sexual feelings that flood his body at this time often undermine an adjustment which he had previously been able to maintain. Many young people find themselves unable to complete their high school studies. Others do so with an effort, but run into trouble in the first years of college. On the surface the problem may appear as described below.

A teenager who had done fairly well at school runs into difficulty with his studies. His marks drop, his interest lags, he becomes restless, and starts running around with "bad" characters. His parents ascribe his behavior to a lack of discipline, poor will power, rebelliousness, or the mood of today's youngsters. They may close their eyes to his difficulties in the hope that he will outgrow them. This rarely happens. They may berate the young person and attempt to coerce him into a more responsible attitude. This generally fails. In the end, they reluctantly accept the idea that seemingly bright children become "dropouts," that some are just naturally "floaters," that many young people from good backgrounds engage in destructive or delinquent activities; and they give up any attempt to comprehend the attitude of their adolescent children.

The schizoid individual cannot describe his problem. As far back as he can remember, he has always had some difficulty. He knows that something is wrong, but it is a vague knowledge that he cannot put into meaningful words. Without the understanding of his parents or teachers, he resigns himself to an inner desperation. He may find others who share his distress and with whom he can establish a rapport based on a mode of existence that is "different." He can even rationalize his behavior and gain some sense of superiority by proclaiming that he is not a "square."

I shall present four cases to illustrate some of the different forms the schizoid disturbance can take and the common elements in all four. In each case the disturbance was severe enough to require therapeutic help. In all cases, it was ignored or overlooked until a crisis occurred.

VARIETIES OF SCHIZOID PERSONALITY
AND BEHAVIOR

1. Jack was a young man, twenty-two years old when I first saw him. He had graduated from high school at eighteen, after which he spent a year singing folk songs in coffee houses. He followed this with two years in the army, then drifted from one job to another.

Jack's crisis occurred after his release from the army. In the company of his friends, he took some mescaline, a hallucinogenic drug. The result was an emotional experience that shocked him. He said:

> I had hallucinations that are impossible to describe. I saw women in every conceivable stimulating position. But when I came out of it, I hated myself. My guilt about sex confuses me. The strange thing is that I claim to be unconventional, left wing, no sex limitations, et cetera. I can reason this out, but I can't get away from the feeling of guilt. It frightens and depresses me.

This experience, induced by the drug, broke down Jack's adjustment. The schizoid tendency in his personality, which he had managed to keep under control, broke through into the definitive symptoms of the disorder. He described them as follows:

a. Fright—"At times the fright is so severe that I can't be left alone. I think I'm just plain afraid of losing my mind."

b. Hypochondriasis—"Every little pimple, scratch, pain, et cetera, scares me to death. I immediately think of cancer, syphilis. . . ."

c. Detachment—"Once I felt like I was slipping from reality, sort of removed; and within the past few weeks, I've felt removed almost constantly, as though I'm somewhere else watching myself."

When the symptoms appear with the intensity described

above, the diagnosis is easy. However, it would be a mistake to assume that there had been no previous evidence of the schizoid disturbance. Jack had experienced severe fright in the form of night terrors when he was very young. And even as a child he struggled with feelings of unreality. He related that:

> As early as I can remember [six or seven years], I've always felt different, but I was constantly convinced by my parents that this was normal. In grade school I usually felt sort of strange—example: sitting in class watching the other pupils and wondering if they felt the same confusion as I did.

The unfortunate aspect of this problem was that no one in Jack's immediate entourage seemed to understand his difficulties. "My parents and friends convinced me that this feeling [of being different and strange] was a normal feeling," he said. Jack's experience in this respect seems to be the rule. Even night terrors are often passed off as "normal" experiences, which the child will outgrow.

Jack's body showed the typical schizoid features. It was thin, tight, and rigid, with an underdeveloped musculature, limited motility, and restricted respiration. It was an unalive looking body, from which Jack had dissociated his ego long ago. He had never seriously engaged in sports or other physical activities. His hypochondriacal anxiety expressed his fear of his body and his lack of identification with it.

2. Peter, a seventeen-year-old boy, was referred for psychiatric evaluation after an alarming incident. He had gotten drunk one night following an argument with his girl friend. Then, to show her how much he cared, he took his guitar to her home to serenade her. Since it was late at night, her parents were disturbed by his actions. To quiet him, they invited him into their home. Once inside, Peter demanded to see their daughter and threatened to cut off his finger or his hand as proof of his affection. He became so unruly that he had to be forcibly restrained and returned home.

Three months before this incident Peter had been involved in other troubles. He stole a car together with some friends. It was returned, and the boys admitted the theft.

But, then, they ran away to avoid involving their parents, so Peter said. They broke into an empty home, stole some provisions, hid from the police, and thus compounded their difficulties with the law. Because Peter came from a good family and had a clean record, he was placed on probation. His delinquent behavior was blamed on his companions by his mother. Not until after the incident with his girl friend did she think that something could be wrong with Peter.

That something was wrong could have been seen earlier. Before any of these incidents occurred, a problem had developed in his schoolwork. After two good years in high school, Peter began to have difficulty concentrating. His studies fell off badly in his junior year. He stayed out late, started drinking, and became unmanageable. But no one seemed to show concern until the crisis occurred.

Peter's body was well built and well porportioned. His face had an innocent expression but was otherwise without feeling. This look of innocence had deceived his family. His eyes had a blank, empty quality. Despite its normal appearance, his body was tight and hard, and his movements were very uncoordinated. His knees and ankles were so stiff he could hardly bend them. His body lacked feeling, and even when he related the incident about his threat to cut off his hand he did so without feeling.

During our discussions Peter said that his sexual contact with a girl provided the only warmth he experienced and that his life was meaningless without it. Seemingly, the need for this body contact was so imperative that it overrode all rational considerations. Without it he felt so empty and unalive that moral principles had no value. I find that this condition is typical of all the delinquents I have seen. Their search for kicks is an attempt to "get a charge" into an otherwise "dead" body. Unfortunately, this search for excitement takes the form of a dangerous escapade or a rebellion against authority. The lack of normal body feeling in these young people accounts for their preoccupation with sex.

If the schizoid disturbance is not understood, delinquent behavior will continue to puzzle the authorities and the families of these young people. It will be blamed on a lack of family discipline or attributed to a moral weakness in the youth. While these explanations have some validity, they overlook the dynamics of the problem. An ego that is not grounded in the reality of body feeling becomes desperate. In its desperation it will act destructively toward itself and others.

3. Jane was a young woman of twenty-one who came into therapy following the breakup of a romantic affair. She felt lost and desperate. She sensed that something was seriously amiss with her personality, but she didn't know what it was or how to handle it. We can gain some idea of her problem from the following story:

> I remember in my teens thinking I was at war with myself. Especially at night, in bed, I felt I was at war with something in me. It was very frustrating and very hopeless. I felt so confused. I didn't know whom to ask.

> At eleven, I discovered my body. Before that I took it for granted. I gained a lot of weight and became self-conscious. I also began my periods at this time. The more inhibited I became, the more weight I gained and the less real I felt. I started masturbating one year later. I thought I would get pregnant or a venereal disease. I felt very guilty about it. But I would also have to masturbate before I could do anything. If I had to write a paper for school, I would procrastinate until I finally masturbated. Then I could do it.

> Throughout this period I had a constant fantasy. I fantasized that I was riding a horse. Everyone else had a horse, but mine was better than theirs.

> Men absolutely terrified me. I had no friends through high school and only one date in college.

Jane was at war with her sexual feelings. She could neither accept them nor repress them. The result was an intense conflict that tormented her and from which she attempted to escape through the world of fantasy. In her fantasy, the horse can be interpreted as a symbol of the body, especially the lower half. Her attempt to deny the reality of her body was only partially successful. Its feelings intruded on her consciousness and demanded satisfaction even at the price of enormous guilt.

The split in Jane's personality was also manifested on

the psychical level, in a very striking way. From the waist down, Jane's body was heavy, hairy, and dark-hued. Her hips and thighs were large and their muscle tone was poor. Above her waist she was dainty: her chest was narrow; her shoulders sloped sharply down; her neck was long and thin; and her head was small, with regular features. The skin tone of the upper half of her body was fair. The contrast between the two halves was sharp. From the lower half of her body one had the impression of sexual maturity and womanhood that was ripe, or perhaps, in view of its flaccidity and heaviness, overripe. The upper half of her body had an innocent, childlike appearance.

Who was Jane? Was she the dainty creature riding regally on the lower half of her body or was she the horse with whom she also identified and upon whom her ego rode like a queen? Obviously, she was both, but she was unable to reconcile these two aspects of her personality.

4. The next case, though less severe in its manifestations of illness, presents another aspect of the schizoid disturbance. Sarah was a divorcee with a five-year-old son. The breakup of her marriage was quite a shock to her and brought on a deep depression. I diagnosed her character structure as schizoid although her superficial behavior gave little evidence of so severe a disorder. She expressed her problem as follows:

> It's not that I'm unreal, yet I feel that my relations to people are not real. I often wonder what people think of me when I am doing something. I have delusions of grandeur. I feel that they must think I'm great. But really, I see that I can't cope. My performance doesn't measure up to my expectations.

I had been aware of an arrogance in Sarah's manner and speech which is typical of certain schizoid individuals. Sarah impressed me as one who thought she had superior qualities or superior intelligence. When I questioned her about the nature of her delusions of grandeur, she replied:

> My delusion is that I have a good character in general. For example, even now, I expect people to say what a good mother I am. How well I treat my son! I

was always the teacher's pet. I never disobeyed. I was a classic "goody-goody."

Sarah was a small girl-woman with a petite, dainty face, square shoulders, and delicate body structure. Her physical appearance suggested a frightened, immature person, while her speech and manner reflected maturity and confidence. This contradiction in her personality suggested a schizoid disturbance. But there were other signs of unreality about Sarah, despite her statement to the contrary. These signs were mostly physical: the lack of contact between her eyes and mine, a frozen quality in her facial expression, a rigidity of the body structure, and a lack of coordination in body movement.

Sarah played a role, that of the "good" compliant child who did what was expected of her and did it well. Her role playing was so unconscious that she expected people to approve of her as if she were a child. Many people play certain roles in life without thereby becoming schizoid. It is a matter of degree. When the role dominates the personality, when the whole is lost in the part (the part acted out), when, as in Sarah's case, the person cannot be seen or reached behind the mask and the costume, one is justified in describing such a personality as schizoid.

In terms of symptoms each of the four cases—Jack, Peter, Jane, and Sarah—was different. In terms of the two variables which determine this illness they were alike. Each one suffered from conflicts that split the unity of his personality, and in each there was some loss of contact with reality. The most important aspect of these cases, however, was that the conflict and the withdrawal were manifested physically. Jack could describe his problems with a verbal fluency that contrasted sharply with the rigidity and immobility of his body. In Peter the conflict was expressed in the contrast between the athletic appearance of his body and its marked incoordination. Jane showed the conflict in the contrast between the two halves of her body while Sarah's sophisticated attitude contrasted sharply with the immaturity of her body.

Withdrawal from reality was manifested in each of the four patients by the lack of aliveness and the emotional unresponsiveness of the body. An observer of the schizoid individual gets the impression that he is not fully "with it." Phrases such as "not with it" or "not all there" are commonly used to describe a *schizzy* quality in a person. We sense his detachment or removal. This impression stems from his vacant eyes, his masklike face, his rigid body, and his lack of spontaneity. He is not absent-minded, like the proverbial professor, who is absorbed in some mental preoccupation. The schizoid individual is consciously aware of his surroundings, but on the emotional or body level he is out of touch with the situation. Unfortunately, we lack an expression to denote the complement of absent-mindedness. Schizzy is the only word that describes a person who is mentally present, but absent on an emotional level.

An air of unreality is the hallmark of the schizoid personality. It accounts for his "strangeness" both to us and to himself. It is also expressed in his movements. He walks mechanically, like a wooden soldier, or he floats zombie-like through life. Ernst Kretschmer's description of the physical appearance of the schizoid individual emphasizes this point.

> This lack of liveliness, of immediately reacting vivacity, of psychomotor expression, is found also in the most gifted members of the group with their hypersensitive inner capacities for reaction.[5]

When an individual's appearance is so bizarre that his unreality is clearly evident, he is called psychotic, schizophrenic, or insane. The schizoid person feels his unreality as an inner emptiness and as a sensation of being removed or detached from his environment. His body may feel alien to him or almost nonexistent, as the following observation indicates.

> Going to work yesterday I didn't feel my body. I felt skinny, like a bag of bones. I never felt so bodiless. I just floated in. It was terrible. I felt strange in the office. Everything felt different, unreal. I had to pull myself together to be able to work.

This graphic description of depersonalization shows both the loss of feeling of the body and the concomitant loss of contact with the environment. In other cases the tenuous contact with reality is threatened when the schizoid individual uses drugs which further dissociate his mind from his body. For example, Virginia took "pot" (marijuana) one night. This is what happened:

> I had the feeling I was watching myself. I felt my body was doing things which were not connected with me. It was very frightening, so I got into bed. I became paranoid. I was afraid I might jump out of the window.

The schizoid may be said to live in limbo, that is, he is not "gone," as is the schizophrenic, nor is he fully "with it." He is often found on the fringes of society, where, with like kind, he feels somewhat at home. Many schizoids are the sensitive persons who become the poets, the painters, and the musicians. Others exploit the various esoteric cults which flourish in the borderlands of our society. These cults are of several kinds—those that use drugs to achieve higher states of consciousness, those in which Oriental philosophies are exploited to find a meaning in life, and those in which various body exercises offer the promise of a fuller self. But it would be a serious error to assume that the schizoid personality is found only in this milieu. He may also be the engineer who runs his life like a machine or the schoolteacher who is quiet, withdrawn, shy, and homosexual. She is the ambitious mother who tries to be very enlightened and do the right thing for her children. She is also the little girl who is bright, eager, excitable, and compulsive. As children, these people are characterized by insecurity; as adolescents by anxiety; and as adults by an inner feeling of frustration and failure. These reactions are more severe than the words imply. Their childhood insecurity is related to a feeling of being different and of not belonging. Their adolescent anxiety verges on panic and may end in terror. Their adult feeling of frustration and failure has an underlying core of despair.

APPROACHES TO THE SCHIZOID PROBLEM

The schizoid disturbance has been investigated along a number of lines, three of which are important to this study. These are the psychological, the physiological, and the constitutional. Psychology attempts to explain behav-

ior in terms of conscious or unconscious mental attitudes.
Physiology seeks the answers to disturbed attitudes in
derangements of bodily functions. The constitutional approach relates personality to body structure.

Psychologically, the term "schizoid" is used to describe
behavior which qualitatively resembles schizophrenia but
is more or less within normal limits.[6] The specific behavior patterns which suggest this diagnosis are summarized
as follows:

1. The avoidance of any close relations with people;
shyness, seclusiveness, timidity, feelings of inferiority.

2. Inability to express hostility and aggressive feelings
directly—sensitivity to criticism, suspiciousness, the need
for approval, tendencies to deny or distort.

3. Autistic attitudes—introversion, excessive daydream-
ing.

4. Inability to concentrate, feelings of being dazed or
doped, sensations of unreality.

5. Hysterical outbreaks with or without apparent provocation, such as screaming, yelling, temper tantrums.

6. The inability to feel emotions, especially pleasure,
and the lack of emotional responsiveness to other people,
or exaggerated reactions of hyperexcitement and
mania.[7, 8, 9]

Schizoid behavior, however, often appears to be normal.
As Otto Fenichel points out, the schizoid individual has
succeeded in "substituting pseudo-contacts of manifold
kinds for a real feeling contact with other people."[10]
Pseudo-contacts take the form of words which are substituted for touch. Another form of pseudo-contact is role
playing, which is a substitute for an emotional commitment to a situation. The main complaints of schizoid individuals, as Herbert Weiner states, "revolve about their not
being able to feel any emotions: they are estranged from
others, withdrawn and detached."[11]

It can be shown that the psychology which characterizes
the schizoid individual is related to his lack of identity.
Confused as to who he is, and not knowing what he wants,
the schizoid individual either detaches himself from people
and withdraws into an inner world of fantasy or he adopts
a pose and plays a role that seemingly will fit him into
normal life. If he withdraws, symptoms of shyness, seclusiveness, suspiciousness, and unreality will predomi-

nate. If he plays a role, the outstanding symptoms will be tendencies to deny or distort, sensitivity to criticism, feelings of inferiority, and complaints of emptiness or lack of satisfaction. There may be alternations between withdrawal and activity, depression and excitement, with rapid or exaggerated mood changes. The schizoid picture presents many contrasts. Some schizoids are highly intelligent and creative, although their pursuits may be limited and unusual, while others appear dull and lead empty, docile, and inconspicuous lives.

Another view of the schizoid personality, a physiological one, is offered by Sandor Rado.[12] According to Rado the schizoid personality is characterized by two physiological defects. The first, an "integrative pleasure deficiency," denotes an inability to experience pleasure. The second, "a sort of proprioceptive diathesis," refers to a distorted awareness of the bodily self. The pleasure deficiency handicaps the individual in his attempt to develop an effective "action self," or identity. Since pleasure is "the tie that really binds" (Rado), the action self that emerges in the absence of this binding power of pleasure is brittle, weak, prone to break under stress, hypersensitive. This pleasure deficiency to which Rado refers has characterized all the schizoid patients I have seen. But where Rado regards it as an inherited predisposition, I explain it in terms of the struggle for survival. Uncertain of his right to exist, and committing all his energies to the struggle for survival, the schizoid individual necessarily bypasses the area of pleasurable activity. To a man fighting for his right to exist, pleasure is an irrelevant concept.

The seeming distortion in self-perception is often the most striking feature of the schizoid personality. How can one explain Jack's remark, "I feel apart from my body as if I were outside watching myself"? Is there a fault in Jack's self-perception or is his detachment due to the lack of something to perceive? When a body is devoid of feeling, self-perception fades out. However, it is equally true that when the ego dissociates from the body, the body becomes an alien object to the perceiving mind. We are confronted here with the same duality we described at the beginning of this chapter. The withdrawal from reality produces a split in the personality, just as every split results in a loss of contact with reality. The significance of body perception can be appreciated if one accepts Rado's remark that "the proprioceptive awareness [of the body] is the deepest internal root of language and thought."[13]

The weakness in the schizoid individual's self-perception is directly related to his inability to experience pleasure. Without pleasure the body functions mechanically. Pleasure keeps the body alive and promotes one's identification with it. When the body sensations are unpleasant the ego dissociates from the body. One patient said, "I made my body go dead to avoid the unpleasant feelings."

The constitutional approach to the schizoid problem is best represented by the work of Ernst Kretschmer, who made a detailed analysis of the schizoid temperament and physique. He found that there is a close connection between the two, and that individuals with a schizoid temperament tended to have an asthenic body build, or more rarely, an athletic body build. Broadly speaking, the asthenic body can be described as long and thin, with an underdeveloped musculature, while the athletic body is more evenly proportioned and better developed muscularly. In addition, Kretschmer and Sheldon[14] have called attention to the presence of dysplastic elements in the schizoid body. Dysplasia refers to the fact that the different parts of the body are not harmoniously proportioned.

The four patients whose cases were discussed at the beginning of this chapter showed these typical schizoid features. Jack's body was elongated and thin, with the underdeveloped musculature of the asthenic type. Peter's body, which seemed well proportioned and muscularly developed, could be described as athletic. Jane showed dysplasia: the upper half of her body had an asthenic quality, while the lower half was amorphous and lacked definition. Sarah's body, too, had a dysplastic appearance: the upper half of her body was asthenic, in contrast to the lower half, which was markedly athletic. Her calf muscles were as developed as those of a professional dancer, although Sarah had never engaged in sports or dancing.

Body structure is important in psychiatry because it is an expression of personality. We react to a large, heavy man differently than we do to a small, wiry one. But to base the personality upon the body type is to accept a static rather than a dynamic view of the relationship between body and personality. It ignores the motility and expressiveness of the body which are the key elements in personality. The asthenic body is a meaningful classification only because it indicates the degree of an individual's muscular rigidity. The athletic body denotes a schizoid tendency only when its movements are markedly uncoordinated. Factors such as vivacity, vitality, grace, spontaneity of gesture, and physical warmth are significant because they affect self-perception and influence the feeling of identity.

Rado's view of the schizoid disturbance rests upon the hypothesis that it results from physiological dysfunctions. This is opposed to the psychoanalytic view, expressed by Silvano Arieti, that the problem is essentially psychological. Kretschmer, on the other hand, states that the schizoid condition is constitutionally determined. Whereas both Rado and Kretschmer believe that this illness has a hereditary origin, Arieti affirms that "schizophrenia [and therefore the schizoid condition] is a specific reaction to an extremely severe state of anxiety, originated in childhood, reactivated later in life."[15]

Rado, Kretschmer, and Arieti have each concentrated upon one aspect of the problem which the others regarded as secondary. Arieti concedes, for example, that "it is a well-known fact that most schizophrenics belong to the asthenic constitutional type,"[16] but he claims that it is a result of the disorder and not its cause. To avoid the argument about which comes first, we must assume that they are interrelated phenomena. The disturbances seen in body structure and physiology are an expression in the physical realm of a process which in the psychological realm appears as disorders of thought and behavior.

Psychologically, the schizoid problem is manifested in a lack of identity and, necessarily, therefore, in a loss of normal, emotional relationships to people. Physiologically, the schizoid condition is determined by disturbances in self-perception, deficiencies in the pleasure function, and disorders of respiration and metabolism. Constitutionally, the schizoid body is defective in coordination and integration. It is either too rigid or hardly held together at all. In both cases it lacks the aliveness upon which adequate self-perception depends. Without this self-perception, identity becomes confused or lost and the typical psychological symptoms appear.

A total view of the schizoid problem should present in a unified concept both the psychic and physical symptoms of the disturbance:

1. The psychological lack of identity.
2. The disturbance in self-perception.
3. The relative immobility and the diminished tone of the body surface.

The relationship between these levels of the personality may be stated as follows: The ego depends for its sense of identity upon the perception of the body. If the body is charged and responsive, its pleasure functions will be strong and meaningful, and the ego will identify with the body. In this case, the ego image will be grounded in the body image. Where the body is "unalive," pleasure becomes impossible and the ego dissociates itself from the body. The ego image becomes exaggerated to compensate for the inadequate body image. Constitution in the dynamic sense refers to the degree of vitality and aliveness of the body.

Their relation to one another can be shown diagrammatically as a triangle.

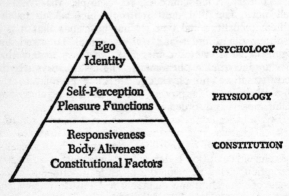

FIG. 5 Levels of Personality

The connections between these levels of personality is illustrated in the following case. The patient was a woman who had an ego image of herself as a superior person, above average in intelligence and sensitivity. In the course of therapy this ego image was dispelled. She reported a dream in which two children, a boy and a girl, hid themselves in the basement of a building and went on a hunger strike. She related:

> In my dream I feel that they are doing this out of spite. I go down into the basement, where I see their bodies lying side by side, as if they were dead, but I notice their eyes are open and their faces seem alive in contrast to the corpselike quality of their bodies. I feel that they represent me. I have often acted spitefully in my life. I wonder if the open eyes symbolize the mind, since I feel that this is the most alive part of me.

This patient had a tall, thin body and a hollow, gaunt face which gave her appearance a cadaverous quality. She experienced her condition one day while walking with her mother in the street. She remarked, "I felt so ashamed of her that I detached myself so as not to be involved with her. I walked beside her, feeling removed from her and from the world, like a ghost." In relating this incident, the patient realized that there was an intimate connection between her dream of the corpselike bodies, her experience of feeling like a ghost, her detachment from her body, and the appearance of her body. And then she asked me, "Why did I have to deaden myself?" The answer to this question requires an understanding of the dynamics, the mechanism, and the etiology of the schizoid problem.

3

The Defense
Against Terror

FEAR AND TERROR

FEAR has a paralyzing effect upon the body. Normally, an individual reacts to fear with fight or flight. He attempts to remove the danger or to escape it. If these reactions are blocked, his self-control is shattered. His personality collapses and his sanity is threatened. In this situation insanity can be avoided by certain maneuvers which deny and repress the fear. Some measure of self-control is reestablished, but the fear is not eliminated. In its repressed state it becomes a vague terror. It is transformed into the fear of losing control or going out of one's mind.

Underlying the fear of insanity is a terror which is all the more frightening since it is nameless and faceless. Its horror is expressed in such images as the snake pit. This terror lurks in the depths of each schizoid individual and can be compared to an unexploded bomb. The explosion of the terror into consciousness is a "world shattering" experience for the individual. It is represented in the schizoid mind as a world-destruction, or *Weltuntergang* fantasy or as a feeling of total annihilation. The schizoid individual reacts to this threat with a feeling of "falling apart" or "going to pieces." Against this terror and its catastrophic effects he erects desperate defenses. If these defenses fail, the only means left of avoiding this terror is the complete escape into the unreality of schizophrenia.

Superficially, the terror appears to be related to the fear of insanity. Jack, whose case was presented in Chapter 2, said, "I think I'm just plain afraid of losing my mind." Most patients experience the terror similarly. However, it can be shown that terror itself is the force that threatens to overwhelm the ego and destroy the sanity of the individual, and that schizophrenia is a final attempt to escape this terror. What is this nameless fright?

Fears become nameless and faceless when they are repressed. In the unconscious, they live on, with the terrifying effect they had upon the child. After a patient has been successfully released from the grip of this terror, some of its elements become clear. These are the fear of being abandoned, the fear of being destroyed, and the fear of destroying someone. But these are specific fears because they are conscious, while the unconscious terror of the schizoid is an amorphous dread whose tentacles chill the bones and paralyze the will. This terror is like the proverbial skeleton in the closet, which become less frightening when the door has been opened and its reality confronted. Before the closed door which hides the unknown, the person trembles with an overwhelming fear that saps his courage and defeats his resolution. Therapy must help the patient gain the courage and strength to face his fears. In the process, he will inevitably experience his terror. With the support and understanding of the therapist, this experience can have a positive effect.

Paul reported such an experience after having been in therapy about a year:

> I've had a strange week. I have been alternating between periods of absolute helplessness and feeling much more alive. Friday I was quite active, but Saturday I just couldn't get on my feet. I felt the whole day slip through my fingers. I got very depressed and I cried a little. Sunday was better. I went out. Monday I felt so completely dead I just wanted to lie in bed the rest of my life.
>
> That night I was coming out of a dream and in a half awake state; I turned over on my back and reached out with my mouth to suck. My lips were trembling, and I became very anxious and almost paralyzed. My arms felt heavy and lifeless, like dead weights which I couldn't move. I had to use all my will power to fight

against succumbing to the paralysis. I felt that if I let myself go into it, something catastrophic would happen. I made myself wake up fully.

The analysis of Paul's experience shows that the terror manifested in the trembling anxiety and feeling of paralysis developed when Paul made a spontaneous gesture to reach out for pleasure. This gesture of reaching out to suck stirred some childhood memories in which a similar activity threatened to have a catastrophic result. As an infant, Paul met with a hostile reaction from his mother when he made a demand upon her. Her hostility was expressed in a look of murderous rage which the child understood as, I've had enough of your demands; if you don't shut up, I will leave you or destroy you! Such parental expressions of hostility are not uncommon. Many mothers scream their rage and exasperation. Some have even told me how many times they felt they could have killed their children. One such experience will not lead to an overwhelming terror in the child, but if it represents an unconscious attitude on the part of the mother, the effect on the child will be one of fear that any demand it makes could lead to abandonment or destruction. In turn, the child develops a murderous rage against the parent, which is equally terrifying.

The overall effect of such experiences is to inhibit the individual's aggression. The schizoid individual becomes afraid to make demands on life that would lead to pleasure and satisfaction. Reaching out to the world evokes a vague sense of terror. He guards against this terror by narrowing his environment and restricting his activities. I had a patient who was very uncomfortable when she had to travel outside of the area in which she lived. In other patients it is experienced as a panic at the thought of going out on the streets alone or making a trip. In all schizoid patients the terror is related to the fear of losing control, since loss of control would allow the emergence of repressed impulses which, as in Paul's case, carry in their wake the possibility of catastrophic results.

The inhibition of aggression, the restriction of activity, and the necessity for control impose a rigidity upon the body that limits self-assertive gestures. Impulses are restrained, and finally, impulse formation is weakened. Having repressed his desires out of fear, the schizoid individual ends up not knowing what he wants. The denial of pleasure leads to a rejection of the body. To survive in the face of terror he deadens his body by reducing his breathing and his motility.

In view of this situation, it is easy to understand the schizoid detachment and uninvolvement as a defense against terror. To the degree that he can keep himself aloof from emotional relationships, he can avoid the terror that might follow the breakthrough of repressed impulses. His physical rigidity serves the same purpose. But detachment and isolation diminish his contact with reality, undermine his ego, and weaken his sense of identity. Noninvolvement also deprives him of the emotional satisfactions which sustain normal relationships and provide an inner feeling of well-being. Finally, rigidity creates an inner emptiness and vacuum which threatens to collapse the schizoid structure.

This defense against terror requires another maneuver. The schizoid individual uses "pseudo-contacts" and "intellectualizations" to maintain contact with reality and support a pattern of behavior which resembles the normal; that is, he plays a role. This unconscious role provides him with an identity and a meaning for his activities. As long as the role can be maintained, the danger of decompensation or of collapse into terror and insanity can be averted. But this maneuver also has its difficulties. Role playing narrows the base of existence. An assumed identity may crumble in the confrontation with the self when one is alone. For this reason, the schizoid is often afraid to be alone. Thus, all aspects of his defense (and maneuvers) render the schizoid vulnerable to the very dangers they are designed to avoid.

Schizoid behavior differs from normal behavior in important respects. It lacks the motivations which determine normal behavior; that is, it is not motivated by the search for pleasure but by the need to survive and the desire to escape the loneliness imposed by emotional detachment. It rests upon rationalizations (May's "technical formulations") and role playing and does not stem from genuine feeling. Thus, while the schizoid is enabled to function, his behavior and actions have the bizarre quality one associates with automatons and creatures who go through the motions of living without a feeling for life.

It would be a mistake, however, to regard the schizoid individual as deprived of all feeling. Behind his defense lies an intense longing for real contact, warmth, and love. These desires are not completely absent from his motivation. Much as he may impress one at times as an automaton, he comes through at other times as a person in trouble. His actions not only resemble the normal, they partake of the normal. The difference from the normal is fundamentally one of degree. To the extent that the desire for pleasure and satisfaction motivates his behavior, he is normal. To the extent that he represses those feelings but acts *as if* they determined his behavior, he is schizoid.

THE DYNAMICS OF THE SCHIZOID DEFENSE

The schizoid defense is an emergency mechanism for coping with a danger to life and sanity. In this struggle all mental faculties are engaged in the fight for survival. Survival depends upon the absolute control and mastery of the body by the mind. If the mind should relax its vigilance, catastrophe would occur. In the normal individual, in whom no terror lurks, the body is not immobilized by the struggle for survival and is free to pursue its natural desire for pleasure.

One of my patients repeatedly saw in a Rorschach test the image of a person hanging on to the edge of a cliff. This vision was a projection of his unconscious awareness that he hovered over an abyss, and that to save life and reason, he must hang on with all his might. It also indicated the magnitude of the terror against which he struggled. The physical effort to hang on, literally, consumed all his energy. His improvement was ushered in by a feeling of exhaustion and a need to sleep. This indicated that his state of jeopardy had passed and that he was able to relax for the first time. In therapy, exhaustion is one of the first signs that the patient is coming into contact with his body in a meaningful way.

The immobilization of the schizoid body results in a lack of aliveness and responsiveness. The schizoid individual perceives this unreponsiveness as an "emptiness" in his body. If the condition becomes aggravated, that is, if there is further loss of feeling, he feels "removed." His mind, as Jack said, feels detached from his body. He feels outside of himself, watching himself.

The mind and body of a normal individual function as complementary systems to further the well-being and pleasurable feelings of the individual. When an impulse arises in the body, the mind determines its meaning, adapts it to reality, and regulates its release. In all higher animals where the mind-body duality exists, the mind functions to control and coordinate movement in the interest of reality, while the body provides the impetus, the energy, and the mechanism for motion. Behavior which has this integrated aspect has an emotional quality. It starts from an impulse, which then gives rise to feeling, thought, and appropriate action. This kind of body-mind relationship is operative in emotional responses motivated by the desire for pleasure.

In the schizoid individual, whose impulses are rigidly controlled because of the underlying terror, there is an absence of feeling upon which the mind can act. In place of feeling, the mind substitutes logical thought as the motivation for action. The body becomes an instrument of the will, obeying the commands of the mind. I explain this difference to my patients as follows. Normally, one eats when one is hungry, but in the schizoid state, one has lunch because it is twelve o'clock. Although many people who are not schizoid are constrained to eat at fixed hours, it nevertheless illustrates the principle to my patients. The schizoid individual engages in sports or does exercises to improve his control over his body and not for the pleasure of the activity or the movement. Lacking the binding power of pleasure, the unity of his personality is threatened. He compensates for this lack by an increase in the direct control over the body by the mind acting through the will. By such a mechanism, schizoid individuals frequently become outstanding actors, dancers, or athletes.

In the normal individual, in addition to regulating and controlling the action of impulses, the mind can also, at times, command the body to act contrary to its natural instincts. Ordinarily, actions are motivated by the desire for the pleasure and satisfaction to be derived from the achievement of a goal. If the activity leading to the achievement of a goal is a pleasurable experience, the behavior of the organism is spontaneous, coordinated, and seemingly effortless. But situations arise where the attainment of a goal excludes the experience of pleasure. Action in the face of danger, such as that of a soldier on a battlefield, is motivated by considerations other than pleasure. The average schoolboy does his homework out of necessity rather than as a pleasure. Many situations require a conscious effort to mobilize the body, that is, an effort of will in which the mind commands the body to act in ways contrary to its spontaneous desires or feelings. The spontaneous desire of a soldier is to avoid the danger. He forces himself to meet the danger by the exercise of will. The schoolboy would rather play than study, but he is taught to submit to the discipline of the mind.

The world has long known the unique quality of the human will. Such expressions as "will power," "the will to live," and "where there's a will there's a way," give some indication of the nature of the will. The will functions as a biological shortcut mechanism of an emergency nature when all other means have failed. The will can achieve a goal which has appeared impossible. The incredible power of the human will resides in its ability to circumvent the natural desire for pleasure or safety and to accomplish the seemingly unnatural. The will acts through the ego's control over the voluntary musculature of the body. Paul used his will to pull himself together in opposition to the tendency of his body to succumb to its paralysis. Because the will can prevail against the feelings of the body, it is of crucial importance in the life of the schizoid individual.

Normally, the will occupies a secondary or accessory position in the psychic economy. Yet, the fact is that many people in our culture are forced to use their will in routine activities. How often one hears the remark, "I had to use all my will power to get to work this morning." If this sounds like a schizoid statement, it should be realized that the conditions of work in modern culture alienate the individual from the creative process and deny him the pleasure and satisfaction of his productive effort. One works under these conditions because of compelling necessity, not desire. To regiment oneself to the mechanization and standardization of a mass production system requires an effort of will. When the will becomes the primary mechanism of action, displacing the normal motivating force of pleasure, the individual is functioning in a schizoid manner.

The schizoid individual is intensely willful. He is willful in the sense of being obstinate and defiant, but he is also willful in that every action is forced and determined. Sometimes he is successful, but more often not. Generally, each effort of will collapses into despair and hopelessness. As one of my patients remarked, "I am always turning over a new leaf, only to find that it becomes brown before I accomplish anything." What is lacking in the schizoid structure is a reliance upon the natural and spontaneous functioning of the body. Another schizoid patient told me, "I can't understand how my body keeps working by itself. I think it will stop at any time. I'm surprised that it keeps going on. I'm always afraid that it's going to get out of control."

THE SCHIZOID BARRICADE

Without a basis for his identity in the normal functioning of his body, the schizoid individual depends on his will to maintain the unity of his personality. To do this job the will must be constantly active. As a result, the musculature is in a continual state of contraction. The spasticity of the muscles explains the characteristic rigidity of the schizoid body, which then serves as a barricade against terror. Loss of control is a threat to the schizoid individual because it may engender a disruption of his personality, a literal falling apart of this barricade. In contrast to the schizoid, the normal individual maintains his unity and identity through the strength of his impulses and feelings. The difference in the two conditions can be contrasted diagrammatically in terms of impulse formation and muscular activity. Figure 6 shows the normal condition; Figure 7, the schizoid condition.

In the normal condition (Figure 6), the impulses that originate at the center of the body and flow to the periphery act like spokes in a wheel to maintain the fullness and integrity of the organism. The constant stream of impulses seeking pleasure through the satisfaction of needs in the external world, charges the periphery of the body, so that it is in a state of emotional readiness to respond. In the alive body the charge at the periphery is manifested in the tone and color of the skin, in the brightness of the eyes, in the spontaneity of gesture and in the relaxed state of the body musculature.

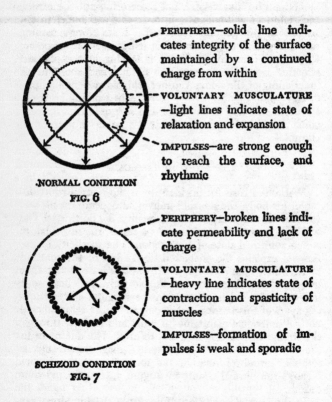

PERIPHERY—solid line indicates integrity of the surface maintained by a continued charge from within

VOLUNTARY MUSCULATURE—light lines indicate state of relaxation and expansion

IMPULSES—are strong enough to reach the surface, and rhythmic

NORMAL CONDITION
FIG. 6

PERIPHERY—broken lines indicate permeability and lack of charge

VOLUNTARY MUSCULATURE—heavy line indicates state of contraction and spasticity of muscles

IMPULSES—formation of impulses is weak and sporadic

SCHIZOID CONDITION
FIG. 7

In the schizoid condition (Figure 7), impulse formation is weak and sporadic and does not reach the periphery of the body, which is therefore relatively undercharged. Since the impulses do not reach the surface of the body with sufficient strength to maintain its integrity, a contraction of the voluntary musculature occurs to hold the body together like a rigid container and to prevent the collapse threatened by the inner emptiness. The reduced charge at the periphery of the schizoid body results in an increased permeability of the surface membranes to external stimuli, which accounts for the hypersensitivity shown by most schizoid individuals. Necessarily, contact with the external environment is tenuous. Action upon the world to gain satisfaction is generally ineffective. The chronic contraction of the deep muscles is responsible for the narrowing of the body which gives it the typical asthenic appearance.

The immobilization of the body musculature in the schizoid condition has a double meaning. On one hand, it is a defense against terror and a means of maintaining some unity in the personality. On the other hand, it is a direct expression of the terror, since it represents the physical attitude of one who is frozen stiff with fear. Paul could not perceive this quality of his body because he was incapable of reacting emotionally. As long as he remained frozen, the terror would be hidden, like a skeleton in a closed closet. He had to thaw and reach out before this perception became possible. Only through the experience of the terror and its resolution into its component fears was there any hope for a significant improvement in his personality.

The collapse of the schizoid rigidity would plunge the individual into a schizophrenic crisis. Collapse brings about a loss of ego boundaries and the destruction of such unity and integrity as the personality has. This cannot happen to the normal individual. Once a strong contact is made with the reality of the external world, it operates to sustain the peripheral aliveness. This difference is illustrated in the reactions of these two types to excessive stress. It is an accepted concept that under sufficient stress the schizoid structure can give way, producing an acute psychotic break. In the normal individual, on the other hand, the breakdown which occurs due to insupportable stress generally takes place in the tissues and organs of the body and reults in somatic illness rather than mental illness. It appears that the forces that bind mind to body are different in the two cases. One can compare these phenomena to the action of certain adhesives. Some are so strong that when a rapture is forced, it is the substance that yields and not the bonding medium. Other adhesives, such as rubber cement, permit the bonded objects to be pulled apart without the disruption of their structure.

What are the forces that unify the personality in the normal and the schizoid individual? In the normal person, body and mind are held together by the integrative function of pleasure. This refers to capacity for pleasure. Since pleasure is a principle of the body, the mind which anticipates pleasure affirms its identity with the body on the deepest level of experience. The capacity for pleasure also guarantees a steady stream of impulses reaching to the world for satisfaction. In the absence of this pleasure function, impulses are tentative and infrequent. The schizoid person therefore depends upon his will to cement mind to body. But the will, though hard as steel, is brittle, whereas pleasure is flexible and pervasive. It acts like the sap in the living tree to provide strength and elasticity.

The idea that there are two different mechanisms for maintaining the unity of a personality suggests that there may be some validity to the concept that somatic illness and mental illness tend to be mutually exclusive and antithetical, and that, broadly speaking, an individual is predisposed to one or to the other, but not to both at the same time. Under conditions of insupportable stress, these two unifying forces may be expected to give way with different results. When the pleasure functions disintegrate, one may generally expect somatic illness, while the disintegration of the will produces mental illness. Thus, one can anticipate an interchangeability of symptoms, depending on the state of functioning of the total organism. Leopold Bellak comments on this same phenomenon, "The low incidence of allergic disorders in psychotics, and the return of allergic complaints after improvements and recovery, is probably one of the best documented instances of such interchangeability."[17]

My clinical experience is that schizophrenics rarely manifest the symptoms of a common cold; when they do, I regard it as a sign of clinical improvement. It is also well documented that states of intense emotional excitement and upheaval may alleviate physical afflictions in normal individuals. An example is the effect of emotional shock upon the condition of rheumatoid arthritis. The remission of this illness due to emotional shock was one of the observations that led to the use of cortisone in the treatment of this condition. Cortisone is similar in action to the corticosteroids which are produced by the adrenal gland in conditions of stress or shock.

The interchangeability of symptoms is dramatically illustrated in the following case of a male schizophrenic patient whom I treated for a number of years. In the course of therapy most of his schizophrenic tendencies and manifestations were considerably reduced. At one point, after what I felt had been a significant improvement, the patient developed an epidermoid cancer at the tip of his nose. Actually, the patient had been aware of this growth for some time, but had ignored it. The patient had a history of X-ray treatments on his face for an acne condition many years earlier. However, the appearance of the cancer at this particular time in the therapy seemed significant to me. Was it possible that when his escape into psychosis as a withdrawal from reality was prevented by the analytic working-through of the schizophrenic mechanisms, he attempted to withdraw from life by developing a cancer? This interpretation was accepted by the patient and proved helpful to his therapy. An operation was successfully performed, which led the patient to comment, "I guess I cut off my nose to spite my face." Following the operation, however, the patient made a big step forward toward building a stable personality.

I do not wish to suggest that physical illness does not occur among schizophrenics or that schizophrenia cannot develop in the presence of somatic disease. We are dealing with tendencies which, while they are mutually exclusive as theoretical postulates, are only relatively so in life. One may hypothesize that once the ego anchors in reality it cannot easily be dislodged.

THE SCHIZOID RETREAT

The schizoid individual defends himself against terror and insanity by one of two strategies. The most common defensive strategy, as has been described above, is a physical and psychological rigidity that serves to repress feeling and keep the body under the control of the ego. It is structured to withstand insults from the outside world in the form of rejection and disappointment. It is a fortress within which the schizoid lives in the relative security of illusion and fantasy.

But not all schizoid individuals show this typical rigidity. Many, including Barbara, whose case was presented in Chapter 1, show in their body structures a superficial flabbiness or lack of muscle tone instead of the rigidity described above. Impulse formation is further reduced—to the point where the body looks more dead than alive, the peripheral charge is very low, and skin color is pasty yellow or muddy brown. Logically, such a condition would follow the breakdown of the rigid defense and lead to schizophrenia. However, in Barbara's case it may be postulated that a collapse occurred in early childhood, before a rigid defense could be structured by her personality. Barbara gave in before she could fight back.

To account for a personality that remains sane yet whose body structure shows collapse, it is necessary that the concept of the schizoid defense against terror be extended beyond that of rigidity. When the terror is extreme, a more desperate maneuver is required. What could be more terrifying than to picture oneself as the victim of a human sacrifice? The feelings which this image evokes would be enough to drive one out of his mind. Yet Barbara and other patients have lived with this terror and have not gone mad. They saved their sanity by believing in the necessity and the value of the sacrifice. They gave up their bodies and accepted their symbolic death, but by this action they robbed the terror of its sting. A body that lacks all feeling can no longer be frightened or shocked.

Thus, the two maneuvers by which the schizoid can defend himself can be described as (1) the rigid barricade, or (2) the retreat from the field of action. In the retreat the schizoid individual surrenders most of his troops (muscular tone) and loses the ability to fight back, although he retains control of the rest of his personality. He may be compared to a general without an army, but he is very much better off than an army in chaos without a general. The schizophrenic condition is one of chaos in which each faculty of the personality abandons the others. The schizoid retreat is a maneuver to avoid a rout.

In both schizoid rigidity and schizoid retreat the defense against insanity is the power of the rational mind to sustain the individual's function in society under all conditions. In schizoid rigidity the mind acts through the will. In the schizoid retreat the will is inoperative, but the mind joins forces with the enemy to avoid a final defeat. Barbara did this by identifying with her demon. Having no will to cope with danger, Barbara avoided disaster by being submissive in every situation. This submission was tolerable, since it could be rationalized as a sacrifice in the interest of survival.

Generally, these two defense maneuvers are mutually exclusive. The individual who has committed all his energies to the rigid barricade cannot retreat if his defense is overrun. His ego lacks the flexibility to rationalize a defeat and the collapse of his resistance could lead to a psychotic break. The schizoid individual whose defense is based on retreat and sacrifice has lost the possibility of making a stand. A further retreat becomes impossible, and if required, decompensation into schizophrenia would occur. Nevertheless, these two defense maneuvers are related to each other logically and historically. Logically, schizoid rigidity is a defense against collapse, while the retreat stems from a breakdown of a previous resistance. Historically, it can be shown that the schizoid maneuver of retreat and sacrifice developed at an early age in the child following an unsuccessful effort to erect a rigid defense against the impact of parental hostility.

BREAKDOWN AND SCHIZOPHRENIA

Since the schizoid defense serves to keep repressed impulses in check, it depends upon a degree of control that taxes the endurance of the individual. Consequently many forces can upset the schizoid equilibrium and bring on a psychotic eipsode. It is not his defense which protects the schizoid person against a nervous breakdown, but the amount of health which persists in his personality. Here follow a few of the common situations that can produce a collapse in the schizoid structure.

1. Often an acute psychotic attack is brought on by the use of a drug which temporarily prevents the mind from exercising its control over the body. Mescaline and LSD function in this way. Under the influence of these hallucinogenic drugs, direct contact with the body is broken. The sensations and fantasies which flood the schizoid mind often produce a feeling of terror so overwhelming that it shatters the ego. It may be recalled that Jack was shocked by his experience with mescaline. The danger of LSD in the treatment of borderline schizophrenics is now recognized.

2. Lack of sleep, as Paul Federn has pointed out,[18] is another factor which may produce a psychotic break in predisposed individuals. It has been shown that sleep deprivation produces hallucinatory phenomena even in normal individuals. Lack of sleep weakens the mind's control of the body. A breakdown may occur in a schizoid individual who spends his nights studying for exams.

3. Emotional situations which the schizoid individual cannot handle may produce a breakdown. Schizoid patients have been known to crack up in the face of an impending marriage, a financial crisis, or following the birth of a child. One of my patients attempted suicide after rejection by a young man.

4. Critical periods of life: adolescence and menopause. Adolescence with its surging sexual impulses is a particularly difficult period for the schizoid personality. Indeed, schizophrenia was formerly called dementia praecox because it occurred most frequently in early adulthood. Menopause is another period when inadequate ego adjustments collapse under the impact of strong emotions, often plunging the individual into an emotional crisis.

A nervous breakdown is a loss of control over feelings and behavior. Its manifestations differ, however, from one patient to another. In some patients it appears as an overwhelming anxiety and confusion. Others become wildly destructive and have to be restrained. Still others develop paranoid delusions. And some become progressively withdrawn and unresponsive. Each reacts according to the dynamics of his personality structure, that is, according to the relative strength of the repressed impulses and the defenses against them. In all cases the experience contains common elements which show that a similar process is at work. These elements are:

1. Confusion and feelings of anxiety verging on terror.

2. Estrangement—a state of partial unreality in which one cannot tell if one is dreaming or awake. In this situation one pinches oneself to tell the difference. Estrangement occurs when a person is overwhelmed by sensations.

3. Depersonalization—the loss of the feeling of self.

4. Finally, schizophrenia—a withdrawal and regression to infantile or archaic levels of functioning as a means of survival.

The person going through a breakdown is not aware that repressed feelings have broken through his defenses. Such an awareness would require self-knowledge and ego strength that the schizoid doesn't have. When he acquires these through therapy he is in a position to release the repression without danger to himself or others. The incident which sets off the breakdown may be almost insignificant. If conditions are right, it acts like the fuse which explodes the dynamite. The catastrophic result can only be explained in terms of the terror which is buried within the personality. On no other basis, can one understand the extreme steps which the person will take if the terror continues.

The schizophrenic state is a denial of reality. If the denial is complete, the terror vanishes. Since one aspect of his terror is the fear of being destroyed, the schizophrenic's condition is a refuge. He can hardly be destroyed if he is not "here," that is, not existing in present time and space. He cannot be punished if he is not himself, that is, if he is really Napoleon or Jesus Christ or some god in disguise. On the other hand, if his terror stems from his fear that he will destroy someone else, then a paranoid mechanism removes his fear. He has no reason to reproach himself, since, by means of the paranoid delusion, he is convinced that others are scheming to destroy him. It is amazing how little anxiety the paranoid individual shows when he recounts his story of imagined persecutions. Finally, not to feel and not to think dispels all fear.

4

The Forsaken Body

THERE is something about the physical appearance of the insane individual that strikes us as strange and bizarre. We sense that he is out of contact with things around him. This impression is conveyed by certain physical signs that distinguish the schizophrenic from the normal.

I saw a girl in my office some time ago who was in an obvious psychotic state. She carried her head to one side, as if her neck were bent at an angle. Her eyes had a wild, distraught look. Her face had an expression of fear and agony. She tore at her hair with both hands, moaned and muttered. Her speech was slurred and I could not understand her. I sensed, however, that she understood what I was saying.

She was the patient of one of my associates who was on a hospital call at the time. Although she had no appointment with him, her desperation brought her to the office. She would not quiet down. Any attempt to calm her was resisted forcibly. She continued to moan and tear at her hair. When her doctor was reached he spoke to her on the phone and she became more tractable. Finally, his arrival ended the episode, for he was able to calm her and drive her home.

The appearance of this patient indicated such an evident disturbance that a glance was sufficient to reveal the diagnosis. However, no diagnosis of schizophrenia should be based simply upon a person's state of agony and torment, for it can be shown that similar agonizing emotions may occur in response to a tragic event. For example, a mother might react in like manner to the death of her child. She would moan, tear her hair, and refuse to move. The agony and torment of the insane is no less real because we are unaware of the reason for their suffering. The two situations differ, of course, in their causative factors. In the case of the mother, the anguish is related and proportionate to a known and accepted cause; the behavior of the insane person appears disproportionate to the apparent stresses of his immediate situation. The observer cannot perceive the cause of his actions; and the insane person, whether he knows the cause or not, cannot communicate it to us.

The opposite situation can also exist in insanity. The cause may be known or visible, but the psychotic person's reaction seems to bear no relation to this cause. The simplest example is the lack of reaction to an obvious loss or injury, as in the case of a schizophrenic parent who kills a child but shows no grief. Thus, the lack of meaningful response to the events of the external situation is an accepted indication that "something is off."

When we say that the psychotic is out of contact with reality, we do not necessarily mean that he is unaware of what is happening around him. The catatonic, for example, is fully aware of what one says or does to him. And the girl in the above illustration, I am sure, knew what I was doing and heard my questions. I asked her what was troubling her. But she couldn't answer this question. She was reacting to a situation inside herself, that is, to certain feelings and body sensations which she did not understand and which were overwhelming her. It is not a question of the intensity of the feeling. The grief of a mother who has just lost a child would be equally intense. She, too, could ignore her environment temporarily. But she would be capable of describing her feelings and of relating them to an immediate cause.

The psychotic person is out of contact with his body. He does not perceive the feelings and sensations in his body as his own or as arising from his body. They are alien and unknown forces acting upon him in some mysterious way. Therefore, he cannot communicate them to us as meaningful explanations of his behavior. He feels terrified, and his behavior expresses this feeling, but he cannot relate it to any specific event.

The schizophrenic acts as if he were "possessed" by some strange force over which he has no control. Before the advent of modern psychiatry it was customary to regard the insane as being "possessed by a demon," or "devil"—for which he was to be punished. We have rejected this explanation of his illness, but we cannot avoid the impression that the schizophrenic is "possessed." No matter what the outward expression of the psychotic—whether comic, tragic, delusional or withdrawn—this impression is always present. It still serves as a valuable indication of the illness for today's observer.

It is significant that we use the concept of "possession" in our language to designate sanity. We describe a person as being "in possession of himself" or "in possession of his faculties," or oppositely, we say that he has "lost possession of himself." Possession in this sense refers, of course, to the control of the ego over the instinctual forces of the body. When possession is lost, these forces are out of ego control. In the psychotic individual the ego has disintegrated to a point where it can be compared to a state of anarchy in which one doesn't know what is going on and is terrified because of it. On the other hand, the loss of control which occurs in a hysterical outburst can be compared to a riot. One knows that ego authority will soon be restored and the rioting emotions brought under control. Self-possession can be gauged by the person's ability to respond appropriately to his life situations. The schizophrenic lacks this ability completely. The schizoid individual is handicapped in his responsiveness by the rigidity of his body.

THE SCHIZOID MASK

The first feature which strikes the observer as odd about the appearance of the schizophrenic or schizoid individual is the look of his eyes. His eyes have been described as "off," "blank," "vacant," "out of touch," etc. This expression is so characteristic that it alone can be used to diagnose the presence of schizophrenia. It has been commented on by a number of writers. Wilhelm Reich, for instance, says that both the schizoid and schizophrenic personalities "have a typical *faraway* look of remoteness.

. . . It seems as if the psychotic looks right through you with an absent-minded but deep look into far distances.[19]" This special look is not always present. At other times, the eyes just look vacant. Reich observed that when emotions well up in the schizophrenic, his eyes " 'go off,' as it were."

Silvano Arieti refers to an "odd look or expression in their eyes," which he credits to many observers. He himself describes a retraction of the upper lid that produces a widening of the eyes. He relates it to the common expression in schizophrenics of "bewilderment and withdrawal." Arieti also comments on a so-called look of "madness" that he attributes to the lack in some schizophrenic eyes of normal convergence and constriction.[20] I believe this look is an expression of terror that can be interpreted as madness because it is unrelated to any known cause. Most commonly, one sees either the "faraway" look Reich describes or an expression of fear and bewilderment. The common denominator in all cases, however, is the inability of the schizophrenic to focus his eyes *with feeling* upon another person. His eyes may be wide with fear, but he does not look at you with fear; they may be full of rage, but it is not directed at you. You are uneasy in his presence because you sense an impersonal force in him that could break out and shatter you without acknowledging your existence.

One of my patients, whose eyes became glassy as he went into a catatonic state, told me later that he saw everything that took place. Though he appeared to be "gone," he saw my hand as I waved it before him. The mechanical function of vision was intact; light entering his eyes impressed his retina in the same way it acts on the sensitive film of a camera. When the patient came out of his catatonic state his eyes lost their glassy quality and resumed a more normal appearance. This patient's catatonic experience developed after an exercise of striking the couch with his fists while saying, "No!" The exercise evoked feelings that the patient couldn't handle and to which he reacted by "going dead." His apparent deadness was a defense against his feelings of rage. He suppressed this rage by withdrawing from almost all contact with the external world; the withdrawal produced the glassiness of his eyes.

The subjective impression that the schizoid is unable to make contact with your eyes is the most disturbing aspect of his appearance. You do not feel that he looks at you or that his eyes touch you, but that he stares at you with seeing but unfeeling eyes. On the other hand, when his eyes focus on you, you can sense the feeling in them; it is as if they touch you.

Ortega y Gasset makes an interesting analysis of the function of vision in his essay, "Point of View in the Arts." He notes:

> Proximate vision has a tactile quality. What mysterious resonance of touch is preserved by sight when it converges on a nearby object? We shall not now attempt to violate this mystery. It is enough that we recognize this quasi-tactile density possessed by the ocular ray, and which permits it, in effect, to embrace, to touch the earthen jar. As the object is withdrawn, sight loses its tactile power and gradually becomes pure vision.[21]

Another way of describing the disturbance in the schizophrenic's eyes is to say that he "sees but does not look." The difference between seeing and looking is the difference between passivity and activity. Seeing is a passive function. According to Webster's New International Dictionary, seeing refers to the faculty of vision "where the element of attention is not emphasized." To look, on the other hand, is defined in this dictionary as "to direct the eyes or vision with a certain manner, purpose or feeling." Because the schizophrenic cannot direct his vision with feeling, he lacks the full possession of this faculty or the normal control of this bodily function. His self-possession is limited.

We look at people's eyes to learn what they feel or to sense their response to us. Are they happy or sad, angry or amused, frightened or relaxed? Because the schizoid's eyes tell no story, we know he has repressed all feeling. In treating these patients I pay very close attention to their eyes. When I reach them emotionally, that is, when they respond to me as a human being, their eyes light up and come into focus. This also happens spontaneously when a patient gains more feeling in his body as a result of therapy. The color of his eyes becomes more vivid, and they look more alive. The blankness or emptiness of the eyes is thus an expression of the relative unaliveness of the total personality. The responsiveness or lack of it in the eyes of the schizoid patient gives me a clearer indication of what is going on with him than any verbal communication. More than any other single sign, the expression in the eyes of a person indicates to what extent he is in "possession of his faculties."

Everyone senses that the eyes reveal many aspects of the personality. The eyes of a zealot burn with the fire of fanaticism, and the eyes of a lover glow with the warmth of his feeling. The brightness of a child's eyes reflects his interest in the world; the dullness which may appear in the eyes of old people indicates that this interest has waned. The eyes are windows of the body. Though they do not necessarily reveal what a person is thinking, they always show what he is feeling. Like windows, they can be shuttered or open, glazed or clear.

If parents, educators, and physicians would look (direct their vision with feeling) at children's eyes, the tragedy of the schizoid child who is not understood could be partly avoided.

The schizoid's inability to focus stems from his anxiety about the feelings which would come through in his eyes. He is afraid to let his eyes actively express fear or anger because this would make him conscious of these feelings. To look with feeling is to be aware of the feeling. The suppression of the feeling requires that the eyes be kept vacant, or distant. The lack of expression in the eyes, like the lack of responsiveness in the body, is part of the schizoid defense against feeling. However, when the feelings break through the defense and inundate the ego, the eyes "go off," as Reich pointed out, or the fear and rage may pour through them chaotically, without focus and direction, as in the case of the schizophrenic girl in my office. Thus, when eyes have either the "far-off" look or a look of wild, undirected rage or terror, they denote schizophrenia. Vacant and distant eyes indicate a schizoid state.

When one moves from the eyes to the total expression of the face, other signs of the schizoid disturbance are seen. The most important is an absence of facial expression, similar to the lack of feeling in the eyes. It has been said that the schizoid face has a masklike quality. It lacks the normal play of feeling that makes the healthy face look alive. The mask takes several forms: it may show the bewilderment of the clown, the naive innocence of the child, the knowing look of the sophisticate, the haughtiness of the aristocrat. Its characteristic feature is a "fixed" smile, in which the eyes to not participate. This typical schizoid smile can be recognized by (1) its unvarying quality, (2) its lack of appropriateness, (3) its unrelatedness to a feeling of pleasure. It can be interpreted as an attempt to relieve the tension of the masklike visage when feelings arise which the schizoid cannot express or communicate. The smile hides and denies the existence of any negative attitude. Harvey Cleckley refers to this schizoid expression as the "mask of sanity."[22]

Behind the mask of the fixed smile and the knowing look one can discern an expression in the schizoid face which I would describe as cadaverous. It is the look of a skull or death's-head. In some cases it can be seen only if a steady pressure is exerted with the thumbs upon the cheekbones on both sides of the bridge of the nose. Under this pressure the fixed smile disappears, the facial bones stand out, the color drains from the face, and the eyes seem to be hollow sockets. It is a ghastly expression and strikes one as the look of death. The patient is not aware of this expression, since it is hidden by the mask, but its presence is another gauge to the depth of his fear. It would be correct to say that the schizoid individual is "scared to death," literally and not just in a manner of speaking. This expression also appears in the figure drawings of some patients, as Figures 2 and 13 (pp. 12 and 139) show.

The schizoid mask is not removable at will. The schizoid's facial expression is frozen by an underlying terror, and the mask is his armor against this terror. The mask also enables the schizoid person to appear before the world without causing the shock reaction his cadaverous expression would otherwise provoke. To remove the mask, the "rigor mortis" must be thawed out, the fear and terror must be made conscious, and their grip upon the personality released.

Kretschmer poses the question that must challenge the

mind of anyone who has had contact with the schizoid personality. "What is there in the deep under all these masks?" he asks. "Perhaps there is nothing, dark, hollow-eyed nothing—affective anemia."[23] He continues: "One cannot know what they feel: sometimes they don't know themselves, or only dimly." If one asks the schizoid individual what he feels, the most common answer is, "Nothing. I don't feel anything." Yet when, in the course of therapy, he allows his feelings to come to the surface, he will reveal that he has the same desires and wants as any other person and that they were always present. His mask and his denial of feeling is a defense against his terror and his rage, but it also serves to suppress all desires. He believes that he cannot allow himself to feel or to want, since this would leave him vulnerable to some catastrophe, rejection, or abandonment. If one wants nothing, one cannot be hurt.

At times, when the schizoid patient is out of control and overwhelmed by his inner feelings, his facial expression becomes so distorted that it looks inhuman. When he allows a feeling of anger to arise, or when he adopts the facial expression of anger, his visage frequently looks demonic. What one sees is not anger but the dark eyes and knit brows of a frightening black rage. In the regressed and withdrawn schizophrenic the face and head often resemble a gargoyle. At other times the face seems to melt and an infantile smile plays about the mouth, without, however, involving the eyes.

This dissociation between the smile about the mouth and the lack of expression in the eyes is typical of the schizoid personality. Eugen Bleuler has commented as follows on the split in the facial expression of the schizophrenic: "The mimic lacks unity—the wrinkled forehead, for example, expresses something like surprise; the eyes with their little crow's-feet give the impression of laughter; and the corners of the mouth may be drooping as in sorrow. Often the facial expression seems exaggerated and highly melodramatic."[24]

Another characteristic feature of the schizoid face is its rigid jaw. This is invariably present. Together with the fixed smile, it creates a marked lack of coordination between the upper and lower parts of the face. The rigid jaw expresses an attitude of defiance that belies the vacant or frightened look in the eyes. The rigidity of the jaw helps to block off any feeling of fear or terror from becoming manifest in the eyes. In effect, the schizoid is saying, I will not be afraid.

I have found that it is almost impossible for the patient to mobilize any conscious expression in his eyes before the tension in the jaw muscles is substantially reduced. This usually happens when the patient gives in to his feelings of sadness, and cries.

If one observes the crying of an infant, one will notice that it begins with a quiver in the chin. The chin recedes, the mouth droops, and the jaw drops as the infant gives way to the convulsive release of feeling in the crying. The rigidity of the schizoid jaw inhibits this release. It functions, therefore, as a general defense against all feeling.

A dynamic interpretation of the tension in and about the schizoid head was suggested to me by a short unpublished monograph on the snarling reflex.[25] Generally, the schizoid patient cannot snarl, that is, he cannot curl his upper lip and bare his teeth. Normal individuals find it easier to make this gesture. The schizoid difficulty is due to the immobilization of the upper half of the face, extending over the scalp to the nuchal region at the junction of the head with the back of the neck. These nuchal muscles are tightly contracted in the schizoid condition. One can appreciate the tension involved if one assumes an exaggerated expression of fright: opening the eyes wide, raising the brows, and pulling the head back. One then feels the muscles at the base of the skull contract. Snarling and biting require a direction of motion exactly opposite to that which occurs in fright. In biting, the head is brought forward, so that the upper teeth inflict the bite while the lower ones hold the object. Since the schizoid is frozen in the state of terror, he cannot execute this movement or make the gesture of snarling.

The schizoid inhibition of snarling and biting relates to a deep-seated oral disturbance which is also manifest in the schizoid reluctance to reach out with his mouth and to suck. This total oral disturbance stems from an infantile conflict with a mother who could not fulfill the child's oral erotic needs. The infant's frustration leads to biting impulses, to which the mother reacts with such hostility that the child has no alternative but to suppress its oral desires and repress its oral aggression.

BODILY RIGIDITY, FRAGMENTATION,

AND COLLAPSE

Another common finding in the schizoid body is the lack of alignment between the head and the rest of the body. The head is often carried at an angle to the trunk, inclining either left or right. This carriage is another indication of the dissociation between the head and the body, but I never fully understood the reason for this position of the head until a patient made the following observation. He was at an interview, under considerable emotional stress. Suddenly, his vision became fuzzy, and objects appeared to lose form. When he put his head to one side, his vision cleared. If he tried to hold it straight, the disturbance recurred. He was able to go through the interview leaning his head on his hand. The probable explanation of this phenomenon is that the inclined position of the head allowed him to use one eye, the dominant one, for vision and to avoid the difficulty of convergence and accommodation required when both eyes attempt to focus on an object.

Rigidity and tension also characterize the remainder of the schizoid body. One almost always sees a rigidity of the shoulders and neck, which seems related to an attitude of haughtiness and withdrawal. I interpret this expression as an attitude of "being above it," the "it" meaning the body and bodily desires and feelings. This attitude becomes generalized as being above people or the bodily pleasure of life. The haughtiness is most clearly manifest in patients who have a long, thin neck which seems to detach the head from the rest of the body. In these cases the shoulders are depressed, accentuating the separation. In other cases the shoulders are elevated, as if the patient were trying to hold himself up by his shoulders. As a result of the rigidity of the shoulder girdle, the arms hang from their sockets like appendages rather than as extensions of a unified organism.

Schizoid rigidity is not the same as the rigidity of the compulsive neurotic, which stems from a tension that contains a strong emotional charge. The neurotic is frustrated and angry; the schizoid is terrified with a suppressed rage. The body structure of the rigid neurotic individual has an essential unity which is lacking in the schizoid structure. The rigidity of the schizoid is like ice compared to the steel of the rigid neurotic. In the schizoid personality the rigidity is as brittle at it is hard, as constricting as it is containing. Kretschmer quotes Strindberg, who became schizophrenic, as saying, "I am as hard as ice yet so full of feeling that I am almost sentimental."[26]

Schizoid feeling is sentimentality because it lacks a direct connection with physical sensation. It can be described as a "cool" feeling which reflects denial of need and rejection of bodily pleasure. Normal feeling is emotional rather than sentimental because it is grounded in physical sensation; emotional feelings, therefore, are warm or hot (passionate). On the other hand, the schizoid is not devoid of feeling or even passion when it is a question of defending the rights of the underprivileged or fighting for a cause. His dedication to principles reflects a selflessness that is at the core of his personal difficulties. This is not to say that the defense of justice is the exclusive domain of the schizoid. What is meant here is that the schizoid, lacking a sense of personal identity, frequently seeks a justification for living in social causes, isms, and panaceas. Schizoid sentimentality is the result of the abstraction of feeling from the self and the body. It denotes a loss of personal identity, which is compensated for through social identifications.

Further examination of the schizoid body reveals several other characteristic disturbances. One commonly finds that the upper half of the body is relatively underdeveloped muscularly. The thorax tends to be narrow, tight, and held in a deflated condition. This thoracic constriction, which is particularly evident in the lower ribs, necessarily limits respiration. In other cases, however, where the illness is less severe, one may find a compensatory inflation of the chest, considered "manly" by some patients and developed through weight-lifting exercises. In the collapsed body, the chest is deflated, soft, and toneless. In all cases, there is a marked constriction of the body about the waist, due to a chronic contraction of the diaphragm.

In many patients the constriction in the region of the waist gives one the strong impression that the body is divided into two halves. It suggests the interpretation that the person is attempting to dissociate the upper half of the body, with which the ego is identified, from the sexuality of the lower half. I treated a patient who was fully developed in the upper half of her body but underdeveloped in her lower half. From the waist up she looked like a woman, from the waist down she had the appearance of a little girl. She told me an interesting story about herself which reflected her problem. The day after an appendicitis operation, she was given a bedpan to use. My patient protested to the nurse that she couldn't use it because her urine flowed forward instead of downward. When the nurse insisted, the patient tried—and wet herself. What she had said was true. Her pelvis retained the forward position it occupies in little girls. In puberty there occurs a downward and backward rotation of the pelvis which brings the vagina between the thighs. This hadn't happened to my patient, as she was well aware.

The downward rotation of the pelvis, together with the broadening of the hips, produces the normal female body structure. The knees approach one another in the midline as the thighs rotate inward and come together. This development is only partial in most schizoid females: the pelvis retains its forward tilt, and there is a noticeable separation between the thighs.

Another characteristic of the schizoid body is dysplasia, that is, the presence of features which belong to the opposite sex. Android features such as narrow hips, slender thighs, and a male distribution of pubic hair are frequently found in the female. In the male, gynecoid tendencies are present in the form of a full, rounded pelvis, an incipient mons veneris (a mound of fatty tissue over the pubic bone in the female), and a feminine distribution of pubic hair in the form of an inverted triangle.

Dysplasia is less commonly found in the long, thin (asthenic) body type. Such body structures have an immature quality which decreases secondary sexual differences. The hips are narrow and small, as in prepubescent boys and girls; the shoulders are narrow; and the musculature is underdeveloped. The muscles are long and stringy. However, in the asthenic body structure the marked constriction in the waist which seems to separate the two halves of the body, greatly reduces the individual's coordination.

The legs and feet of schizoid individuals also show certain disturbances. The knees are stiff, the ankles are frozen, and the feet are contracted, decreasing the flexibility of the legs. The resulting limitation of motility is most evident in the inability of these patients to bend their knees fully when their feet are flat on the ground. On the other hand, most schizoid patients are able to extend the leg and foot in a straight line and curl the toes in a prehensile manner. I interpret this condition as an indication that the schizoid foot seems more adapted for grasping and holding than for plantar locomotion.

In many patients the feet are inverted, that is, each is turned toward the other. This inversion shifts the weight of the body to the outside edge of the feet and produces a slight bowing of the legs. The inverted foot suggests the prenatal and early infantile condition, in which the feet face each other. It is evidence of a failure of development and indicates a fixation at the infantile level. In this condition the muscles of the foot are chronically contracted to support the weight of the body, thereby greatly exaggerating the normal arch.

Infantilism is also seen in patients whose feet are unusually small. Generally these feet belong to the petite and dainty child-woman. Sometimes, however, they belong to a large, heavy body; in such cases they may be interpreted as a sign of infantile tendencies in the personality. Where the lower half of the body is heavy and flabby, the muscles of the feet also lose their tone. The arch is collapsed, and the weight is thrown to the inside of the foot. I presented a patient at a clinical seminar in my office who weighed 235 pounds. His feet were small and tight and he was unable to spread or curl his toes. His feet had a bluish tint indicating some degree of cyanosis. One of the doctors present commented on their appearance, "I think he lacks contact with the floor, and I believe this is why his ideas float in the air and are not grounded. His legs and feet do not seem strong enough to carry his body."

The patient replied to this comment with the statement,

"I feel that being rooted to the ground is an adult function I don't have."

Two observations by patients relate the disturbance in the function of the legs and feet to that of the eyes. One patient reported, "It seems that when I can't stand on my feet I can't focus my eyes. I wasn't able to focus them today, so I bent my knees, and after a while, my eyes focused better." The patient's remark about bending her knees refers to the therapeutic practice of keeping the knees bent to soften the rigidity of the legs and provide a better contact with the ground. This practice counters a general tendency in the schizoid patient to stand with locked knees and rigid legs.

Another observation was made by a different patient about her experiences in a dance therapy class.

> I was on my knees and bent forward to stretch my neck and back. I could feel my whole backbone except for one or two blank spots. I could breathe easily and fully without conscious effort. I felt connected all over. I got up to stand on my feet, and my legs began to tremble. My eyes kept crossing. I couldn't focus them. The trembling increased until it reached my belly and pelvis, when I began to sob involuntarily.

This observation shows that focusing the eyes depends on the ability to *stand* the body feelings. The concepts implied in the terms "standing on one's feet" and "standing the feeling" seem related. The first patient gained the ability to focus her eyes when she felt her feet on the ground; the second lost this ability when she couldn't stand the sensations in her body.

It has been pointed out that the schizoid body is frozen with fear. How terror affects the body is shown in the following report. A patient related that as she was walking through her house one afternoon she anticipated coming face to face with a grandfather clock which stood in the corridor. As she thought of the clock she pictured a head from which the skin was peeling. The image terrified her. She said:

> My body became rigid. I felt my shoulders rise and stiffen; my head became wooden; my eyes glazed over;

and my ankles froze. I couldn't breathe. It required a tremendous effort to move. For several days after this experience I walked awkwardly and my balance seemed uncertain.

Rigidity functions as a defense as long as the rigidity is unconscious, that is, as long as the person is unaware of his rigidity or its meaning. While the observer sees terror in the immobility of the schizoid body, the schizoid, who is out of contact with his body, senses only his desperate need to hold himself together. The collapse of the rigidity allows the terror to reach consciousness.

When the condition of the schizoid body is one of collapse rather than rigidity, the dominant mood of the personality is fear. Generally, such cases are closer to the schizophrenic end of the spectrum than the rigid types. I had a patient who had anxiety attacks of such severity that they bordered on sheer terror. During an attack her eyes went out of focus, she became confused, and she moaned. At times she hid in the kneehole of my desk or in a corner of the room, curled up like an infant.

Her body did not show the common schizoid rigidity and tightness. Her superficial muscles felt flabby and lacked normal tone. Under the superficial softness, however, one could palpate the tension in the deep muscles at the base of the skull, in the root of the neck, about the diaphragm, and in the lumbosacral and pelvic regions. These tensions were so severe that they literally choked off the flow of blood and energy to the surface of her body. Thus, her skin was tender and dry and had a yellow-brownish coloration. Her eyes lacked feeling, and her legs and feet appeared weak.

The anxiety attack was manifested by a trembling of her whole body. Repeated shudders passed through her. She shook as if she might actually fall apart. These attacks lasted about five to ten minutes and subsided spontaneously when the patient realized that she would come to no harm. After such an episode was over, she always felt better. With further therapy the attacks lessened in severity and decreased in frequency. She learned that they occurred whenever she "opened up," that is, whenever she allowed any feeling of warmth to come through to me, and this knowledge reassured her. But more than anything else, it was my presence and support that sustained her through the difficult periods. She slowly gained the ability to tolerate and accept her feelings, and her skin color changed. She became "pink," as she called it. When she felt good she described herself as being "in the pink." Her deep muscle tensions also relaxed somewhat, and her body became warm whereas previously it had been cold.

As this patient became able to stand her feelings she also gained the ability to stand on her own feet. This development brought her therapy to a dramatic close. When I declined to continue the role of a supporting and protective mother figure she asked me, "Do *you* want me to get well? Do *you* want me to live?" If I said Yes, it would mean (to her) that I would assume responsibility for her welfare. On the other hand, I couldn't say No. She was afraid to sever the umbilical cord that had sustained her through the crises and to depend upon her own resources. I could only answer that the decision to live and get well was hers to make. Reluctantly, she accepted my answer and decided to stand on her own. I followed her progress for more than six years after the termination of our relationship. She continued to improve in both her ability to stand her feelings and to stand on her own feet without help.

The above approach to personality through the interpretation of bodily expression depends upon the ability of the analyst to relate the physical characteristics of an individual to his attitudes and behavior. All people unconsciously interpret personality from physical expression. The analyst has to make these interpretations consciously. He has to know the significance of the physical distortions that a patient's body presents. Kretschmer possessed this ability. Indeed his work is more important for its clinical descriptions than for his attempt to classify patients by body type. These descriptions are the products of a discerning eye, a clinical mind, and a creative imagination. The following is a good example:

> She is very fair, and looks ethereally transparent, with a thin nose and blue-veined temples. There is an atmosphere of "distance" about her. Her movements

are slow, refined and aristocratic, with a few awkward-
nesses here and there. If anyone speaks to her, she
draws herself slightly back and leans against the cup-
board. There is something strange and very dreamy
about her. Her hair is thin, long and very flexible.
When she is greeting you, she reaches out the tips of
her fingers, which are cold and quite transparent. She
smiles distantly, confusedly and uncertainly.[27]

This description illustrates the extent to which the withdrawal and dissociation from the external world is paralleled by withdrawal and dissociation from the body.
Kretschmer's picture of this delusional schizophrenic
shows the transformation of the living body into a disembodied spirit and a forsaken body. She is ethereal, blue,
transparent, and distant as the sky. One misses in her
physical appearance and in her personality the qualities of
redness, earthiness, and corporeality of flesh and blood.
What remains is the transparent shell of a person.

Kretschmer observed and noted the quality of the skin,
the distribution of hair, the shape of features, etc. He
writes, "The complexion of schizophrenics of all ages is
generally pale, often with a dash of yellow or cheese-like
pastiness on the one hand, or with a tendency to sallow
brown pigmentation on the other."[28] He commented
often on the frequency of dysplastic features: infantilism
(small hands), feminism in the male (narrow waist, big
buttocks, enlarged hip measurements, and feminine distribution of hair), and eunichoidism (underdeveloped
genitals). Despite his fine attention to detail, Kretschmer
advised that one should direct his "attention to the total
picture."[29]

Only the total picture in each case enables one to make
the diagnosis of schizoid personality. The details may vary,
because each person is an individual with a unique life
experience, which is reflected in his body. But when these
details are summarized one gains an impression of the
degree of an individual's self-possession. The look in the
eyes, the expression of the face, the carriage of the head,
the posture of the body, the color of the skin, the tone of
the muscles, the timbre of the voice, the stance of the legs,
the motility of the pelvis, the spontaneity of gesture—

these, and many more indices add up to the total picture we are seeking. When this total picture is one of unity, integration, and self-command we regard the person as being "all there," in possession of his faculties and emotionally healthy. The schizoid body lacks these qualities. The schizoid picture is that of a forsaken body from which the psyche has fled in terror.

5

The Body Image

A HEALTHY individual has a clear mental image of his body which he can reproduce verbally and graphically. He can describe his facial expression, his posture, and his bodily attitudes. He can draw a figure which is a reasonable facsimile of a human body. The schizoid individual cannot do this. His figure drawings are often so bizarre and stylized that the weakness of his body image is readily apparent.

In the first chapter I discussed the conflict between the ego image and the reality of the body's appearance as it looks to the observer. The subject of this chapter is the disparity between the way a person sees himself as a social being (his ego image) and the way he sees himself as a physical being (his body image). The disparity between these two images is a measure of the schizoid disturbance. The weakness of the body image is compensated for by an exaggeration of the ego image. This exaggeration becomes apparent to a patient when his ego image is contrasted with his body image as it is revealed, for example, in his figure drawings.

Figure drawings reveal many aspects of a person's body image. They tell us the degree of integration, the state of harmony among the body parts, the feeling for the body surface, the acceptance of sexual characteristics, the basic mood quality of the body, and the overall attitude toward the body. One reason why figure drawings are so revealing is that the person doing them has no model but his own body image to follow as a guide. He will, therefore, express in his drawing the way he perceives his own body. If a person lacks the feeling of pleasure in his body, he will

71

be disturbed about drawing the human body and block out many of its features.

How does a body image become distorted? To answer this question one must know how the body image develops. Research has shown that the body image is formed through the synthesis of sensations which derive from innumerable physical contacts between parents and child. These sensations have a positive or negative sign as they are felt to be pleasurable or painful. Positive sensations favor the formation of a clear and integrated body image. Negative sensations lead to distortions or gaps in the body image.

It should be realized, as S. F. Fisher and S. E. Cleveland point out, "[Parents'] attitudes towards him [the child] are expressed in how they go about satisfying his hunger sensations, how they pick him up and handle him, and how they try to regulate such body processes as excretion and defecation."[30] The "how" refers to the quality of the touch, the look in the eyes, the gentleness of the manner, all of which are registered in the child's consciousness as body sensations that will affect his body image.

When a body image is defective, it always denotes a disturbance in the mother-child relationship, since the mother is the person most involved with the child's physical needs. A rejecting mother deprives the child of the opportunity to experience the pleasure of its body in the close physical intimacy of the mother-child relationship. A possessive mother denies the child the right to experience its body as its own by usurping its body for her personal pleasure and satisfaction.

Since the child's identity in early life is mainly a body identity, the quality of the physical contact between mother and child will determine its feeling for its body and the nature of its responses to life. Warm, tender, and supporting arms give the child a pleasurable feeling in its own body and reinforce its desire for further contact with the world. The way a mother looks at her child will have an important effect upon the responsiveness of the child's eyes. It makes a big difference whether the mother's eyes are soft and loving or hard and hateful.

The body image serves two important functions in adult life. It serves as a model for the performance of conscious motor activity. Consciously directed motor activity is sub-consciously rehearsed before an attempt is made to per-form the activity. The sequence of movements is visualized in terms of the body image. An inadequate body image will handicap the performance. The body image also serves to localize sensation. The ability to define the location of a sensation depends upon a well-formed body image. Young children cannot describe the exact location of pain because their body image is too nebulous. For the same reason, schizophrenics are confused about the location of their bodily sensations.

A body image may facilitate one type of activity and impede another. For example, a baseball player can clearly see himself hitting a ball with grace and coordination, but he may be unable to picture himself doing a tango with equal grace. In this case, one would expect his body image to show a deficiency in those qualities that relate to dancing. This is not a question of coordination. Each of these activities has a different emotional meaning. Hitting a baseball has an aggressive connotation, while doing the tango implies sensuality and sexuality.

The body image of the schizoid individual is deficient in those qualities which relate to the expression of feeling. The schizoid sees his body as inexpressive and unrespon-sive, and his figure drawings reflect this limitation. How-ever, his ego image may be quite different: he may imag-ine himself as sensitive, understanding, and sympathetic. What he cannot do is reconcile his sensitivity with his lack of warmth, his sympathy with his detachment, his under-standing with his impotence. The figure drawings of schizoid patients show certain common characteristics: the figures are unalive, often grotesque, stylized or sketched. They look like statues, clowns, dolls, specters, zombies or scarecrows.

THE MASK OF THE CLOWN

A common distortion of the body image is seen in figure drawings which portray the body as clownish. Figure 8 is typical of this kind of drawing by schizoid patients. It was made by Paul, whose terror was described in Chapter 3.

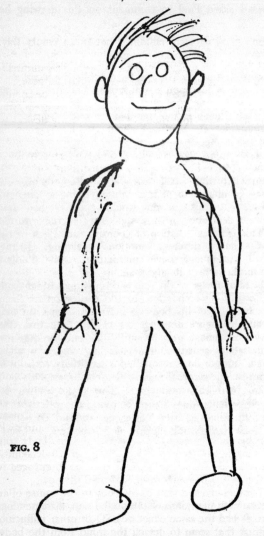

FIG. 8

When I asked Paul to comment on this drawing he said:

> He's good natured, childlike, but in an empty way. He's trying to say, I mean no harm.
>
> He plays the fool so people will think he's unintelligent, one dimensional. This would serve his purpose.
>
> I played the fool for so long. Now I try to be sophisticated in a philosophical way. I've never gotten away from playing the fool though I've used many devices to cover it up.

What is his purpose? What is the clown trying to hide? It is a fair guess that behind the masquerade of the clown is a deep sadness and a poignant longing. This was certainly true of Paul, who experienced a temporary paralysis when he tried to express his longing. I have found this to be true of all other patients who played the fool or adopted the role of the clown. However, Paul's figure drawing also shows a repressed hostility, which is expressed in the fingers drawn as thorns, or needles. Paul described the arms of the figure as "cut off and dangling," indicating their inadequacy as aggressive organs and his dissociation from the feeling of hostility in them.

The "fool" and the "intellectual" denote a split in Paul's personality. He was an intelligent young man, well educated and well read. His ability to discuss philosophical ideas was impressive. Yet he appeared foolish. In social situations he was shy, timid, and awkward. He didn't know what to say to a girl. Thus, he was emotionally clubfooted, as his figure shows, despite a keen mind. Two bodily characteristics determined the fool. He had an insipid grin, which he wore constantly, as if to say, I mean no harm. And he was physically uncoordinated and awkward in his movements. The clumsiness of his body contrasted sharply with the facility of his mind. Understandably, he rejected his body as "foolish" and never engaged in physical activities or sports until he started therapy.

Paul got a detached view of his body in the course of an experience with marijuana. He took, he said, a tremendous amount. It had the same effect as LSD or other hallucinogenic drugs that seem to detach the mind from the body, so that one sees oneself as if from the outside. The result is often a clearer perception of the body's disabilities. I shall quote his experience.

> My eyes became very alive, excited, relaxed. I saw things clearly.
>
> I felt very much out of it. I sat on a chair which didn't seem to rest on the floor. I felt I was floating above the ground. I seemed to feel the pattern of tension in my body: bands of tension around my head, across my chest, down my legs, and around my armpits. My arms felt detached from my body line. I was like in a straitjacket without arms. My left leg felt shorter than my right one. [Notice the difference in the two legs in the figure drawing.]
>
> I played piano effortlessly. I experienced incredible longing and also the feeling that I could do anything. It was a very split feeling, overwhelmingly positive towards the piano, where previously I felt very negative to it. But I sensed that it wasn't me playing. I was outside myself, observing the action. I sensed that there was another person in the room besides me and my friends. I felt an evil genie in me, a Mephistophelian force hovering over me and directing me. It seems I played flawlessly, but this was due to the fact that if I made a mistake, it was deliberate or willed.
>
> The experience was basically unsatisfactory. It ended with a headache, and I became very lethargic.

The similarity between Paul's self-perception under the drug and his figure drawing is striking. His awareness of his arms as cut off and dangling, of his legs as being different in size, and his body as being in a straitjacket parallels the identical distortions in the figure drawing. The impotence he feels in his body is portrayed in the figure of the simpleton or clown. The sense of power is perceived as a dissociated force outside the body.

Paul was impressed with the power that the genie represented. It seemed omnipotent in contrast to the feeling that his body was in a straitjacket. While playing, Paul felt possessed by the genie. Later he realized that this power was within him somewhere, and if he could possess the genie rather than be possessed by it, he could achieve great things.

As Paul gained more feeling in his body the mask of the clown disappeared. He emerged as a sad young man, aware of his unhappiness, but serious in his desire to live and find pleasure.

The spirit of the schizoid individual is trapped in a frozen body. While he dreams of personal fulfillment, his energy is unavailable for personal pleasure. His energy is bound in chronic muscular tensions, his spirit is locked in repressed feelings. It is part of the therapeutic task to help the patient free himself from his restrictive tensions. It is also part of his task to help the patient uncover and grapple with his repressed feelings. This involves a voyage to the underworld (his unconscious) and a struggle with its demons (his repressed feelings) if he is to recapture the "power" that is life.

THE DOLL

Another common distortion of the normal body image is revealed in figure drawings which picture the body as a doll. Also the physical appearance of an individual, usually the female, often suggests a doll-like quality in the personality. Mary as a young woman in whom this quality was manifested both in her figure drawings and in her body structure. She could best be described as petite. She was five feet tall and weighed about a hundred pounds. Her body looked very youthful, to the point of being almost childlike, despite her 33 years. She impressed me as immature and underdeveloped, that is, as a child-woman. Structurally, her features were trim and youthfully proportioned. Functionally, her body was rigid. Her skin was pale, dry, and unalive-looking. Her face was expressionless, her eyes tended to become vacant, to lose focus and feeling. Nevertheless, there was something attractive and appealing about Mary.

What image did she have of her body? What was her attitude toward it? The male and female figure drawings reproduced here in Figures 9 and 10, together with her comments on them, provide some information.

The fact that she spontaneously drew three figures to represent her concept of the female body is significant. It

FIG. 9

indicates a three-way split in her personality. The top figure in Figure 9 is extremely childlike and boyish, without hands, feet, or sexual characteristics. The middle figure, the matron with her head detached from her body, suggests Mary's womanly aspect; however, it is an unintegrated body image. The lower figure, which shows only a head with a sophisticated expression, represents her dissociated ego.

All the figures are stylized, which denotes a poor conception of the human body. They look unreal and lack human feeling. Mary's comment on these drawings was: "They look a little like me. All my women are very tailored, the way I would really like to look."

Figure 10 is Mary's conception of the male body. After she drew it she remarked:

> Instinctively, I wouldn't draw a penis on a man. I don't draw arms either, or hands. I can't make hands look like hands. No hips and no sex. Too good-looking. Face and head too boyish. That's the way I used to want to look—like a fag [homosexual]. I used to like them. He doesn't have any feelings; he's intellectual and tasteful.

When I asked Mary to describe her feelings about hands, she remarked, "Hands are like claws, especially when the fingers are long, tapered, and brightly red—like my mother's." Then she added, "I'm terrified of cats. My fantasy is that a cat will spring at me and claw me to death. My blood turns to ice when I look at its eyes."

Evidently, Mary identified her mother with a cat, and her fear of cats is a reflection of her fear of her mother. The identification of mother with cats suggests the cat-and-mouse game in which Mary felt herself to be the helpless object, a plaything of her mother. The lack of hands and feet in her drawing denotes her impotence to fight or flee.

From the foregoing I drew the conclusion that Mary's body image was that of a doll. Her drawings are doll-like, she has been described as a doll by others, and she regarded herself as a doll. She said one day, "I am a kissy doll, pretty, asexual, and unalive." But if her body image was that of a doll, her ego image was that of a sophisti-

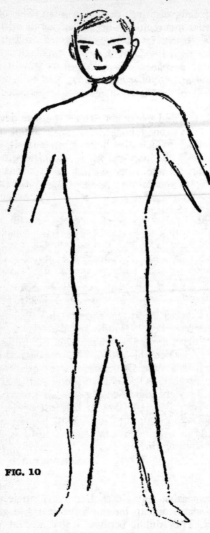

FIG. 10

cated, sexually exciting, mature woman. She often complained that men couldn't keep their hands off her. Many men find themselves strongly attracted to this doll-like, child-woman quality, which poses no challenge to their manhood. Thus, Mary had a split personality: her ego image, which determined her conscious behavior, was at variance with her body image, which reflected her true feelings.

In the schizoid personality the ego image develops as a reaction to the body image. The ego cannot accept the negative value which the body represents. It creates its own image of the personality, in opposition to an unacceptable body image. However, the two contrasting images develop simultaneously in response to the external forces which split the unity of the personality. The elucidation of these forces requires an analysis of the patient's character structure with reference to infantile experiences.

What identifications shaped Mary's personality? What experiences transfigured her body? During one session, while discussing the symbolic meaning of her body structure, Mary said:

> My mother always used to say that she loved having a doll which she could dress up and show off. I remember that it made me feel I didn't belong to myself. And her hands touching—it made me crawl. My body belonged to my mother as if I were her doll. If I said No, and she pursued me, I became paralyzed.

Mary abandoned her body because her mother had taken possession of it. Her body became possessed by a spirit, so to speak—the spirit of her mother. From Mary's reaction, it can be assumed that it was a malevolent spirit, but its exact nature was still unknown. At this point all Mary could say was that in her role as doll and plaything for her mother, she was a "faggy little boy-girl."

On another occasion, Mary related the following:

> I remember very clearly that every single night they would stand me up on the toilet seat and give me an enema. They did it because I screamed at night and they thought it was gas. I was naked, and if their friends dropped in, they would watch. My mother is a very phallic person.

Then, in a hysterical voice, Mary cried out:

> I just can't stand the feeling in my body. I feel I am being violated all the time. I am constantly aware of my pelvis and vagina. I feel like there are things crawling around in it. I feel that I don't want to breathe. I don't want to move.

She began to sob hysterically, then continued:

> I made my body go dead. I made it just freeze. I've just done it now. I want to be a boy.

The "doll" can be explained as an unconscious maneuver to cut off and repress sexual feelings which are perceived as alien and threatening. By becoming a doll or a mannequin (a full-size doll), a person deadens his body and depersonalizes. Mary's rejection of her body and her femininity, apparent in her figure drawings, is related to the strange feelings in her belly and her genitals. From her statement it is evident that her tendency to go dead, that is, to depersonalize, is a reaction against these sensations which she perceived as a threat to the integrity of her personality. I have found the same phenomenon in every case of split personality I have treated.

DEPERSONALIZATION

The mechanism of depersonalization is the inhibition of respiration and movement. But this maneuver is not really as consciously made as Mary's statement seems to imply. Lurking in the background is a feeling of terror perceived consciously as a "strange sensation," against which the organism defends itself by "going dead." In the face of this terror, the body freezes, the breath is held, and all movement stops.

Once depersonalization occurs and the ego is split from the body, a vicious circle develops. As long as the body is cut off from perception, its sensations are experienced as strange and terrifying. Without an adequate body image the mind cannot correctly interpret bodily events. This is why hypochondriasis is such a common symptom in individuals with schizoid tendencies. Where a normal person could understand and therefore tolerate such phenomena as a throat constriction, a heart palpitation, or butterflies in the belly, the schizoid individual reacts to these happenings with exaggerated alarm. The schizophrenic actually "sees" them as the result of external influences, even though they occur within his own body, through no outside interference.

Eugen Bleuler offers a number of examples of the distortion in self-perception which characterizes the depersonalized state.

> The patients are beaten and burnt; they are pierced by red-hot needles, daggers or spears; their arms are being wrenched out; their heads are being bent backwards; their legs are being made smaller; their eyes are being pulled out, so that in the mirror it looks like they are entirely out of their sockets; the head is being squeezed. . . . They have eyes inside their head; they have been put in the refrigerator. Boiling oil is felt inside their bodies; their skin is full of stones. Their eyes flicker, as do their brains.[31]

Two reasons explain the frightening quality of these sensations. First, they occur in a body that is otherwise relatively without feeling. The contrast between the "deadened" body and the spontaneous sensation partly explains their abnormal intensity. Second, the schizophrenic lacks the ability to integrate his feelings and impulses into goal-directed activities. In the normal individual, impulses are organized into action patterns which channel the energy of the impulse into expressive or aggressive actions directed toward the outside world. This the schizophrenic cannot do. As a result, the chaotic impulse remains locked in the interior of the body, where it overexcites the organs and produces sensations which are perceived as strange and threatening.

Psychologically, the alien and disturbing body feelings reported by patients are unconsciously associated with frightening infantile and childhood experiences. The strange feelings Mary reported in her pelvis and genitals recalled similar sensations experienced in early life. Generally, this association has to be elucidated through the analysis of dreams and memories. However, simply making the association conscious does not relieve the anxiety.

As long as the ego is split off from the body, the genital excitations which occur in adulthood will be experienced with anxiety. This anxiety leads to a further cutting off of total body feeling.

The lack of an adequate body image based on an alive and responsive body surface explains promiscuous sexual behavior. Genital excitation is felt as a strange and disturbing force which has to be eliminated or discharged. This results in a compulsive sexuality which is nondiscriminating and devoid of affection. Such sexuality serves to release genital excitation, but since the total body is emotionally uninvolved, it fails to provide any positive pleasure or satisfaction. Homosexuality, in particular, is characterized by this kind of sexual feeling, as I pointed out in my book *Love and Orgasm.* Every homosexual I have treated shows this disturbance, which is related to an inadequate body image.

Experience reveals that when the body becomes alive, compulsive sexual behavior and promiscuity cease. Sexuality assumes a new meaning for the patient. It represents the desire for bodily closeness rather than the need to discharge an unpleasant tension. It becomes an expression of love and affection. In his new state of being, the patient experiences his genital excitation as part of this overall feeling, and therefore, as pleasurable.

In the course of therapy, as Mary gained more feeling in her body and better contact with it, she became aware of the childhood experiences which had forced her to abandon her body. She related such a memory:

> Many times, now, I lie in bed and feel my whole body. It feels so good to know it is all there. But even then I am aware of the tensions which cut off the lower part of my body. That's where parents tickle children. My father used to tickle me there until I couldn't stand it. I felt I would die if he wouldn't stop. It seemed he never stopped in time. He used to grab me by the knees. It was horrible! Now, I can't even touch myself there.

There is a perverse element in a parent who would bring a child to the point of hysteria in the name of affection. Such behavior suggests an unconscious sexual involvement with the child. In one sense, the giving of an enema can also be interpreted as a sexual violation. The insertion of the nozzle into the anus parallels the sexual act too closely to be free of this significance even if parents are unconscious of such a meaning. In fact, parents who give repeated enemas to their children are unconscious of the sexual symbolism of the act, but this parental blindness reflects their insensitivity to the child. In view of the behavior of Mary's mother and father it is not surprising that she should feel violated. Following a visit to her parents one weekend, she reported her reaction:

> I realized my mother was a lesbian. She touched me and I wanted to kill her.
>
> That evening my body felt horrible, and I had sexual sensations in my pelvis which were very unpleasant, wrong. I felt bad, as if I had something in me I had to get out. So when I went to bed I masturbated. The feeling was only in the clitoris. I found myself masturbating in a violent way, as if I was trying to rub something away. The orgasm was tight, tense, and angry. It only helped a little bit.
>
> I had the same feelings as a teenager. I used to masturbate the same way—wanting to get rid of those bad sexual feelings. Once I tried to give in to these feelings with homosexual thoughts about my mother. It was very exciting, but horrible. Terribly unsatisfactory. At this time I had a short affair with a girl, but it was no good.

Then Mary added:

> My father's mouth does the same thing to me. When I was a child, he used to lick me and suck on me in play and affection.

Mary called her mother a lesbian because she perceived that her mother derived a sexual thrill from touching her daughter's body. Her mother confided to Mary that she only tolerated sex and never had an orgasm. Mary described her mother as an aggressive, masculine woman who dominated her home and husband. While her mother played a masculine role in the family, her father took a passive, feminine position.

SEDUCTION AND REJECTION

Mary was seduced by both her mother and her father. A child is seduced when a parent takes advantage of its need for closeness and warmth to obtain an unconscious sexual excitement from the relationship. Seductive parents are unaware of the sexual significance of their actions, as when they kiss their children on the mouth or when they expose their bodies to children. Such behavior is rationalized as affection or liberalism, but the child senses the sexual overtones of these actions. Another element in the seductive situation is that the child is placed in a submissive position. Seductive behavior is initiated by the adult and the child cannot resist since he cannot reject the overtures of a parent on whom he is dependent. In seduction the child is enticed into the intimacy by being sexually excited and is bound to the parent by this excitement.

Seduction places a child in a serious dilemma. He gains a feeling of closeness but loses his right to self-assertion and to make demands for the satisfaction of his own pleasure striving. Physically, the effect of seduction is equally disastrous. The child is sexually excited, but because of his physiological immaturity, he cannot fully discharge this excitation. He cannot focus the excitation strongly on the undeveloped genital apparatus with the result that the excitation becomes an unpleasant body sensation. At the same time sexual guilt couples the excitation to anxiety. The child is left with no choice but to cut off body feeling. He abandons his body.

The seductive parent is also a rejecting parent. To use the child's body as a source of sexual excitement is to violate his feelings of privacy and to deny him the respect and love his developing personality needs. In effect, the child so used is rejected as an independent person. It is not generally appreciated that the rejecting parent is also seductive. Rejection is often based on the parent's fear of intimacy because this arouses the parent's sexual guilt. Such parents are afraid to touch and fondle the child, and when they do, it is with an awkwardness which the child senses as a manifestation of sexual anxiety. The child perceives this anxiety as an expression of an inhibited sexual feeling and reacts with an exaggerated sexual interest in the rejecting parent. Yet the child becomes afraid to approach the parent because of the hostile reaction he arouses, which he later associates with his own sexuality.

Parents who are out of contact with their bodies are not aware of how seductive they are with their children. On the other hand, the child, who lives closer to his body, is extremely sensitive to all nuances of feeling and picks up the hidden sexual interest. Generally, a mother will seduce her son into a seemingly innocent erotic intimacy with her, while a father by look, word, or deed will express his sexual interest in his daughter. Obviously, these relationships are incestuous.

One female patient told me that her mother exposed her genitals to her when she was six years old in the interests of a liberal sex education. The young girl was repelled by the sight and ran out of the room. She felt repulsed by her mother's body and revolted by the idea of her own genital organ. A child is more shocked by the insensitivity of a parent who could do such a thing than by the act itself. Another example of this insensitivity was related by a patient who told me that when she was ten years old her mother noticed that her breasts were beginning to develop. "She came over and put one hand under my breast and said in a leering tone, 'Oh, I see you're developing.' I felt so repulsed. I felt myself leave the ground."

This patient went on to say, "The thought of my mother touching me made me shrink. I wanted to withdraw from her touch. I felt it was sexual. Her breasts and her body repelled me. Once, when I was fifteen years old, she came into the room with split pants. I said innocently, 'You have a hole in your pants.' She answered, 'You have one too.' I almost became nauseous. She was so perverted, dirty, and seductive."

In Mary's case, her parents' seductive and rejecting behavior caused her to reject her body and her femininity. Mary's personality—the doll-like quality, the lack of mature femininity, and her homosexual passivity—derived from her submission to her mother's phallic aggressiveness and her father's oral seductiveness. As a result, submission to a man became impossible for her. "I can seduce them; this gives me control. The opposite situation frightens me." Mary became seductive in self-defense. At the same time, she was terrified of spontaneous sexual feelings, which would make her into a woman and a threat to her mother.

There was a split in Mary's personality between sexuality and genitality. The more she tried to avoid the sexuality of her body, the more preoccupied she became with genitality. She remarked, "I realize I am aware of genitals all the time. I feel inhuman. Do I want to see them or am I trying to defend myself against them?" This obsession with genitals was fed by both a repressed sexual curiosity and anxiety. The answer was Yes to both points of Mary's question.

Repressed sexual anxiety reduced her perception of her body, especially of the lower half. In a session one day, Mary said, "I don't feel my legs. I don't feel they are part of my body." The loss of feeling in the legs which Mary noted is a common and basic disturbance in the schizoid body image. Their figure drawings often lack legs or show them poorly drawn. Gisela Pankow, whose work with schizophrenics consists fundamentally of the dynamic reconstruction of the body image, relates the "split between the head zone and the leg zone" with the rejection of the "notion of a sexualized body."[32] There is a direct connection between the legs and the sexual function. Genitality implies maturity (standing on one's own feet), and vice versa. By divorcing the ego (head zone) from his genitality (leg zone), the schizoid denies his independence and maturity and retreats into a helpless and infantile position. In other words, by splitting off the image of the lower part of his body to avoid sexual feeling, the schizoid dissociates himself from the functions of his legs, which represent independence and maturity. Mary expressed this schizoid tendency.

> I don't allow any feelings below the waist. If some feeling develops in my pelvis, it's an agony. I fear I will go out of my mind. I want to be a mermaid.

Mary had a dream in which she was lying in bed with her father, who was naked. She tried to avoid the contact between the lower halves of their bodies so "it wouldn't get sexual." Thus, Mary's denial of her sexuality stemmed from a fear of sexual involvement with her father. This would arouse her mother's jealousy and wrath, of which Mary was terribly frightened.

Unable to accept herself as a female, Mary tried to identify herself with her brother. As a girl, she asked herself, How do they know I am a girl, not a boy?

"I thought of the penis," she said, "and I felt for it, but I didn't have one. If I was a boy, I would have one." Her final identification was neither male nor female; she became the "boy without a penis," the young homosexual.

We have traced some of the experiences and identifications which determined Mary's attitude toward her body. These attitudes, manifested in both the body image and her physical appearance, are reflected in her figure drawings. As a result of the analysis of her attitudes, the work with her body, and my acceptance of her as a human being, her body image changed. One day she reported, "You know what I feel today? I feel the confines of my body more. It doesn't feel so vague to me."

The withdrawal of feeling from the periphery of the body is the mechanism of the schizoid defense. The loss of charge in the surface of the body reduces the awareness of the body outline and renders impossible the correct drawing of the human figure. It lowers the barrier to external stimuli and makes the schizoid extremely sensitive to outside forces.

There is a functional identity between the body image and the actual body. To achieve an adequate body image requires a mobilization of total bodily feeling. To experience the body as alive and healthy, it must function that way. In addition to removing the psychological blocks to the acceptance of the body, therapy should provide some means for a patient to experience his body "immediately." He must be encouraged to move and breathe, for if these functions are depressed, feeling is lost. My own work with Mary involved a considerable emphasis upon these activities. Among other things, she kicked her legs, beat the couch, stretched, and breathed. The effect of her improvement is shown in the following observation.

I bought a bikini, and despite my fears, I wore it at the beach. I felt so sexual and so womanly. You know how I feel about my body. This was a marvelous feeling. I don't know when I've ever felt so good. I felt like another person.

In the foregoing discussion of Mary's case I have emphasized the development and function of the body image. In Chapter 13 I shall discuss another aspect of her therapy, the unmasking of her role as a "kissy doll."

The schizoid individual is a person whose feelings are bottled up like the genie in Aladdin's lamp. But the schizoid seems to have forgotten the magical formula that could release the genie. If the story of Aladdin and the magic lamp is interpreted as a metaphor, the lamp corresponds to the body, the incantations are words of love, and the act of rubbing the lamp is the equivalent of a caress. When the body is caressed, it lights up like a lamp and exudes a potent emanation, the aura of sexual excitation. When the body is "lit up," the eyes shine and the genie of sex can effect his magical transformations. Actually, the schizoid has not forgotten the magical formula; he talks of love and engages in sex, but the lamp is missing, cracked, or broken, and nothing happens. In desperation, he turns to the perverse, experiments with drugs, or becomes promiscuous. None of these desperate maneuvers releases the genie of love and sex.

6

The Psychology of Desperation

SELF-DESTRUCTIVE BEHAVIOR

MANY individuals engage in activities which they recognize as harmful to themselves but which they continue to repeat despite this awareness. At times, one gets the impression that the person, specifically the schizoid individual, is driven by an evil demon into actions which peril his life or his sanity. Even in less severe cases there is a self-defeating tendency in the personality that is often very difficult to overcome in therapy.

It is normally assumed that if a person becomes aware that certain activities or patterns of behavior are self-destructive, he will change his actions. Even experienced therapists make this assumption and are surprised and disappointed when the patient fails to respond positively to the analysis. This situation, which is known as the negative therapeutic reaction, led Freud to postulate the concept of a "repetition compulsion," that is, the need to repeat painful traumatic experiences. It can be illustrated by the example of the person who has an inner feeling of rejection yet continually exposes himself to situations in which he is rejected, often sensing in advance that he will be rejected. The idea of the repetition compulsion was later extended by Freud into the hypothesis of a "death instinct."

True, all the patients I analyzed had self-destructive tendencies. That was why they were in treatment. But I found no evidence in any of my patients to support Freud's hypothesis. Many expressed death wishes, but a death wish is not a death instinct. Self-destructive behavior can often be radically modified. The fact that people are self-destructive indicates the presence of a force in the personality that dissipates the life energy of the organism. Such an anti-life force appears in the schizoid personality, but it is the direct result of the schizoid split, not its cause. Since all aspects of the schizoid personality are subject to the dissociative process, his existence itself becomes divided into life and death forces.

A common example of the self-destructive tendency is the addiction to tranquilizing and sedative pills. One of my patients had been warned by her physician that these pills were detrimental to her health. They decreased her energy, maintained her condition of anemia, and left her generally listless and tired. She remarked, "I know I die a little every time I take the pills." She had made a number of attempts to abstain from the pills. Each time she did, she felt better, more alive, and more positive toward life. Strangely, however, she turned back to the pills just when she felt good. And no sooner did she resume her dependence on the pills—to curb her anxiety and ensure her sleep—than she lost all her good feelings.

Her anxiety, like that of all schizoid personalities, increased when things went well and she felt good. Good feelings, she said, lead to the awareness of pain and doom. Finally, the anxiety becomes unbearable. "I don't want to feel so good because I will have to pay for it later," she remarked. The pills diminished the anxiety by producing a kind of oblivion. The association of good feeling with anxiety seems so strange to normal thinking that one has to meet this condition many times to accept it without surprise.

I treated an alcoholic woman whose response in the therapeutic session was positive. She discussed her problems and feelings openly and easily. At the end of each session she remarked about how much better she felt, yet when she returned home after treatment she could not resist the temptation to take a drink. Another patient, who had made significant progress in therapy, suddenly expressed a strong fear of death. Previously, his desperate struggle to survive precluded this anxiety. He became consciously afraid of dying the moment he felt he had something to live for. Such anxiety arises from the fear of being punished for the good feelings. If the anxiety becomes too strong, the individual is left with no choice but to destroy his good feelings.

The anxiety that becomes attached to life-positive feelings stems from an underlying sense of doom. Generally, the individual is unaware that he labors under a sense of doom, although unconscious feelings of despair may occasionally erupt into consciousness. These feelings, however, are quickly repressed in the interest of survival, and the person continues his futile struggles. When, in the course of therapy, the pattern of his self-destructive behavior is analyzed, the patient admits that he had a precognition of failure. On some level of awareness, he knew that he couldn't succeed, even that he mustn't succeed.

Why should success be so feared, or what success is so feared? The feared success is the sexual possession of the parent, but it often requires a long analysis before the patient gains this insight. At first he is unaware that the sense of doom hanging over him is the terror of committing incest, the danger of breaking the awesome taboo, and the fear of the grim reprisal that would inevitably follow. In his defense against this terror the schizoid individual sacrifices his right to enjoy his body and to experience the warmth of human contact. Thus, he feels banished from human society by his inability to share the pleasure of erotic desire and gratification. Since his exile is psychological, the barrier is guilt—not the guilt of sexual intercourse (which the sophisticate can rationalize), but the guilt of pleasure in erotic intimacy. Divorced from feeling, the sexual act does not evoke the oedipal conflict because the body functions mechanically. Pleasure, however, demands the loosening of restraints, the lifting of repression, and the acceptance of incestuous longings and desires. The acceptance of these sexual feelings permits their integration into the personality and their transfer to others in a mature relationship.

The doom that hovers over the schizoid individual is the threat of being abandoned or destroyed for violating the incest taboo. To avoid this doom, he repressed his sexual feelings and abandoned his body. Now, as an adult, he finds that the normal avenue to human relationships is blocked because of this repression. Thus, his defense isolates him, alienates him from human society, and sentences him to the very doom he feared. The schizoid dilemma is that he cannot go forward to a satisfactory relationship because of terror, and he cannot stay as he is because of loneliness and isolation.

But the oedipal conflict is never fully quiescent as long as the repression exists, for repression is never total. Sexual feelings constantly threaten to break through, and the fear of the dreaded punishment is never absent. The schizoid individual struggles with the feeling that doom is inevitable no matter which way he turns. In view of this feeling, his only recourse is to learn to live with it.

If a person can accustom himself to the idea of catastrophe, its sting is eliminated and its terror blunted. If one has nothing to gain, there is no risk of losing anything. A punishment that is self-inflicted is intended to avert a greater punishment by outside agents. This is the explanation of the beating fantasies or the actual beatings sought by masochistic individuals, as Wilhelm Reich showed in his analysis of the masochistic character.[38] In masochism, the actual punishment is always less than the feared punishment, which is castration. Similarly, a self-imposed isolation is less frightening than abandonment and death.

The self-destructive behavior of the schizoid individual has a survival value in his unconscious. It is a survival technique, anachronistic in his present situation, but valid in terms of his infantile experiences. It is a type of defense that is occasionally seen in the animal kingdom, playing dead or possum in the presence of danger. I had a patient who literally acted this out in the course of a session. He was lying on the couch in a relaxed position when I noticed that his eyes were rolling up in his head, with the whites of the lower part showing. His breathing diminished; he lay there motionless; and he looked as if he was dying. When I pointed out to him the meaning of his bodily expression, he told me that he used to adopt this pose or attitude when he was a small boy and was threatened by his parents. They became frightened when they saw his death look, and their behavior changed from threats to solicitude.

The suicide attempts that young people make with increasing frequency these days are subject to the same interpretation. Despite the obvious self-destructive element in such actions, they are also a dramatic appeal for help. Many parents awaken to the seriousness of a child's emotional condition only when confronted with such drastic actions. It is unfortunate that manifestations of the schizoid problem often pass as personal idiosyncrasies, lack of interest, or willful resistance. Parental insensitivity often drives the young person to overt self-destructive behavior to force a serious consideration of his difficulties.

The danger in such drastic measures is that one can go too far. Each time one dies a little, the way back to life and health becomes longer. Finally, despair may reach a point at which one doesn't care, and the line that separates life from death may be breached. How long can one call for help that is not forthcoming? How long can one live in the shadow of doom without invoking the doom? In the end, the desperate maneuver has a desperate outcome. The desperate individual provokes his fate.

THE TECHNIQUE OF SURVIVAL

An example of the psychology of desperation is the case of a young man who consulted me because of prolonged depression and the inability to work. Bill was a mathematician with a cool, precise mind that could analyze a problem clearly except where he was personally concerned. In the course of therapy his problem became focused on the feeling that "nothing happens." This feeling emerged sharply during an analysis of two dreams, in both of which, he remarked, "nothing happens." He then realized that it was the dominant feeling of his life and that it underlay his depression and inability to work. The feeling became accentuated when the therapy, after a propitious start, seemed to go nowhere. At the beginning, as he mobilized his muscles in various exercises, he experienced strong involuntary vibrations in his legs and body. He became excited because something seemed to be happening to him. But aside from some release of feeling in crying, these preliminary involuntary movements led nowhere. His initial enthusiasm subsided, and his depression deepened. He had more difficulty working. I had warned him about this development, since experience has shown that patients must confront their inner fears before they get better. We both recognized the possibility that he could lose his job because of his inability to work. This would mean that "something would happen" to him, and he conceded that perhaps this was what he was looking for, although it certainly would be an unfavorable development.

Physically, Bill was a young man with a thin, tight body which could be described as asthenic. He had broad shoulders, a narrow pelvis, and extremely tight, tense legs. His chest, which was rather large, was depressed in the region of the sternum, and his abdominal musculature was severely contracted. Owing to this, his breathing was limited to his thorax. While his arms and legs were strong, they were not integrated with the rest of his body. Despite an apparent strength there was a weakness in his body. The split in his personality was also manifested in his facial expression. In repose his face looked sad, tired, and old, but when he smiled he brightened like a young boy. The conflict between optimism and dejection led him into dangerous activities, in which, fortunately, nothing happened.

Bill was a rock climber; one of the best, he said. He had made many ascents of steep cliffs without any fear or hesitation. He had no conscious fear of heights or of falling. He was not afraid because in one part of his personality he didn't care if he fell. He related an incident about a time when he was climbing alone and lost his foothold on the cliff. For moments he dangled, holding on with his hands to a narrow ledge. While he groped for a toe hold, his mind was detached. He wondered, What would it be like if I fell? There was no panic.

The conflict in Bill's personality was between his desire for something meaningful to happen and his fear that if it did, the result would be catastrophic. This conflict drove him to accept the challenge of situations which posed a danger, specifically, the danger of falling. When he was near a cliff he forced himself to its very edge to prove that he was not afraid. He reasoned that the presence of the void should make no difference, since he was standing on flat ground. This reasoning was determined by the psychology of desperation. The desperate person exposes himself to unnecessary dangers to prove that he can survive. Bill's desperation was revealed by some strange fantasies. He had impulses, well contained at the moment, to touch high-tension electric cables and to step in front of speeding cars to see what would happen. He remarked that if he committed suicide, it would be by jumping off a cliff. "If," he said, "I could do it safely." Bill wanted the excitement of danger with the security that nothing would happen.

It can be shown analytically that people who have a fear of falling from heights are also afraid of falling asleep or falling in love. Against the fear of heights, the ego can erect defenses which repress the fear and permit the person to function in the threatening situation. It may even, as in Bill's case, force him to challenge his unconscious anxiety. But the ego cannot help a frightened person fall in love, since this feeling is beyond ego control. I was not surprised to learn that Bill suffered from insomnia and that his sleepless nights were recurring more frequently. Nor had Bill ever really been in love. A person capable of loving would not complain that nothing happens. Love is an event of transcendent significance.

It became obvious that Bill was terrified of falling. His defense against this fear was to subject himself to situations in which this could happen, to prove that he had nothing to fear. Such a tactic required an exaggerated control of his body, especially his legs. His legs were tight and tense, he could hardly bend them; his ankles were frozen, and his arches so contracted that contact of the feet with the ground was greatly reduced. In view of his physical handicaps, he was the last person one would expect to climb rock walls, but he compensated for his handicaps by a strong will. Thus, he lived on an emergency basis, fighting each challenge with all his strength to prove that nothing would happen.

As long as this charade continued, nothing would happen to bring Bill out of his depression. He had to learn to let go; his will had to weaken its grip on his body. At this point in his therapy I asked Bill to assume a position of stress which is used by skiers and other athletes to strengthen their leg muscles. Such body exercises have the effect of concretizing emotional attitudes and making the patient aware of his problems through the perception of his physical rigidities. In Bill's case, the exercise was designed to make him conscious of his fear of falling.

Standing at the edge of the couch, Bill bent his knees and leaned forward so that all the weight of his body was on the balls of his feet. He could maintain his balance by arching slightly backwards and touching the couch with his fingers. Athletes generally hold this position for a minute or so. When I asked Bill how long he could remain in it, he said, "Forever." Since this meant indefinitely, I asked him to try. He held the position for more than five minutes while his legs trembled and the pain increased. When the pain finally became too great, Bill didn't fall. He threw himself down on his knees, as if indifferent of consequences. He repeated this exercise several times, until it became apparent that he was afraid to let the sensation of falling develop. Bill sensed that his legs would not let go. I interpreted this physical attitude as Bill's unconscious resolve to stand on his feet at all costs. Psychologically, this meant that he would "stand alone." He unconsciously rejected any dependence on others and denied his need for contact and intimacy.

At our next meeting, Bill reported the breakthrough of a strong feeling.

> That night, after our last session, I had my first nightmare. I awoke thinking there was someone in the room. I must have screamed. Awake, I thought I saw a figure at the door. I was scared to get out of bed. Finally, I heard my cat, and when I called to it I felt better. This experience reminded me of my childhood fears. I realize now that my going to bed late is due to my fear of falling asleep.

Prior to this dream Bill had no recollection of his childhood anxieties. The incidents he recalled lacked emotion. Following the dream, we discussed his relation to his mother and father, and Bill realized that he had repressed all feelings about his parents. He had suppressed his love for his mother and his fear of his father. Thus the taboo against the sexual involvements of the oedipal situation was extended in Bill's mind to mean that "nothing must happen." For a taboo to have such extreme consequences the oedipal situation must pose a real possibility of incest and an imminent threat of disaster. In this circumstance, severe measures are adopted to prevent a catastrophe. These measures are a denial of the body and its feelings, and the isolation of one member of the family from another. Bill had felt very much alone as a child and continued to be alone as an adult.

Bill's nightmare was the first breakthrough of his repressed feelings. He recognized that the strange figure in his dream represented his father, and that he must have been in awe of him as a child. As he grew up, this awe was covered by an attitude of arrogance since "nothing did happen"; he was neither punished nor cast out. However, the underlying feeling of doom persisted in Bill's unconscious mind and was transferred to his work situation. His psychology of desperation demanded that he challenge the authorities to see if they would retaliate, while at the same time he was terribly afraid of losing his job. Bill had devoted his life to mastering the technique of surviving on a precipice.

The psychology of desperation stems from conflicting attitudes: an outer submission covering an inner defiance, or an outer rebellion hiding an inner passivity. Submission means that one accepts the position of the "outsider," the minority, the dispossessed, or the rejected. It entails a sacrifice of the right to personal fulfillment and satisfaction, in other words, the surrender of the right to pleasure and enjoyment. The inner defiance demands that the desperate individual challenge his situation. Defiance forces him into provocative behavior, which tempts the doom that he fears. But survival requires that the provocation must not go to the full limit, and in this way the doom is evaded.

Bill was a "loner." His outer attitude was one of rebellion. He challenged all situations, but they were challenges that could not succeed because they were negated by his inner passivity. As long as Bill accepted being alone as his necessary state of existence, he had to forego the pursuit of pleasure and devote all his energies to strengthening his ability to stand alone.

Shortly after the nightmare, Bill reported another dream. He was in a room with another man. Both were naked. The other man, who Bill thought might also be himself, bent over a window to look outside. Bill then approached him from behind and inserted his penis into the man's anus. Bill remarked, "I had no feeling. I just wondered what it would be like."

When I suggested that the other man represented Bill's longing for contact and his need to be given something, he burst into agonized crying. Bill had suppressed the passive side of his personality, which contained his feelings because it represented homosexual submission. Bill's fear of falling was also related to his fear of homosexual submission. He had to work through these feelings to resolve his difficulties, since his inability to function on his job represented his fear of submitting to his employer.

The self-destructive behavior seen today in alcoholism, drug addiction, delinquency, and promiscuity reflects the degree to which individuals in our culture have become isolated, detached, and desperate beings. Whether the depression is real or imagined makes little difference, except that in real desperation the defensive strategy stops when the emergency passes. The schizoid individual, however, lives in a continuous state of emergency. The specific fate which he fears can be determined from his behavior, since this behavior is both a challenge to his fate and an attempt to inure himself to its consequences. When the schizoid individual has acted in such a way as to force the hand of fate, he can then say, "See, I was right. You hated me. You rejected me. You crushed me." He can thus explain his isolation, worthlessness, and emptiness. And he can set out to prove to himself and to the world that he can rise above his doom.

The following case illustrates the complex forces underlying self-destructive behavior which consisted of promiscuous sexual activity following a night of drinking. Penny, as this patient will be called, often ended her evenings in bed with some man whom she had met in a bar where she spent the evening drinking. When she awoke the next morning after such an episode, she could not recall what had happened the night before. Under these circumstances, Penny became pregnant several times, and had to undergo illicit abortions, which she dreaded. Penny's only explanation for this behavior was that she could not stay home alone in the evening. But this explanation was only a rationalization. Penny was twenty years old when I first saw her, and this pattern had been going on for a number of years. She was one of the desperate people, cut off and moving about in the limbo of half existence. When I used that expression to describe her condition, she remarked that she had just written about it.

> Listen.
> Lay off and leave me alone.
> Left not to rest in peace
> But to linger and roam
> In limbo,
> Where I'm known,
> Not loved and loving,
> But known
> And left alone,
> Lost
> Among lifeless
> Slabs of stone,
> Gray and cold
> And lacerated
> With the foam
> Of my madness.

Then she asked me:

What happened to me? Why have I spent my years tied up in one knot or another? Whatever will be able to penetrate the thousands of days and nights that have made me what I am? And how will it be done? I don't believe it can be done, but I have to try—and trust your ability, knowledge, and I hope, your good feelings about me. Otherwise, what is now unbearable would soon become impossible, and that would be the end of that.

Penny had come to New York from a Midwestern town and worked as an executive secretary. She was intelligent and sensitive, which made her behavior all the more irrational. But its irrationality was more apparent than real. If to be alone threatened her sanity, she had no alternative but to find companionship at any cost. Why was Penny so afraid to be alone? Aloneness meant to be unloved and unloving, and a desperate sexuality seemed preferable to this fate. Yet every desperate attempt Penny made to find love left her feeling more rejected than before. In her desperation she could not refuse any overture. There was always the possibility, she said, that this one might be it.

When I first saw Penny she had the typical schizoid look: her eyes were dull and vacant, her skin was pale and pasty, and her body was frozen in rigidity. Her breathing was very shallow. When she tried to breathe deeply she panicked. For a minute, she couldn't catch her breath; then she began to cry. She realized how frightened she was and how much she was out of contact with her body. I pointed out that the way for her to get out of her misery was through an acceptance of and an identification with her body. This made sense to Penny because she realized she was ashamed of her body and that her promiscuous sexual activities were desperate attempts to gain some contact with her body.

Desperate people like Penny often engage in sexual activity to gain body feeling. This compulsive activity may give the impression that these persons are oversexed. They are, if anything, undersexed, for the activity stems from a need for erotic stimulation rather than from a feeling of sexual charge or excitement. Sexual activity of this kind never leads to orgastic satisfaction or fulfillment, but leaves the person empty and disappointed. Later in her therapy Penny spoke of the "excitement of disappointment." She meant by this remark that every adventure had at its core the hope that it could be meaningful and the fear that it would be disastrous. This mixture of hope and fear underlies the psychology of desperation. It blinds the individual to reality and forces him into situations which can only have a destructive effect upon his personality.

Penny did not accept herself as a woman. She remarked, "I can accept being a woman, but I doubt if I could ever enjoy it." But without the pleasure, acceptance denotes submission to one's fate. For Penny this fate was to be humiliated, degraded, and finally, rejected and destroyed. She submitted to this fate because she felt damaged and defiled in her being. In view of what she had been and done, she felt no one could respect her, least of all, herself. She commented, "I feel like second-hand merchandise, like a china bowl with a crack in it." Then she caught the meaning of her Freudian slip and exclaimed, "What did I say!"

A person does not choose his fate; he only fulfills it. He is bound by his fate as long as he accepts the values which determine it. If to be a woman means to be inferior, then Penny was a lost cause. But she was too sophisticated and too intelligent to accept this value judgment. It was not femininity that placed a stigma upon her but feminine sexuality. Marriage and motherhood were virtues, but sexual pleasure was sinful for a girl. Penny was not aware of thinking this way; she considered herself a modern sophisticate who accepted sex. However, her promiscuity was a sign of sexual guilt. This combination of sophistication and guilt was responsible for Penny's desperate sexual behavior.

Penny's true feelings were exposed when I questioned her about masturbation. "Masturbation" was a word she could not bring herself to utter. The very idea of it disgusted her. A further analysis of her feelings showed that she regarded the vagina as dirty, untouchable. Like Mary, she rejected the lower half of her body, and in the process, denied her whole body as a meaningful source of pleasure. Ashamed of her body and afraid of its sensations, Penny could not be alone with herself. She could not turn to herself—that is, to her body—for comfort and assurance. In her desperation, she was forced into sexual experiences that increased her guilt and her shame.

Satisfaction in masturbation is an indication that a person can "do it for himself." Lacking the ability to do it for oneself, a person becomes desperate and must find someone else to do it for him. Since beggars are not choosers, the person is often forced to desperate measures. Bill's need to climb rock walls was no less desperate a maneuver than Penny's recourse to sexual promiscuity. Danger was courted to provide an excitation that neither could obtain through the self-experience of the body. The problem is not masturbation per se, but sexual guilt and the rejection of the body. The inability to masturbate with satisfaction is the main symptom of this guilt.

Penny's survival technique was to immerse herself in her guilt until it lost its horror, which it never did. Yet there is some strange salvation in this behavior. A person that he can survive a seeming depravity. The aftermath is never quite as bad as had been anticipated. One is not struck dead for one's sins. The dread of sexuality is somewhat diminished, and sanity is preserved despite the torments of the experience.

The individual who loses contact with his body faces the threat of schizophrenia. The desperate maneuver is an extreme means to provide this contact. Penny's promiscuity enabled her to displace her feeling of shame from her body to her action. Bill's challenge of heights displaced his fear of his body to the rock wall. Shame and fear become bearable if they can be projected upon external events. The desperate maneuver is a means to preserve sanity by transferring the terror to actual situations. The mind can cope with specific fears; it feels vulnerable before the unknown. If this maneuver fails, the last desperate move to avoid the doom is suicide.

Sex and death are inextricably entwined in the split personality. The fear of sex is the fear of death. When one is fighting to stay alive, anything that threatens to undermine one's self-control is a mortal danger. The sexual feelings pose such a danger. Another patient expressed it clearly. She said, "I'm fighting to stay alive. If I let go, something is going to take over and drive me off a cliff." Bill tried to make sure that he couldn't be driven off a cliff. Penny was continually going off the deep end. In each case the impelling force was sexuality. Occasionally this demon shows his face, as in the following remark: "I felt strong sexual feelings and I was scared to death." This remark, made by a married woman, does not express a fear of sexual activity but only of sexual feeling. In this sense, Penny's promiscuity had the effect of decreasing her sexual feelings and thus saving her from a greater terror. This terror occasionally came to the surface. She related:

> Something happens to me which frightens me terribly. As I awaken, but before I am fully conscious, I become aware that my heart is beating loud and fast, and I can't breathe. I realize that if I don't breathe, in a minute or so I will die. It feels as if I am dying. My head is bursting and my chest feels as if it will explode. It reminds me of a description I read of a person having a heart attack.

Later, Penny reported a dream that provided some explanation for the terror:

> I was in a bedroom looking across an obstacle to another room, in which I saw myself. I was terrified, and I awoke with my heart pounding. Awake, I thought about the dream, and I realized that the obstacle was my parents in bed having sex. It filled me with horror.

Why should such a vision terrify a child? Why is the idea of parental intercourse so difficult for children to accept? If physical intimacy is associated in a child's mind with fear and shame, the sexual act will be viewed as an assault upon the ego and the body. The child sees it as a violation of privacy, an insult to the personality. On a deeper level, the child's reaction to the sight of sexual intimacy mirrors the 'parents' unconscious feelings about the sexual act. Penny's horror reflected her mother's conscious or unconscious dread of sex. Penny described her mother as unattractive, indifferent in her physical appearance, and as a woman who found no pleasure in her body. Her father, she said, was detached and unable to express affection. To such a man sex is a need to discharge a tension. To such a woman sex is submission to an unpleasant duty.

The quality of the physical intimacy between mother and child reflects the mother's feelings about the intimacy of sex. If the act of sex is viewed with disgust, all intimate body contact is tainted with this feeling. If a woman is ashamed of her body, she cannot offer it graciously to the nursing infant. If she is repelled by the lower half of her body, she will feel some revulsion in handling this part of the child's body. Each contact with the child is an opportunity for the child to experience the pleasure of intimacy or to be repulsed by the shame and fear of it. When a mother is afraid of intimacy, the child will sense the fear and interpret it as a rejection. The child of a woman who is ashamed of intimacy will develop a feeling of shame about its own body.

The fundamental trauma of the schizoid personality is the absence of pleasurable physical intimacy between mother and child. The lack of erotic body contact is experienced by the child as abandonment. If the child's demands for this contact are not met with a warm response, it will grow up with the feeling that no one cares. It may even find that insistence upon this need for body contact evokes a hostile reaction in parents. It will suppress its desire for intimacy to avoid the pain of an unfulfilled longing. And it will learn that survival demands the suppression of feeling and desire. By the same token, to feel the longing is to sense the abandonment, which to the child is the equivalent of death. Since intimacy is the aim of this longing, the avoidance of intimacy serves to keep the fear of abandonment in repression.

When a child's need for intimacy, body contact, and oral erotic gratification is not fulfilled in the first years of life it becomes transferred to the sexual feelings which develop during the oedipal period. This development explains why the oedipal conflict assumes such intensity in these children. The sexual attachment to the parent of the opposite sex is charged with the unfulfilled infantile longing for intimacy and oral gratification. This overcharged attachment creates a real danger of incest as far as the feelings of the child are concerned. In analysis, we speak of a displacement from the mouth to the genitals. The mixture of orality (infantile longing) and genitality (preliminary budding of sexual feeling) is so confused that the child cannot distinguish between these desires. The need for body contact could lead the child to accept a sexual intimacy forbidden by the strongest taboo.

The parents' role in this conflict is the combination of rejection and seduction. By rejecting the child's oral needs for contact and intimacy, they drive its longing into a sexual channel. By seducing the child, they add to the intensity of its oedipal conflict. To avoid violating the incest taboo, the child sacrifices all feeling. Bill made sure that nothing could happen. Penny desperately hoped something would happen; she wanted to fall in love and get married, but she couldn't allow it to occur.

Unfortunately, the child is made to assume the burden of guilt for its desperate condition. The parents hide behind a moral code that often makes no distinction between the infantile desire for erotic gratification and intimacy and adult genitality. They condemn infantile masturbation out of fear that it will arouse the child's sexual feelings, thereby blocking the one avenue that could diminish its tensions. In their fear of the oedipal situation, they deny the child the body contact that could prevent its desperation.

Finally, the child's doom is sealed with the warning that erotic gratification leads to a bad end. Overtly or insidiously, a girl is made to feel the sharp line that separates the virgin from the loose woman, the matron from the prostitute. Every move by the young girl toward erotic pleasure is deemed a step toward perdition. If the girl is rebellious, she is categorized as worthless, a tramp, and sometimes, a whore. In desperation, parents have humiliated their daughters with the remark, "No good man will ever want you." In their fury, they have cursed their daughters with the malediction, "You will end up in the streets."

This was Penny's upbringing. She was launched into life burdened with a strong sense of shame and guilt about her body and her sexuality. Any contact with a man on a pleasurable basis evoked these feelings. That is why she had to become drunk in her pursuit of erotic gratification. She drank to diminish the intensity of these feelings and to permit some ease in her approach to the opposite sex. By her drinking, however, she reinforced these feelings. In this conflict with her guilt, one desperate move provoked another, one drink led to another, and in the end she defied her fate by sexual acts that bound her to it ever more closely. The fears of her parents were confirmed, and the fate they predicted threatened the daughter they sought so desperately to protect.

The desperate person reacts to every situation as if it is a "matter of life or death." Every issue poses the question of survival. Every problem is viewed as a choice between black and white. Every decision is burdened by the alternatives of all or nothing. The result is that the desperate person gets nothing; he manages to survive, but fails to satisfy any of his wishes.

Schizoid desperation cannot be overcome until the individual is assured of his ability to survive. This means that he must plumb the depths of his despair and accept his doom. It is significant that some schizophrenic patients do not recover until they have made a sojourn in the most disturbed wards of the psychiatric hospital. Having found that they can survive in this most desperate situation, they dare to confront reality; they dare to accept their desire for physical intimacy. In an environment where shame is meaningless they overcome their shame of the body. When they realize that they have nothing further to lose they lose their fear. They gain the conviction that survival itself is an empty achievement without the pleasures and satisfactions that intimacy provides.

7

Illusion and Reality

DESPERATION leads to illusions. The desperate person creates illusions to sustain his spirit in his struggle for survival. This is a valid function of the ego, as William V. Silverberg pointed out in his analysis of "the schizoid maneuver": "It would seem, then, that what I have called the schizoid maneuver may perform a definite and needful function in blunting the edge of terror in situations in which a person is helpless in the face of inevitable injury or destruction."[34] As an example of this mechanism, Silverberg quotes a poem by Rainer Maria Rilke in which a young soldier facing death in battle transforms the sabers of the enemy into a "laughing fountain," into which he plunges. With this illusion, "the terrifying reality of annihilation is evaded, not, to be sure, in actuality, but in the young man's mind." Recourse to illusion is fostered by helplessness in the face of external reality. It becomes pathological, however, when the helplessness is due to feelings of inadequacy unrelated to the external reality.

DESPERATION AND ILLUSION

The danger of an illusion is that it perpetuates the desperate condition. One of my patients remarked, "People established unreal goals, then keep themselves in a constant state of desperation attempting to realize them." An example of an illusion, or an unreal goal, is the desire to be "the perfect wife." This secret wish places a woman in a desperate situation. Her behavior will be compulsive; she must prove by her actions that she is the perfect wife. Her attitude will be hypersensitive; she will interpret every ex pression of discontent on the part of her husband as a sign that she has failed, and therefore, as a personal rejection. At the same time, she will be insensitive to her husband's feelings, since she is preoccupied with her ego image; and her behavior will force her husband into the very reactions of displeasure that will threaten her image. As her desperation increases she will strive even more compulsively to fulfill her illusion, further entrapping herself in a vicious circle.

Few people are so naive as to believe consciously in the illusion of being the perfect wife, the perfect mother, or the perfect friend; but people's actions often indicate the presence of these illusions in their unconscious minds. The hypercritical person betrays his own need to be considered perfect. His inability to accept others as they are reflects his inability to accept himself. His search for perfection is a projection of his own demands upon himself. Perfectionism is perhaps the most common of all illusions and, certainly, one of the most destructive to human relationships. The illusion of being a perfect mother demands a "perfect child" and leads to the rejection of the human child, who needs his mother's understanding and support. The perfect mother becomes a desperate and destructive woman.

Desperation and illusion form a vicious circle, in which one leads to the other. The more the illusion rejects reality the more desperate becomes the struggle to support it. When, as in the schizoid condition, the illusion becomes the very basis of existence, it must be guarded and sustained against reality.

In Chapter 6, I described the desperate sexual behavior of a patient named Penny. Her promiscuity was seen as an attempt to cope with the feeling of rejection. It is also possible to view this behavior as the product of an illusion. Despite the implications of a sexual attitude that could be called loose and irresponsible at best, Penny clung to an illusion of purity and virtue. Hers was not an ordinary virtue, but a superior virtue, one that remained untarnished by promiscuity and drinking. The fantasy associated with this illusion was that one day she would meet her prince, who would discern her nobility and superiority through the dross and shame of her life. He would then proclaim her his princess and honor her in the eyes of the world. It is a modern version of the Cinderella story in terms of sexual morality. By covering herself with shame, Penny would put the prince to the test. If he failed to recognize her quality, he was not a true prince. And only a prince was worthy of a princess in disguise.

The Cinderella dream is found in all schizoid girls. It is a compensation for the feeling of worthlessness from which these girls suffer. However, it should also be interpreted as a manifestation of the inner feeling that there are untapped resources in the personality. The schizoid is split between an unrealized potential, magnified by illusion to grandeur, and an experienced self, reduced by disillusionment to despair. Another version of this story is the Sleeping Beauty theme. In this version, the sleeping potential is awakened by the courage and ardor of a prince who overcomes the witch's curse by reaching the princess through the briars and thorns which hide her. Unfortunately, fairy tales rarely come true in real life. As long as the illusion is operative, Cinderella will continue to remain in her scullery, covered with rags, and Sleeping Beauty will stay hidden behind the impenetrable thicket.

The reality which the illusion distorts is the inner feeling of despair and hopelessness. Penny's illusion that she was a princess was designed to counter the conviction that no man would want to marry her. By means of her illusion, she could pretend that she was doing the rejecting. As therapy progressed and her desperation diminished, she realized that she had been running away from her despair.

This realization emerged with clarity following a visit home during which her father voiced his disapproval of her. Penny became irrationally angry and stormed out of the house. His rejection was the final blow. It shattered her illusion. Her image of the prince had been a transfiguration of her father, who, she believed, loved her in spite of all. This illusion grew out of a deep belief that no matter what, she would always be a princess in his eyes.

The incident produced two effects. Immediately after it happened, Penny felt a strength and power such as she had never known before. It was as if a chain which bound her had been sundered. This new strength stemmed from the anger she felt against her father, a feeling she had previously repressed. However, her anger did not last long, and her mood then became one of despair, which was only relieved by the analysis of her relationship to her father.

In her early childhood, this relationship had been an involved one. Penny had transferred to her father all the longing for intimacy, affection, and support which a child normally demands from its mother. This transference was necessitated by the mother's failure to satisfy the child's needs and facilitated by the father's positive response to the girl. But his response was ambivalent. He could not satisfy the child's need for body contact, since this aroused his own strong guilt feelings about physical intimacy. He accepted her as an intelligent and thinking being but rejected her as a sexual and physical being. This compounded the rejection Penny experienced as an infant with her mother.

A child cannot survive without some feeling of parental love and acceptance. In the interest of survival, Penny accepted her father's requirement that she dissociate from her body and its sexuality on the implied promise that by doing so, she would become his "special one." But this dissociation placed her in a desperate condition. Having forsaken the pleasure of her body, Penny needed something to sustain her spirit. She had to believe that her father truly loved her and that he only made this demand to protect her from a difficult oedipal situation. To guard her sanity, she had to believe that someone loved her, and having turned to her father, she had to believe in him. Each disappointment at the hands of her father only strengthened this illusion, for the alternative seemed to be a despair unto death.

Penny's childhood sitution contained another element which strengthened her illusion. Her relation to her father brought her into competition with her mother and created a dangerous rivalry. In the child's mind, it was the mother who prevented the father from responding fully to the love of his daughter. The mother thus becomes the wicked witch or stepmother who casts a spell upon the girl to prevent the fulfillment of her desire. Penny's older sisters, who sided with the mother, took on the role of the jealous stepsisters in the fairy tale. All of the conditions for the myth were present to a degree that made it difficult to separate illusion from reality.

The differentiation of illusion from reality is not always

easy. Penny's mother and father did love her. There was some element of reality in her belief that she was considered "special." Every child has a feeling of being special to its parents, which is replaced in maturity with a sense of self and a feeling of identity. The child feels itself to be the focus of its parents' love. This feeling becomes an illusion, however, when the love is made conditional upon the child's surrender of its instinctive or animal nature. The illusion is then used to sustain the ego and deny the sacrifice; and it cannot be surrendered in maturity. Consequently, the individual is fixated in his childhood situation.

The schizoid illusion of superiority and specialness is also found in young men. One of my patients described such an illusion in himself.

I suddenly became aware that I had an idealized image of myself as an exiled prince. I related this image to my dream that some day my father, the king, would come and claim me as his heir apparent.

At my graduation from grade school, I recall waiting for my father to appear. He never did. I always tried to prove myself worthy of him in sports, achievements, and scholarship. He never took notice. Then he died.

I realize that I still have the illusion that someday I'll be discovered. Meantime, I have to maintain my "pretensions." A prince can't demean himself by ordinary work. I have to show that I'm special.

The patient's pretenses of nobility and superiority contrasted with the reality of his struggles and failures. The disparity between illusion and reality forced my patient into a desperate condition. Since he was an actor, the dream of being discovered seemed particularly appropriate. Yet the harder he tried, the more he failed. His auditions were always impressive, but his performances rarely measured up to his initial promise. All his effort went into the audition, in the hope that his illusion would be fulfilled. When this did not happen he lost heart during the rehearsals and his performances suffered. He learned later that his effort during rehearsals was not wholehearted. Finally, in one set of rehearsals his acting ability deteriorated and he was released from his contract.

He behaved the same way in therapy. At the beginning he made a great effort to mobilize his body to show me how well he could do. However, the compulsion behind this effort increased his tension, and the good feelings which he had initially experienced disappeared. Since this development occurred at the same time that he lost his job, he sank into a deep despair. During this crisis his illusions were unmasked. Then he realized that he had never done his best. "If you don't do your best," he said, "you can't fail." What he meant was that you could always excuse your failures. The illusion prevented him from confronting reality.

DESPAIR AND DISSOCIATION

Although the renunciation of illusion is a step to health, it is invariably accompanied by despair. This despair stems from the fear of abandonment. Yet the despair is irrational, for, like the fear of abandonment, it represents the persistence into adulthood of infantile feelings. When the illusion collapses and the despair which it covered breaks through into consciousness, it becomes possible for a patient to understand his illusions and his desperation as an outgrowth of his underlying despair.

The deeper an individual's despair the stronger and more exaggerated will his illusions be; the more powerful the illusion the greater is the desperation. As an illusion gains power it demands fulfillment, thereby forcing the individual into conflict with reality which leads to desperate behavior. To pursue the fulfillment of an illusion requires the sacrifice of good feelings in the present, and the person who lives in illusion is, by definition, unable to make demands for pleasure. In his desperation he is willing to forego pleasure and to hold life in abeyance in the hope that his illusion-come-true will remove his despair. The psychology of desperation explains why a schizoid individual lives on the brink of disaster. By his desperate and destructive behavior, he challenges his doom, hoping to minimize its terror; and by his illusion, he denies his doom, hoping to avoid his despair.

The connection between these different elements in Penny's personality can be described as follows. The repeated denial of her childhood need for physical intimacy created a feeling of rejection, which developed into despair. In the interest of survival, Penny repressed the longing for erotic gratification by dissociating from her body. This process (rejection—despair—dissociation) resulted in a split in her personality that led to the formation of an illusion and a feeling of desperation. This can be pictured diagrammatically.

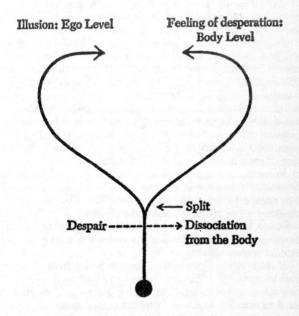

FIG. 11 The roots of this process lie in the experience of rejection in infancy and childhood

The swing between illusion and desperation cannot be prevented as long as the split in the personality persists. The split is healed through the ego's identification with the body. This identification reduces the desperation and exposes the illusion. The collapse of the illusion reveals the underlying despair, which then opens the way for the reconstruction of the infantile situation. At this point the traumatic experiences of infancy and childhood can be abreacted and released.

Illusion and desperation form a noose which slowly strangles the life of the individual. Surprisingly, despair offers the only way out of this stranglehold of unreality. Consider the alcoholic. He doesn't drink because he is in despair. His drinking is a denial of despair, a running away from his feelings, an avoidance of reality. To admit his despair would lead him to seek help. But as people dealing with alcoholics know, this is the hardest thing to get him to admit. The alcoholic is a desperate person who cannot face his despair or concede the possibility of hope. His illusions sustain him. His biggest illusion is that he could stop drinking if he wanted to—if he made up his mind to it. Nothing is further from the truth, as experience has shown. The very nature of an addiction is that one is helpless in the grip of its power. What a conceit of will to think that one can control a pattern of behavior in the face of innumerable experiences of failure!

What is true of alcoholism is true of all self-destructive behavior. If one could control such behavior, one would not engage in it in the first place. The illusion of will constitutes the strongest barrier to effective help. An alcoholic can be helped when he admits his impotence to help himself. A schizoid individual concedes his need when he seeks therapeutic help.

If desperation is the illness, despair is the crisis that can lead to recovery. Is there a despair so black that it doesn't contain some ray of light? Is there a despair so deep that it leads to suicide? The answer to the second question is that suicide is an act of desperation, not despair. It is self-destruction in the extreme; it is the final challenge to one's fate. Despair may lead to death, but it will not be by conscious action. Despair denotes an attitude of resignation, but this resignation is never total so long as life persists. Whereas the person in despair gives up, the desperate individual struggles to escape what appears to him an inevitable doom. If this doom is truly inevitable, his desperation is rational. But, as Silverberg suggests, the judgment that one is doomed or helpless is a subjective one.

Hope is realistic even in the deepest despair, since it admits the possibility of disappointment. Illusion, on the other hand, permits no doubts, allows no challenges. The person who has the illusion that he is totally well-intentioned in his actions will become irrational when his motives are questioned. The individual with an illusion of self-importance can crack up if his ego image is strongly challenged. The desperate person feels that he is hanging on the edge of a cliff, terrified that if he lets go, he will plunge into an unremitting despair. Yet when he does let go of his illusions in therapy, he finds, surprisingly, that he is not destroyed and that hope exists.

Illusions yield slowly. The commitment to therapy is at first only a gesture behind which the ego marshals its defenses against its inner despair and helplessness. Every patient comes to therapy with the secret wish that it will enable him to translate his illusions into reality. Resistances arise which are often difficult to overcome because they hide the illusions from the patient and the therapist. Slowly, in the course of therapy, desperation gives way to despair as the patient stops running away from himself. In his despair—as he realizes that he will never fulfill his illusions—he feels that his therapy has failed. Only at this point does he reveal his illusions. The yielding to despair is accompanied by feelings of fatigue and exhaustion such as a soldier may experience after the battle is over. But the fatigue and exhaustion also serve to impede any desperate behavior.

The working through of these problems is illustrated in the following case history. In her darkest moment, one of my patients, Joan, said, "I feel so desperately tired. I feel so tired I could crawl into a hole and lie there for the next ten years. I feel I can't cope with life any more." The fact is that Joan was never able to cope with life. She had spent her adult years trying

> . . . to be so strong that I could cope with anything. There wouldn't be any problem I couldn't solve. I could mold my life. I could shape the events that happened to me.

I always pictured myself as a sophisticated debutante going to El Morocco, giving fabulous parties, having a career, and being a perfect mother at the same time.

I would be happily married because I would be the perfect wife—devoted, loyal, understanding. My children would reflect my selfless love, patience, and understanding.

Somewhere in all this I thought I would also be a great intellect, a scholar or teacher.

The harsh realities of Joan's life strengthened her fantasies rather than undermined them. She could not accept reality. She was naive to a degree that paralleled her imagined sophistication. On one occasion, her naïveté almost cost her her life: she allowed a strange man to accompany her along a deserted road and was assaulted by him. Later, although she was warned, she entered into a marriage with a psychopathic man who abused and mistreated her. Two years after this marriage ended in divorce she still entertained the illusion that she would be happily married one day because she could be the perfect wife. Joan was a lonely and desperate woman who adopted the role of the clown to avoid her humiliation and clung to her illusions to avoid despair.

Joan's illusions contained basic contradictions, which became evident when they were fully analyzed. She had never questioned her ideal of the sophisticated socialite, although it conflicted sharply with her ideal of perfect motherhood. Her own mother had attempted to reconcile these opposing roles and failed. But Joan had no choice, for she knew no other way of functioning. Her illusions had their roots in the unreality of the family ideology, which is the only reality a child knows.

The illusion has a desperate quality and a compulsive element. Joan's fantasies expressed what she believed to be her needs rather than her desires. She believed she had to be competent, sophisticated, intelligent, devoted, and understanding. When she looked at her illusions objectively, she saw that they corresponded to her father's image of womanhood. Her ego identification with this image was motivated by her desperate need to gain his approval and love. She would prove to him that she was superior to her mother. She would be competent where her mother was inadequate, be devoted where her mother was indifferent, be successful where her mother was a failure. When her illusions collapsed, Joan realized that she was no better than her mother. Joan failed as a person in almost the same way her mother had failed, and for the same reasons. She had spent her energies trying to fulfill an ego image that was unrelated to her true needs.

Realistically, Joan needed a stronger identification with her body and a stronger sense of self. She worked hard through breathing and movement to gain more contact with her body. She improved to a point where people commented on the change in her appearance. But her relations with her father deteriorated. The more she improved, and the more she tried to assert herself as a person, the more critical of her he became. The intensity of this conflict with her father made Joan realize that she could only gain his approval by submission, which she could no longer do. The price was too high. This realization forced her to examine her illusion.

The second factor which undermined her illusions was the realization that her child had problems and that these problems stemmed from her anxieties. This confrontation of reality weakened the sustaining power of the illusions, and Joan slowly went into a deep despair.

Joan had a habit of moving her head from side to side when she was discouraged. When I asked her the meaning of this gesture, she replied, "It's no use. It's no use. I will always be lonely. No one will ever love me." Then she burst into heavy sobs and exclaimed that the therapy had not changed this condition. "I have been lonely all my life," she remarked. Her despair at this moment was profound.

Despite her despair, the destruction of her illusions resulted in Joan's becoming a more human individual. In her despair, she could see her child as an independent personality not as a projected image of her ego. She could understand his difficulties as a reflection of her own anxieties. And she could view his resistance to her as meaningful behavior. Whereas before, she was trying to cope with a difficult child and failing, now she was relating to another person with understanding. She could also see a man as a person with whom to share the pleasures and pains of life, rather than as someone charged with fulfilling her dreams.

PARENTAL UNREALITY

The conflict between self-assertion and the need for approval produces an attitude of rebellion against parental values. This rebellion, however, is powerless to alter the underlying feeling of submission and serves only as a form of protest. The powerlessness of rebellion to change parental values is seen in the case of the person who, as a child, rebelled against a strict parental discipline but turns out to be equally strict with his own children. Barbara, whose case was presented in Chapter 1, observed that she treated her children the way she was treated by her mother, despite her conscious resentment of her mother's attitude. Many people forget when they become parents how they felt as children. They forget how they fought against being made to eat food they disliked, going to bed early, and being restricted in dating, and they impose similar restrictions on their own children. This forgetting of their childhood rebellion can be understood as a repression of their hostility against their own parents, which leads to an unconscious identification with them.

Most children grow up with the illusion that their lives will be different from those of their parents. Each child is convinced that he will achieve happiness where the parent knew misfortune. The need for this illusion is evident. The unhappiness in many homes would produce despair if it were not counteracted by illusion. But the illusion blinds the individual to the forces which create failure and unhappiness. Its promise is unreal. Helping a patient gain insight into the illusions by which his parents lived—in order that he may finally understand his own—is an important part of the therapeutic process.

One young man described this insight as follows:

> When I got home I saw in a little more perspective the unworldly influence of my mother. She does not think of the army as real; it is a nightmare to her. She doesn't accept the unpleasant things of life, such as getting old, dying, my failures, our limited means. I see

that I have to become more objective and detached from the unreality my parents' love foisted on me.

The basic unreality neurotic parental love foists upon a child is the negation of the life of the body. The life of the body is the pursuit of pleasure through movement and body contact. With many parents this value is subordinated to achievement, obedience, and intellectuality, and the importance of bodily pleasure is ignored. The result is a loss in the ability of the individual to be self-assertive and aggressive in his demands for pleasure. To the neurotic parent the life of the body is irrational, unpredictable, and full of danger. His anxiety about the body stems from his fear of his own repressed violence and sexuality, which he projects upon the external world. Survival seems to demand that the animal in the newborn organism be tamed. This is accomplished by a constant pressure on the child, expressed in such injunctions as "Behave!" "Be good!" "Be quiet!" "Be still!" The result is to force the child to dissociate from his body and to suppress his feelings. The following observation by a patient describes the effect of this parental attitude.

There is no active thing in my body. I have always felt incompetent in my body. My parents were always afraid I would fall. They were always afraid I would drop things, and when they screamed, I did drop them. I never trusted my body, so I developed my intellect to cover up my feelings of lifelessness and emptiness.

Then she added, "When you reject your body, you become a naked spirit seeking a body to get into." A person who doesn't live in his own body has to live through the body of another. This is the reason why so many mothers become overinvolved with their children and subvert the relationship for their own needs.

The rejection of the body produces a common schizoid illusion, the illusion of nonaggression. One of my patients described her husband in words which fit most schizoid individuals. "He doesn't see why there should be any unpleasantness in life. He thinks the world should be without hostilities. Everybody should be agreeable." Such a world doesn't exist and never has. The person who attempts to function on this basis is living in unreality. A person creates this illusion to compensate for his own lack of aggression. Without an adequate action-self, to use Rado's term, the schizoid individual feels helpless to secure the satisfaction of his desires. His personality remains fixated at an infantile level. Carried one step further, this illusion leads to the belief that one should be taken care of without the need to exert oneself. It is the familiar tale of the unfulfilled infant who clings to the illusion that someone will satisfy his infantile wants without his effort.

The renunciation of aggression reduces the pleasure capacity of the organism. In adult life, pleasure is an active process, the satisfaction of desires through activity. This is not to say that there are no passive pleasures in adulthood, but passive pleasures are never sufficient to sustain a healthy emotional life. On the other hand, passive pleasure dominates the life of the infant. The longing for passive pleasure which characterizes so many individuals in our culture is a reflection of their fixation at infantile levels of functioning. The illusion that such pleasure can fulfill adult needs prevents the mobilization of aggressive attitudes. Thus, Rado's concept of a pleasure deficiency in the schizoid personality is valid, but this deficiency is determined by the renunciation of aggression and the denial of the body.

In psychological thinking the word "aggression" bears no relation to the result of the movement. An aggressive movement can be constructive or destructive, loving and tender or hateful and cruel. The word itself merely indicates that the movement is directed "toward" rather than "away from." Aggressive actions bring an individual into relationship with persons, things, or situations. For this reason, aggressive actions are ego-syntonic. Their aim or goal is the satisfaction of needs. The psychological opposite of aggression is regression. In regression, one gives up the need and reverts to a level of functioning where this need is no longer felt as imperative. Since needs are satisfied in the external world, aggression denotes that the individual is oriented toward reality. In regression there is a turning away from the world, a withdrawal from reality, a retreat into illusion.

THE REIGNING ILLUSIONS

Two illusions are fairly widespread in our culture, one related to money and the other to sex. The illusion that money is omnipotent, that it can solve all problems and bring its possessor all joy and happiness, is responsible for the worship of money. Similarly, the worship of sex stems from a belief in the omnipotence of sex. In the opinion of those who share these illusions, sex appeal, like money, is a power that can be used to open the gates of heaven. For many people money and sex have become the reigning deities.

Every schizoid patient I have treated has the illusion that sex is omnipotent. Each schizoid girl, though aware that she is not an acclaimed "love goddess," has a deep conviction of the irresistibility of her sexual appeal. Some "act it out," in others the feeling is covered by fear and anxiety. This illusion places an undue importance upon sex, to the neglect of the total personality. In my previous book *Love and Orgasm* I pointed out that sex and personality were two sides of the same coin. The attempt to divorce sex from its basis in the total personality leads to an illusion of sexual "sophistication."

The sexual "sophisticate" uses sex as a means of relating or as an instrument of power. This use of sex distorts its function. Instead of being an expression of feeling for the sexual partner, it becomes a maneuver to bolster one's ego or establish one's superiority. The male who plays the role of the irresistible "Casanova" tries to fulfill an ego image of himself as the "great lover." The woman who sees herself as "sexy" believes that her sex appeal establishes the superiority of her femininity.

How far the illusion of sexiness may be from reality is seen in the figure drawing shown on page 124.

The patient who made this drawing commented on it as follows: "She looks blah. Her body looks bored. She has a phony smile. It's an expression I feel I have sometimes. I have the same kind of figure, sexy and feminine."

How is it possible for a person to see a figure as "blah" on the one hand, and "sexy and feminine" on the other? The thinking that can unite such opposites is based on a view of the female as a round, soft, empty body with big

FIG. 12

breasts and big hips for man's enjoyment. The flat chested, hipless, straight female body, on the other hand, implies a masculine identification and suggests a homosexual approach to sex. That sex is an expression of feeling and that a body without feeling is devoid of sexuality are truths that the schizoid individual denies. The illusion of sexiness mistakes the appearance for the content and confuses sexual "sophistication" with sexual maturity.

This illusion, like many others, develops as an exaggeration of the childhood situation. It represents a fixation at the oedipal level and is a magnification of the incestuous feelings between parents and children. A girl will develop this illusion if she becomes aware of her father's interest in her as a sexual object. She will respond to this interest out of her desire for affection and support, and she will unconsciously adopt the role of sexual object as a means of winning this affection and support from other men.

The woman who views herself as a sexual object believes in the irresistibility of her sex appeal. She may feel repelled by her own body, but she is convinced of its power to attract the male's interest. After all, if her father could not resist her charms, what man can? Her energy will be devoted to the elaboration of her sex appeal, as if this was the meaning of her total personality. In manner and appearance she will express a superficial sexiness that belies her inner feelings. She will attract men whose immaturity corresponds to her own. With these men she will again experience her irresistibility, but complain at the same time to her psychiatrist that "men can't keep their hands off me." Because "sexiness" is so much a part of her personality, she is unaware of her seductive behavior. She flirts too easily, rolls her hips too freely, and dresses too provocatively. Since her illusion depends on the man's response, she will necessarily be promiscuous in her desperate need to maintain the illusion.

The sexually "sophisticated" female fails to find fulfillment as a woman. Her sexual activities fail to provide satisfaction. She is orgastically impotent, and her image of femininity is constantly being shattered by her sexual frustration. Her despair of finding the love through sex increases her desperation and completes the circle.

Normally, a father's feeling for his daughter is guided

by his respect for her youth and innocence. If he is sexually happy with his wife, his affection for his daughter is free of unconscious sexual desire. But in sexually unhappy families the girl unwittingly becomes an object upon whom the father projects his unfulfilled sexual desires and upon whom the mother projects her sexual guilt. The mother sees the daughter as a harlot, while the father sees her as his princess. Feeling rejected by her mother, the girl turns in desperation to her father, and receives love mixed with sexual interest. She has no choice but to accept her father's interest. This situation is further complicated by the fact that her personality between the ages of four and six is particularly vulnerable to sexual excitation, due to the preliminary budding of sexuality which occurs at this time. Her response to her father takes the form of a fantasy in which the girl pictures herself replacing her mother in her father's life. The fear of incest, however, causes her to dissociate from the reality of her infantile body and leads to the illusion that she is sexually irresistible.

The conflict of modern man stems from the opposing values represented by his ego and his body. The ego thinks of achievement, the body of pleasure. The ego functions with images, the body functions with feelings. When image and feeling coincide, the result is a healthy emotional life. When, however, the feeling is subordinated or suppressed in favor of the ego image, the result is a life of illusion and desperation. The illusion contradicts the reality of the body's condition, the desperation evades its needs.

Behind every illusion is the desire for freedom and for love. The desperate individual strives for freedom and love through the illusion of power. In his mind, power is the key to freedom and love. Although this illusion serves to sustain his spirit in its despair and helplessness we have seen that it also maintains the despair and helplessness when the critical period of childhood has passed. To overcome the illusion of power, the reality of freedom and love must be experienced as bodily feelings. This is accomplished by concentrating upon the physical tensions of the body. When a person feels the rigidity of his body, he will know that he is not free, regardless of his rebellion and defiance. If he feels that his body is frozen, he will know that he is shackled, whatever his external situation may be.

If he becomes aware that his respiration is inhibited and his motility reduced, he will realize that he is not able to love.

The emotional significance of muscle tension is not adequately understood. The unresolved emotional conflicts of childhood are structured in the body by chronic muscular tensions that enslave the individual by limiting his motility and capacity for feeling. These tensions, which grip the body—mold it, split it, and distort it—must be eliminated before one can achieve inner freedom. Without this inner freedom it is illusory to believe that one can think, feel, act, and love freely.

8

Demons and
Monsters

THE DESPERATE INDIVIDUAL is not generally aware that he harbors a demonic force within himself. He rationalizes his behavior or excuses it on the grounds of his helplessness and desperation. He is identified with his demon and unable to see it objectively. The demonic force, at this stage, is part of the person's character structure which the ego is committed to defend. It is like a Trojan horse within the city walls whose insidious danger the ego fails to see. Thus, it is not until the horse has disgorged the enemy and the city is threatened with disaster that the nature of the deceit becomes apparent. When self-destructive behavior threatens the life or sanity of an individual he may realize that such behavior is due to an alien entity in his personality. Where formerly he would justify his actions as a natural response to frustration and disappointment, he is now in a position to see them as a compulsion and therefore as a symptom of his illness. At this point, the therapist can expose the demonic force behind the compulsion and by analyzing its elements, dissolve it as an active entity. Since there is a demonic component in every schizoid personality, it is necessary to know how the demon arises if the split in the personality is to be healed.

The demonic is the negation of the illusion. The demonic force acts to destroy the illusion and reduce the person to the level of his despair. Its weapons are cynicism and doubt. Cloaked in the guise of rationality, the demon hides its irrational nature. When the illusion collapses as the demon predicted, it goes on to say, Show them you don't care. Its counsel is self-destruction—since nothing really matters and no one really cares. It mocks the ego and weakens its stability. In effect, it says to the ego, So you thought you could live without me! You thought your illusions could sustain you! The effect is like an uprising of the slaves upon whom an economy depends. The demon's voice is the voice of the rejected body taking its revenge upon the ego that denied it. The ego, having put its faith in the illusion, is helpless when the illusion collapses. The body which was forced to serve the illusion reacts destructively when the controlling force is released. It overwhelms the helpless ego and temporarily takes possession of its faculties. It erupts as a hostile and negative force, destroying all that the illusion aimed to achieve.

A child is born without illusion and without a knowledge of good and evil. He is born an animal organism whose behavior is geared to the satisfaction of his physical needs and his desire for pleasure. Good and bad become meaningful concepts when he is taught to resist the lure of bodily pleasure and to curb his aggression. The good child obeys and is submissive, the bad child rebels and is assertive. If the parental authority is overwhelming, the child will reject his animal instincts in the interest of survival. He will bury them in the pit of his belly and encapsulate them by muscular contraction. His abdominal wall will become flat and hard, his buttocks tight, his pelvic floor pulled up, and his diaphragm frozen. Isolated and enclosed, the instincts of sexuality and aggression slowly smolder into perversion and hate. Cut off from participation in the life of consciousness, the rejected bodily passions create their own domain of hell. In this process a devil is born.

Human demons arise through the same psychological mechanisms that created the original devil, Lucifer. Lucifer was originally one of God's angels, who was cast out of Heaven into Hell because he rebelled against God's authority. Prior to Lucifer's rebellion all was peaceful in Heaven, which was Paradise. Lucifer's expulsion corresponds to man's fall from grace for succumbing to the temptation of the serpent and eating the fruit of the tree of knowledge. Both Lucifer and man transgressed against God's will, but Lucifer was cast into the pit, while man, expelled from the Garden of Eden, was suspended between Heaven and Hell.

There is an interesting parallel between the ideas that assign the devil to the bowels of the earth and my concept that the human devil resides in the pit of the belly. The flames of hell also have a parallel in the fires of sexual passion that are located in this region of the body. Carnal pleasure is the main temptation the devil uses to lure the ego into the abyss of hell. Against this catastrophe the terrified ego strives to maintain control of the body at all costs. Consciousness, associated with the ego, becomes opposed to the unconscious or the body as the repository of the dark forces. Yet the temptation cannot be removed or the devil overcome so long as the body is alive. In this unending struggle, the ego's illusions are constantly undermined by the activity of the repressed feelings.

The interaction between illusion and demonic force can be seen in the case of the woman who has the illusion that she is the perfect mother, yet who often acts in such a way as to destroy her child and negate the illusion. This is not done consciously. On the contrary, her conscious desire is to be perfect and to have a perfect child; but no child is perfect, and she becomes frustrated at her child's human failings. Under the maxim that mother knows best, she denies her child the opportunity to develop his own personality through self-regulation. His resistance to her domination is viewed as an obstructionist tactic and is blamed on the natural perversity of the child. As her irritation mounts over the child's continued failure to respond positively to this treatment, she turns on him with rage and hostility. It is amazing how self-righteous the mother can feel behaving in this manner.

The conflict between a child and its parents can only have a negative outcome for both parties. The child cannot win against its parents, upon whom it is dependent for survival and growth. But parents also cannot win against the child, for while the child may become outwardly submissive, he remains inwardly rebellious. The rebellion flares again in adolescence, when the surge of sexual feeling stirs the desire for independence in the young person. The old struggle is renewed, only this time the hostility is more overt on both sides. In such a situation, when a truce is finally reached, the young person has lost his identity and the good feelings of his body. He becomes quietly or actively desperate and develops the schizoid personality. The parents have lost the love of their child, a development which they cannot understand.

The demonic aspect of the mother who acts in this way to her child is seen in the relentless and compulsive manner with which she pursues her goals. The conflict between mother and child soon loses the superficial justification of what is best for the child and becomes a clash of wills. Not infrequently this clash degenerates into a state of war; violence or the threat of violence is present. I have seen mothers turn on their children in my office with such a look of rage and hostility that I instinctively recoiled. It seems that the mother is determined that her child shall conform to her image of it, or she will destroy it. This image which the mother projects upon her child fulfills the mother's ego at the expense of the child's happiness. Since this image is a projection of the mother's image of herself, it appears that the mother acts to prevent her child from having more freedom or joy than she herself knew. All of this occurs on the unconscious level, while on the conscious level the mother is still obsessed with her illusion of perfect motherhood. The force which drives a mother in this direction against her conscious intentions is demonic.

The demonic aspect is actually visible at times in the facial expression of the mother when she becomes enraged at the child. Her brow clouds over, her eyes look black, her jaw sets, and her voice becomes hard. The total expression is one of suppressed rage, a murderous rage, which creates the impression of a demon let loose from hell. In the face of such an expression, what child would not become terrified? It is said that "Hell hath no fury like a woman scorned." But while such a rage can be faced by an adult, it is devastating to the personality of a young child, whose dependence on his mother makes him helpless to counter it. The image of the witch derives from the child's experience of this demonic aspect in his mother.

The demonic action, as distinguished from the normal, is not ego-syntonic; it is expressed against the ego's will, in opposition to the ego's wish, and is not, therefore, an open expression of feeling. In demonic rage, for example, the brows lower as if to contain the destructive force or to deny it; the result, however, is an undisguised look of hostility, of which the person is unaware. Anger, as opposed to rage or hysteria, embraces the total personality and is accepted by the ego. The demonic action is linked to a denial mechanism: the ego disclaims the deed at the same time that the body is doing the action. The term *devilish* denotes a behavior in which there is a simultaneous acting out and denial of the intent of the action. The person who is only identified with his ego is unconscious of this dishonesty. Such behavior stems from a strong sense of guilt which produces a dissociation between the conscious mind and the body's feelings.

The mother who turns against her child is actually committing a self-destructive action. The projection of her image upon the child reveals her unconscious identification with the child. Her hostility against it is therefore a reflection of her own self-hatred. In rejecting the child's individuality, she is unconsciously rejecting her own individuality. The child is an extension of her own body, which has now gained an independent life. Cutting off her child from affection and warmth is a symbolic cutting off of her own body or her hand. The child is not only an extension of her body, it is also an expression of her sexuality. All her repressed guilt about her sexuality and all her negative feelings about her body become focused on the child, who will react to this projection by a hostile attitude which the mother interprets as perverse.

If little children act like demons, it is because the natural qualities of the child have become distorted by the parents into negative forces which the child must deny. Too frequently, the normal demand of children for erotic contact with the parent is viewed as a tactic to harass the parent and gain attention. In his irrepressible spontaneity, the child is said to be "full of the devil." His natural interest in sexuality is considered a perversion by some parents. His overriding desire to be free and have fun is commonly regarded as an irresponsible attitude. If he doesn't eat what his mother chooses, he is said to be stubborn. All of a child's actions are determined by the fact that he lives the life of the body, much as an animal does. His actions are governed by the pleasure principle. He does what feels good and avoids what is painful. But this is intolerable to a parent who has denied his own body. According to many parents, a child must be controlled and taught to obey, he must adopt adult values, and he must forsake his body, that is, he must deny his natural instincts. It is not surprising, therefore, that some children become little demons and act perversely. The perverse attitude will develop in a child who loses hope that his parents will respond with understanding to the open expression of his feelings.

A mother's response to her child is conditioned by her personality. If she is relaxed and satisfied with her function as a woman and a wife, she will pass these good feelings on to the fruit of her marriage. If she is tense, frustrated, and bitter about her feminine role in life, she will react to her children with the same feelings. In a previous book, *Love and Orgasm,* I pointed out that a woman cannot fully separate her feelings about a child from her feeling for the act which gave rise to its being. Her feelings about sex will determine her attitude to the child. Regardless of her conscious desire, her sexual guilt and anxieties will influence her behavior toward the child. How she handles the child's body reflects her feeling about her own body. I saw a young mother become horrified when her young infant regurgitated on her dress. She pushed the child away from her as if it were an unclean thing. The expression of disgust which may appear on a mother's face when she has to change a child's diaper will be felt by the child as a rejection. The intolerance some mothers show toward a baby's crying reveals the degree to which they have suppressed their own feelings.

The mother who relates to her child as to an object or a possession is acting demonically. Such an attitude denies that the child has any feelings, and grows out of the mother's denial of her own feelings. In place of feeling as a determinant of behavior, such a woman manipulates other people in order to fulfill her ego image. She will also treat her husband as an object, and her sexual relations with him will represent a performance instead of an expression of love. In this behavior a woman expresses her contempt for the man, which her ego, of course, denies. Her repressed feelings of hostility and sexuality become a demonic force that compels her to act destructively. Just as she unconsciously rejects her husband as a man, she will also reject her child as a person. The demonic in a mother always derives from repressed sexuality. This was illustrated in Barbara's case, which was discussed in Chapter 1. Barbara considered herself an emancipated woman—artist, bohemian, liberal. Her emancipation took the form of perverse sexual behavior. Barbara's justification of this behavior was that "it shows you can be above sentiment when sentiment is meaningless." The sentiment she discarded was one which views sex as an expression of love. Her behavior was an act of rebellion against an ideal which, obviously, had lost meaning for her. This ideal was the purity and dignity of the human body. Starting with the illusion of emancipation, Barbara ended with a feeling of emptiness, a loss of her identity, and the collapse of her body. Her pretended sexual emancipation was a denial of her need for love, and as such, it was a demonic expression.

The idea that a repressed and alien sexuality is the disturbing factor in the personality is not new to psychiatry. Wilhelm Reich points out that since 1919, it has been known that genital sensation is the persecutor in schizophrenic delusion.[35] The difference between illusion and delusion is one of degree and reflects the difference between the schizoid state and the schizophrenic condition. In the schizoid personality this genital excitation gives rise to the illusion of emancipation, sophistication, and sexiness. In the schizophrenic delusion, the isolated genital excitation gives rise to paranoid ideas with a homosexual component.

The other element which goes into the makeup of the demonic entity is suppressed rage. Every schizoid individual has a layer of suppressed rage in his personality which breaks through occasionally in demonic form as an overwhelming and destructive impulse. It differs from anger, which is ego-syntonic and ego-directed. The rage is like a volcanic explosion which demolishes everything in its path. The schizoid individual sitting upon this explosive force feels constantly threatened by the possibility of its eruption. His defense against this inner rage is rigidity and immobility, which is also the defense against his terror.

The fact that the same defense is used in both cases indicates that the terror and rage are intimately connected. Schizoid terror is the fear of the murderous and destructive impulses in the personality. Schizoid rage is the reaction to the terror.

Terror and rage arise in the personality through the experience of parental rejection. The child reacts to the denial of its rights as unique, inviolate, and independent being with anger. But the expression of anger by a child is often met with a hostile reaction from the parents, increasing the child's fear and changing his anger into the irrational response of rage. Unfortunately, such patterns of action and reaction tend to become chronic, with the result that the child feels more and more alienated, increasingly frightened, and overtly negative. For the child there is no way out of the conflict but the suppression of his rage and superficial submission to his parents. Depending on the severity of the conflict, his personality will show the typical features of the schizoid structure: terror, rage, desperation, illusion, and finally, a perverse behavior in which his negative feelings find their outlet.

In adult life, the suppressed rage finds expression in self-destructive actions, which may be directed either against the self or against one's children. It may also erupt against a spouse with whom one is identified, but only very rarely against others. The schizoid individual acts out his rage upon those who are dependent on him, thereby reversing the original situation in which he, as the helpless, dependent child, experienced his mother's rage. In dreams, however, the original object of the rage may become apparent. Thus, a patient discussing a dream about her father, said, "I can't cope with the bloodiness in me. I was so angry I felt like a cat. I could have scratched him to pieces, put his penis in a meat grinder, and crushed it to a bloody pulp."

The existence of this suppressed rage as an explosive force in the schizoid personality limits his responses. Rado suggests that "The absence or paucity of 'between' responses renders his ambivalence extreme and keeps him shifting from excessive fear to excessive rage, from blind obedience to blind defiance and back."[36] The point is, of course, that a bomb allows no "between" responses. Either it explodes or it doesn't; there is no way it can be discharged by degrees. The absence or paucity of proportioned responses is due to the suppressed rage rather than the other way around. The suppressed rage, with its murderous impulses, is also responsible for the schizoid attitude of "all or nothing." Every decision is a matter of life and death, since on a deep level the question of whether to act or not touches the problem of this buried violence. To open the door to feeling, even a little, risks the release of the inner storm.

The demonic force which results from the combination of repressed sexuality and suppressed rage is seen in sex murders. The sex murderer is described as a fiend. He is also a very sick person, for such actions denote insanity. But murder in general is often linked to sex. Or, to put it differently, sexual conflicts in the emotionally unstable person often lead to murder.

In the schizoid personality, the demonic force is hidden, and "acted out" in more subtle form. Since the ego denies its existence, the superficial appearance of the individual is one of sweetness and goodness. The demonic hides behind the mask of the angelic. But the angelic is suspect in a person with a rigid body and a fixed smile. The therapy of this type of character structure often requires considerable time before the patient feels secure enough to drop the mask and express a negative attitude. Later it turns out that this attitude was present all along as a lack of faith in the value of the therapy. This lack of faith may not seem to be much of a demonic force, but nothing is more destructive to relationships than a deep-seated negativity that is masked by seeming cooperation.

The destructiveness of this character structure lies in its dishonesty. A relationship with the schizoid individual is always frustrating because despite his seeming cooperation, he denies his feelings. The effect of his smile and superficial sweetness is to make the other person feel guilty when there is a conflict. Even though one senses the negative attitude underneath the mask, one feels powerless to expose it. In the end, one becomes openly negative and hostile oneself, without always being able to justify it. The schizoid individual withdraws in self-defense, unaware of his role in provoking the dispute.

"Acting out" is a more deliberate tactic. It involves the denial of a person's own lack of faith and the projection of this bad faith upon another. Under the cover of the accusation of bad faith ("I love you, but you don't love me!" "I give and you only take!"), demands are made that the other person cannot possibly fulfill. With seeming justification, then, the schizoid individual makes the other person feel responsible for all his unhappiness. Behavior may be described as "acting out" when it is rationalized and ascribed to another person or external force.

The person who is in contact with his body is aware of his own hostility and doesn't project it on others. He is aware of his own lack of sexual feeling and doesn't accuse his partner of emasculating him. But when the body is rejected and denied, this reality function is lost. The repressed feelings become a demonic force which negates all hopes and aspirations.

The tactic of placing blame on others constitutes the essence of what is called paranoid behavior. In paranoid behavior the individual projects upon another his own negative feelings, specifically his repressed sexuality and his repressed hostility. When this tactic meets with resistance, the paranoid individual reacts with an irrational rage completely devoid of any feeling of responsibility for his actions.

The paranoid individual presents the true picture of the devil when he is in one of his rages. His eyes take on a malevolent look, his brows arch upward, and his lips are drawn back in a half smile, half snarl. The pictures of devils and witches are derived from such expressions. At other times, his face assumes an angelic appearance that somehow fails to be convincing. The withdrawn and rigid schizoid, on the other hand, is really a "poor devil," or rather, a frightened devil, which is, I suppose, the same thing.

The demonic is, unfortunately, the voice of the body's experience. If it doubts every sincere intention, it is stubbornly clinging to a childhood tactic which ensured survival. If it cynically rejects all positive feelings as meaningless sentimentality, it is voicing the disappointments of childhood. Unless this fact is appreciated, the demonic force in the schizoid personality cannot be overcome.

The quality of the monstrous has a different meaning and a different function. I would define as monstrous a human body that lacked human feelings. For example, one of my schizoid patients described her figure drawing (see Figure 13) as a "ghoulish apparition." Then she added:

> She doesn't look alive. She's strange, tough, yet she seems to be running away. She has a blank staring look, like I get sometimes. She looks like a monster. It's a very schizzy expression. Sometimes I catch myself in the mirror and I'm shocked. I get this look of ghoulishness, like I don't know who I am or what I should be doing. I don't know what I want.
>
> If I eat, I feel better. But then my body is ugly, grotesque, misshapen. When I'm thin my body becomes languid and lovely. I like it. When I eat I get passive and indolent. All I do is eat, sleep, and go to the bathroom. When I don't eat I become intense. I can't sleep or move my bowels. I become frantic. There is nothing in between these extremes for me.

The split in this patient's personality is clearly revealed in her remarks. While she feels better when she eats, her appearance revolts her. It contradicts her ego image of a languid, lovely woman which, however, is only a mannequin, unable to sleep or move its bowels. Her definition of a ghoul was "an organism that lives off other people," but her description of the ghoul as an organism that eats, sleeps, and defecates suggests that it is also an infant. An infant, of course, lives off its mother when nursing. Could my patient have gotten this feeling of being a ghoul from her infantile experience at the breast?

This patient was a twin born to a small woman who was only eighteen years old at the time. She related that her mother told her that her milk had turned sour very early and "we couldn't get enough to eat." My patient could not recall her infantile feeding experiences, but it is a fair assumption that she went through a difficult period. As the stronger of the two girls, she was pushed aside by her mother in favor of her weaker sister. It is conceivable that in her struggle for the breast she was regarded by her mother as some kind of monster who couldn't see that her mother was doing what was best. Mothers have a strange

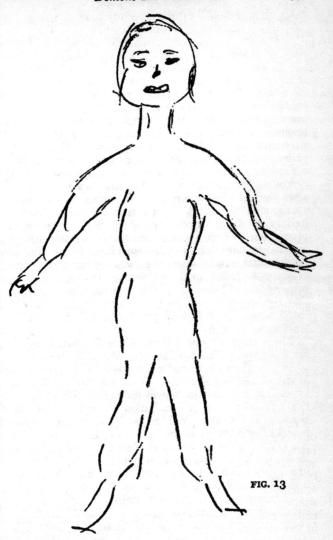

FIG. 13

habit of regarding the natural demands of the child as monstrous when they cannot fulfill them.

It is easy to picture the conflict that could arise from such an experience. To indulge her appetite was to feel like an animal, an infant, a monster. Not to eat was to reject her body's desire and to find her fulfillment on some other level. The other level is the ego level. My patient found that she could derive a temporary satisfaction from her work as an actress. As an actress, she lived on her own resources, was excited with her image, and as she put it, ate off herself. How long can a person eat off himself? My patient discovered that after a few exciting performances, her acting lost its intensity. Another alternative seemed necessary. My patient found that she always felt better when she was sexually involved with a man. But, as in her acting, after the first flush of excitement passed, her old feelings of dissatisfaction and ghoulishness returned to plague her. Within a short time her relationship with a man degenerated into a sado-masochistic "acting out" of hostility and recriminations. Sex was for her a repetition of the old conflict in a new setting. It was a form of sustenance, and her need for this sustenance made her feel that she was living off another person. In the end, she hated herself for this feeling and despised the man for yielding to her need.

This patient became a ghoul when she turned against her body and its animal instincts. Her difficulties began when she was made to feel guilty about these instincts. If to eat, sleep, and defecate is immoral, the result is an impossible confusion in human feelings. People caught in this confusion seek self-realization through creative activity, as if the way out is to be found in non-physical modes of satisfaction. In all cases where the creative effort is a substitute for the life of the body, it provides only an image, not a self. Creative activity is satisfying and meaningful only when it enriches and enhances the life of the body from which it draws its inspiration.

To overcome this patient's feeling of being a monstrosity, it was necessary to get her to identify with her body, to accept her physical sensations, and to think in terms of her body. Six years of verbal therapy had ignored this need. Her breathing was severely constricted due to the early inhibition of the sucking reflex. Her first effort to breathe deeply produced a strong panic reaction. For a few moments she was unable to catch her breath and she became very frightened. Then she began to cry, and her panic subsided. She had to mobilize her body through aggressive movements. This was done by getting her to kick the couch while lying on it and to strike it with her fists. At the same time her guilts and anxieties were analyzed. The result was very positive. One day the patient reported:

> I suddenly feel like I never felt before. I feel myself. I feel my face, my feet, my body. I know who I am. I know now what I look like, I'm not so frightened. I don't feel panicky. I don't feel guilty. I'm being very direct and honest, and I find it pays. When I breathe will, I get a surge of good feeling.

The monstrous in human beings takes many forms: spooks, zombies, statues and ghouls. One of my patients was a young woman in her twenties who consulted me because of a severe panic reaction due to difficulty in breathing. She had been in a verbal therapy for eight years previously, but the central problem of her relation to her body had not been touched. When I first saw her, her face was twisted to one side, her body was frozen with fear, and her eyes were large and frightened. After normal breathing was re-established and panic subsided, she told me the following story:

> I was at my sickest at sixteen years of age. I remember making the decision to give up needing anything or anybody. I stopped relating to people, and I lived in an atmosphere of unreality. I tried touching a piece of wood, but I couldn't get the feeling that it was wood. When I crossed the street I had the feeling that the cars couldn't touch me. I was a spirit.
>
> At seventeen and eighteen I had my first love affair. It was very satisfactory. I experienced vaginal orgasms, but I broke the relationship because I felt too guilty. When that affair ended I went through a severe reaction. I developed a condition the doctors called "nervous exhaustion." After that I didn't have sex for years.

At twenty-two I moved away from my home town. In the next several years, I had the most "hellish" sex relations. I didn't have any sexual feelings, but sex was compulsive. My body changed. It became tight and hard. All the bones stood out. My hips became narrower. I lost weight and became thin, since I stopped eating compulsively.

I believe that I gave up my sexual feelings when I left home. My unconscious justification for this promiscuous sexual behavior was, It's okay as long as I don't enjoy it.

This case shows the intimate connection between sexual feeling and body perception. The repression of sexual feeling undermines the ego's identification with the body. With the loss of sexual feeling, the individual becomes desperate. This patient, in a desperate attempt to regain some sense of self, resorted to compulsive sexual activity without feeling. But, as her recital indicates, sexual activity without pleasure fails to maintain the ego's contact with the body. Compulsive and mechanical sex transforms the body into a mechanism, robotlike in its actions—that is, it dehumanizes the body.

Another form of the monstrous in the human being is the statuesque body, that is, the body that is immobilized in a pose. The monstrous quality in such a body is the contradiction between its apparent unaliveness and the fact that it houses a real human being. Analysis of this personality structure always reveals that the human being in the statue is a little lost child. The statuesque body is his defense against the pain and disappointment he anticipates if the feelings of the child for love and understanding were to be allowed expression. It is also his desperate attempt to gain approval by the sacrifice of his feelings. In effect, the statue is saying, I have become what you wanted me to be; now you will be proud of me and love me. But this illusion runs counter to the reality of life. Who can truly love a statue? The frustration and disappointment the individual experiences in his pose increases his desperation and furthers the illusion that the pose must be made more perfect. It also increases the inner anxiety that the pose will fail and that the underlying despair will break through to overwhelm the personality.

Occasionally, one runs across an individual whose appearance is truly monstrous. At a clinical seminar in my office, a young man was presented whose physical appearance strongly resembled the pictures of Frankenstein's monster. He had the same stiff, mechanical walk, square shoulders, deep-set, unalive eyes, and facial expression as the monster of the movies. The similarity was so striking that once seen, it was as difficult to dissociate the patient from this image.

The surprising thing about this young man was that he was the exact opposite of what his appearance suggested. He was sensitive, intelligent, and artistic. A deeper analysis of his personality revealed that his appearance was a kind of costume and mask to hide and protect an acute sensitivity. He reminded me of the Halloween outfits little children wear, which are designed to hide their identity and frighten the observer. In fact, under his exterior, this patient was a delicate and frightened child who had somehow developed this unusual appearance to protect himself from an insensitive world.

The monstrous in human form is the forsaken body which takes on this form to avenge its denial. I do not mean that this happens consciously or by intention. The body has no motive in its development. I am merely attempting to give some meaning to a phenomenon that is otherwise incomprehensible. A living body that functions without feelings is monstrous, just as is a machine that functions like a living being. The monsters we create in our imagination are caricatures of the life we see about us. The different expressions that a body assumes are determined by the experiences it undergoes. The person whose body functions like a puppet has been conditioned to behave that way since infancy.

In contrast to the demon, the monster has a heart of gold. It is as if all the negative feelings became embodied in the exterior aspect, leaving the interior pure and untouched. In every case I have seen in which the appearance could be characterized as monstrous, the inner personality was of an innocent child. The demonic, on the other hand, wears the outer aspect of sweetness and light. Just as the child hides behind the monster, so the devil hides under an angelic demeanor. In both cases we are dealing with a split in the personality. The normal human being is neither angel nor devil, monster nor frightened child, Dr. Jekyll nor Mr. Hyde. These dissociations emerge only when the unity of the personality is split, creating the categories of good and evil, civilized mind and animal body.

John Steinbeck, in his novel *Of Mice and Men*, made a penetrating analysis of the phenomenon of the monster. Lennie was a giant with the feelings of a child. This discrepancy in his personality eventually cost him his life. The child could not control the strength of the giant, and the giant could not express the feelings of the child. When Lennie tried to hold a rabbit in his hands, he held it too strongly and squeezed the life out of it. Then, one day, Lennie tried to touch the golden hair of a girl. She became so frightened at his appearance that she screamed. In his effort to quiet her, he inadvertently crushed her. So Lennie had to die.

The tragedy of the monster is that his appearance defeats his desire. His defense isolates him and may lead to his doom. I have been impressed over the years by the fact that the classic monsters pictured in the movies often turned out to be the true heroes. The Hunchback of Notre Dame is the perfect example. The monster's heart is touched when someone responds to his unspoken appeal for love and understanding and is not frightened away by his appearance. Given this circumstance, the unbelievable strength of the monster can become a force for good.

9

The Physiology
of Panic

It takes energy to drive the machine of life. The schizoid, whose vital functions are handicapped by inner terror and despair, is never free from an underlying fear that his energy supply will prove inadequate. Occasionally, this fear reaches consciousness and the patient panics because of an inability to breathe, with the terrifying feeling that his life hangs for the moment in the balance. When this happens it makes the patient realize how dependent his life function is upon a sufficient amount of oxygen, and he becomes aware of the connection between his reduced respiration and his unalive body.

Many clinical observations support the view that schizoid individuals have difficulty in mobilizing and maintaining an adequate supply of energy. Psychomotor activity —work output, emotional responsiveness, and sexual activity—is some indication of the energy output of an individual. These energy indices are generally low in schizoid patients. Further, the failure of the schizoid individual to respond adequately to certain stresses (marriage, work, etc.) suggests an inability to mobilize the extra energy needed by the increased demands of these new situations. Paul Federn writes, "One frequently observes how a schizophrenic episode is set off by the transition to a higher school level, or from school to job, or to the responsible state of marriage."[87] The frequency with which mental and physical fatigue, sleeplessness or excessive unsatisfactory sexual activity will trigger a psychotic episode indicates that the ability of the schizoid ego to maintain contact with reality is undermined by the depletion of the energy reserves of the organism.

The energy of life is derived from oxidative reactions of which the final step is the coupling of electrons to oxygen either through a process known as oxidative phosphorylation or by slower but more direct transfer mechanisms. The importance of oxygen to the production of energy in the living process is self-evident. Therefore, it seems highly significant that clinical experience corroborates a direct relation between the schizoid condition and a disturbed respiratory function.

RESPIRATION

The schizoid patient doesn't breathe normally. His breathing is shallow, and he doesn't get enough air. Physiologists and others working with schizophrenics have reached similar conclusions. E. Wittkower, who is quoted by Christiansen, says, "Often the respiration of the schizophrenic is abnormally shallow."[38] W. Reich,[39] R. Malmo,[40] and R. G. Hoskins report identical observations. The significance of shallow breathing is described by Hoskins as follows:

> . . . the results of deficient oxygen assimilation are at least of the general order of the symptoms of schizophrenia. These include limitation in the field of attention; perseveration; apathy; depression of spirits; inappropriateness of affect, with silly laughter; poor judgment; obliviousness to danger; loss of self-control; anxiety; excitement without apparent cause; uncontrollable emotional outbursts; insidious loss of the power of decision and unwillingness to bear responsibility; tangentiality of associations; and gradual failure of sane judgment and a sense of the fitness of things.[41]

Many symptoms of which the schizoid complains appear on Hoskins's list; but the patient is not aware, of course, of any relationship between his psychological disturbance and his physiological functions. In fact, the schizoid is not conscious that he inhibits his respiration. By reducing his demands on life, he has adjusted his body to a lower level of energy metabolism. Ordinarily, his deficient oxygen intake is not perceived as a handicap. Occasionally, however, a patient may become spontaneously aware of this inhibition and remark, "I realize that I do not breathe." He means that he breathes very inadequately. Such observations become more frequent after the patient's attention has been directed to his breathing.

Surprisingly, many patients express a conscious reluctance to breathe deeply. One patient made a significant observation about her reluctance to breathe which, I believe, has general validity for many schizoid individuals. She said:

> I am very sensitive to smells, especially body odors. I can't stand perfume on another person, and I don't use it. That is why I don't breathe. I am afraid that if I breathe, I will inhale the smells and odors of other people, that they will get into me.

The neurotic individual frequently expresses the opposite fear. He holds his breath because he is afraid that his "odor" will get out, that is, he is afraid to offend other people. This anxiety about bad breath is found in many neurotic patients, who often have to be convinced that their breath has no unpleasant odor. Anxiety about body odor and bad breath reflects the feeling that the body's emanations are disgusting and "dirty."

Schizoid patients give another reason for their reluctance to breathe deeply. Many say that the sound of the air as it passes through the throat is repulsive. Breathing sounds have been described by patients as "revolting," "animal-like," "uncivilized." In many patients, such sounds are associated unconsciously with the heavy breathing of sexual intercourse. Audible breathing makes one conscious of the body, which the schizoid finds repugnant. It also calls attention to his physical presence, which he finds embarrassing. One technique of survival used by desperate individuals is to be inconspicuous; this tactic fails when one breathes loudly. Playing dead is another defensive maneuver which the schizoid uses and which eventually leads to an inhibition of respiration.

The most important reason for diminished respiration is the need to cut off unpleasant body sensations. This need is not conscious in patients until such sensations develop in the course of therapy. This is especially true for the feelings in the lower part of the body. Shallow breathing prevents any feelings from developing in the belly, where the schizoid has locked his repressed sexuality. Every attempt to get the patient to relax his abdominal wall and release his diaphragm meets with resistance. His objection is that it is "poor posture" or that "it looks sloppy." The first objection is meaningless, since any chronic muscular tension is an unnecessary strain on the body which impedes good posture. The second objection means that it looks "too sexy." The natural posture with a relaxed abdominal wall runs counter to the current fashion of small hips and flat bellies (which, incidentally, represents a rejection of pelvic sexuality in favor of oral-breast eroticism).

At first, letting out of the belly so that breathing can become more deeply abdominal feels unnatural to the patient. He complains of unpleasant sensations. These are of three kinds: sensations of anxiety, feelings of sadness, and feelings of emptiness. As one patient said, "It makes me feel real scared in my belly. It makes me want to cry." In fact, deep abdominal respiration will often release a pent-up crying that has been blocked from expression for many years. After such crying, the patient always reports that he feels much better. The feeling of emptiness is set forth in the following note sent to me by one of my patients:

> I have been having a lot of trouble breathing lately. I took two lessons from the singing teacher I told you about. Wonderful. I think I learned something about my breathing problem. Frozen diaphragm? I breathe with my chest, and so I get choked. He has me breathe by relaxing my lower belly and filling up from there, then contracting in reverse. Is that right? If yes, then I have never used my diaphragm. Anyway, I've been trying it during the day. It is uncomfortable (I feel hollow), but it seems to alleviate the suffocation sometimes.

In some patients the sensation of emptiness in the belly is so frightening that they recoil from the attempt to breathe deeply with the abdomen. They report a sensation in the pit of the stomach that feels like the "bottom dropping out." The frozen diaphragm is like a trap door, the release of which threatens to plunge them into an abyss. I point out to these patients that the sensation of emptiness results from the repression of sexual feeling (pelvic feeling) and that if they would "let go" in breathing, they would recover these feelings. Watching them, one gets the picture of a person hanging from a ledge seven feet above the ground but afraid to let go because he cannot see the ground under his feet. In his first moment of falling, his panic is the same as that of a person suspended one hundred feet above ground. When he does let go of his breathing and hits bottom, which in the body is the pelvic floor, he is surprised at the feelings of pleasure and security which develop. When this happens, the patient becomes aware that his panic stemmed from his fear of sexuality and independence.

The respiratory difficulty of the schizoid is due primarily to an inability to expand the lungs and take in sufficient air. His chest, as I pointed out, tends to be narrow, constricted, and tight. It is fixed generally in the expiratory position, that is, it stays relatively deflated. By contrast, the neurotic suffers from an inability to expel his air fully. His chest tends to be expanded and over-inflated and to stay fixed in the inspiratory position. Broadly speaking, this difference reflects two different personality attitudes. The schizoid is afraid to open up and take in the world; the neurotic is afraid to let go and express his feelings. But this distinction between schizoid breathing and neurotic breathing is not absolute. Neither is the distinction between the two personalities as clear cut as I have indicated. Schizoid tendencies such as the dissociation from the body and the inhibition of respiration exist in neurotic individuals, and neurotic problems are frequently found in the schizoid personality. However, in this study, we are less interested in clinical distinctions than in the dynamics of the schizoid dissociation from the body.

Generally, as soon as respiration deepens in the schizoid patient, his body begins to tremble and develop clonisms, that is, muscular contractions. Tingling sensations appear in his arms and legs. He begins to perspire. If he becomes frightened at the new sensations in his body, he may become anxious. This anxiety seems related to his fear of losing control or "falling apart." Should the anxiety become too strong, the patient may become panicky. He will stop breathing to avoid the sensations and freeze up. The result will be an inability to get air, which, of course, is enough to panic anyone. Panic is the direct result of the inability to breathe in the face of an overwhelming fear. The schizoid's inhibition of respiration leaves him constantly vulnerable to the onset of panic when feelings arise in his body. He is therefore caught in a trap. If through therapy the patient is phsychologically prepared for the new experience, the result of deep breathing may be a revelation of what life can offer. Here is one patient's reaction to this experience:

> God, I could just feel my skin come alive. And my eyes—amazing, fantastic! I feel like I can open them. Things look brighter. Geez, my legs are loose! They're generally like rocks or like violin strings.

The next time I saw him he continued his report of the experience:

> After last session I felt so alive in my body. I was vibrating all over. It took me an hour or two before I was able to walk. It was like relearning how to walk on relaxed legs. I felt I was cured. The thing is, it didn't last more than twenty-four hours.

The respiratory disturbance in the schizoid patient is most evident when he is engaged in active movement. In such an activity as kicking his legs rhythmically on the couch, his breathing becomes labored and does not seem to provide sufficient oxygen to sustain his effort. He tires rapidly and complains of heaviness in his legs and pain in his abdomen. He stiffens the upper half of his body and disengages it from the activity of his legs. The rhythm of his breathing is not synchronized with that of his legs. His pattern of breathing becomes predominantly costal, his abdomen remains flat or contracts further. The effect of this maneuver is to set up tensions in the diaphragm and abdominal wall which prevent the full expansion of his lungs at the moment when he needs more oxygen. The patient has to be advised to let his whole body "go" with the movement.

There are some schizoid patients who can continue kicking longer because of a compensatory overdevelopment of the chest. In these individuals, the ribs are forced outward to create a greater lung capacity without mobilizing the diaphragm. The chest develops the configuration known as "chicken breasted" or "pigeon breasted," because the sternum remains depressed by the chronic contraction of the diaphragm and the rectus abdominis muscle. This condition permits an exaggerated expansion of the lungs in a sideward direction.

The average neurotic person in an identical situation will develop what is known as "second wind," which enables him to prolong his effort. This generally fails to happen in the schizoid patient. To understand why this does not happen, one must understand the mechanics of the respiratory movements.

In normal breathing, inspiration results from an expansive movement of the chest and abdomen. First, the diaphragm contracts and descends, pushing the abdominal viscera downward and forward. The displaced viscera are accommodated by the anterior-posterior expansion of the abdominal cavity. Second, continued contraction of the diaphragm about its central tendon elevates the lower ribs slightly, thus expanding the lower part of the chest. This produces an expansion of the lungs downward and outward, in which directions they have the greatest freedom of motion. Such respiration, called diaphragmatic or abdominal breathing, produces the maximum quantity of air intake for the least effort. It is the type of respiration seen in most people.

In sustained muscular activity, where a greater quantity of air is required to meet the stress of the effort, additional muscles are brought into play. The intercostal muscles (between the ribs), the small muscles which join the ribs to the sternum and to the vertical column, and the scalenes, which hold the first two ribs fixed, are mobilized. These muscles, acting in concert with the diaphragm, produce an expansion of the upper part of the chest cavity, adding additional space for the expansion of the lungs. This further action is dependent on a fixation of the diaphragm in its contracted position which steadies the lower ribs to allow the upper ones to move outward. The

expansion of the upper part of the lungs is limited, however, by their fixation at the hilum where the blood vessels
and bronchi enter and by the immobility of the first two
ribs. Costal breathing, the name given to this type of
respiration, is normally employed to supplement abdominal breathing in situations of stress or emergency,
when additional oxygen is required. Used alone, costal
breathing does not provide a substantial volume of air. In
contrast to abdominal breathing, it yields a minimum air
intake for a maximum effort.

The "second wind" of the neurotic person results from
his ability to mobilize the accessory mechanism of costal
breathing to supplement and deepen his abdominal respiration. When the two types of breathing become integrated,
the diaphragm contracts and relaxes fully, and respiration
takes on the unitary quality seen in infants, animals, and
healthy adults. The key to unitary respiration is the release of all tension in the diaphragm to allow the total
body to participate in the respiratory movements. The
movement of unitary breathing is like a wave which, in
inspiration, begins in the abdomen, where it shows its
greatest amplitude, and moves upward. In expiration, the
wave descends from the chest to the abdomen.

The schizoid individual cannot release the tension in his
diaphragm and abdominal muscles. This tension serves the
purpose of keeping his belly "empty" or "dead"; it prevents any feelings of pain, longing, and sexuality from
reaching consciousness. Schizoid breathing is, therefore,
predominantly costal except when the breathing becomes
very shallow, in which case the distinction between costal
and abdominal breathing is hardly discernible to an observer. When the schizoid person is engaged in activities
which involve the lower half of the body, such as sex or
kicking or in conditions of emotional stress, his diaphragmatic tension increases. As a result, he is forced to rely
almost exclusively upon the accessory method of costal
breathing when his oxygen requirement mounts.

In some patients this phenomenon becomes exaggerated,
and one sees a type of breathing that I have called "paradoxical." In paradoxical breathing, inspiration is produced
by an upward movement rather than an outward one. The
rise and expansion of the chest is aided by an elevation of

the shoulders which pulls the diaphragm upward and contracts the abdominal wall. Thus, the expansion of the chest is accompanied by a narrowing of the adbominal cavity. Sometimes one observes that the belly is sucked in during inspiration and let out in expiration. This type of breathing is only seen in stress situations. The paradoxical nature of this breathing lies in the fact that despite the person's greater need of oxygen to meet the stress, he is getting less than in his relaxed state.

The schizoid inability to mobilize extra energy to meet stress situations is thus directly related to his faulty respiration. His regular use of costal breathing reflects his reliance upon an accessory or emergency method of respiration to meet his normal needs. The same phenomenon was observed in his use of the "will" in everyday actions as opposed to the normal individual's motivation by pleasure. Functioning ordinarily on his reserves, the schizoid is in a constant state of physiological emergency from which he cannot be released as long as he depends on an emergency type of breathing. An underlying sense of panic is always present even in those cases where a compensatory overdevelopment of the thorax permits more sustained effort.

The emotional significance of schizoid respiration is most clearly seen in "paradoxical" respiration. Breathing upward by raising the chest and shoulders and pulling in the belly occurs in fright. If one duplicates this type of breathing, one can sense that it is an expression of fright. The frightened person pulls in his belly and limits his breathing to the upper half of his body. He may hold his breath, or his breathing may become rapid and shallow. When the fright passes, he will sigh with relief, let his chest down and his belly out. The persistence of a raised chest, elevated shoulders, and contracted abdomen indicates that the fright has not been resolved even though the feeling of fear has been repressed and is beyond consciousness. The schizoid type of costal breathing is the physiological manifestation of this repressed fear. It is another sign of the underlying terror in the schizoid body. The defense against this fright and terror is a reduction of respiration. To breathe little is to feel little.

Schizoid individuals have another difficulty with breathing, which stems from neck, throat, and mouth tensions.

These tensions are so severe that schizoid patients frequently complain of choking sensations when they try to breathe deeply. Their throats close when they try to take in more air. When one encourages the patient to open his throat to let the air through, he becomes frightened. He feels vulnerable, as if he had opened his inner being to the world. When this fear is eliminated as the result of therapy and he can keep his throat open while breathing, he reports very pleasurable sensations flowing through his body and into his genitals. His feeling of being choked is therefore—the result of an unconscious act of tightening his throat to cut off threatening feelings.

These throat tensions in the schizoid individual are tied up with his inability to make the strong sucking movements of a healthy infant. The mouth reaching and sucking of the normal infant involve all the muscles of his head and neck. It reminds one of baby birds whose beaks open so wide to receive food that their bodies look like round sacs. When the schizoid reaches out with his mouth, the movement is generally limited to his lips and doesn't include the cheeks, head, or neck. In therapy, when he becomes able to mobilize his whole head in this gesture, his breathing spontaneously deepens and becomes more abdominal. The close connection between breathing and sucking becomes clear when one realizes that the infant's first aggressive movement in life is to "suck" air into his lungs. Its next big move is to "suck" milk into his stomach. Sucking is the primary mode by which the infant obtains his energy supplies. Any disturbance in the function of sucking will have an immediate repercussion upon the function of breathing.

Margaret Ribble points out in her book *The Rights of Infants*[42] that the inadequate respiration of many infants is due to the inhibition of sucking movements. When these movements are encouraged, breathing becomes easier. Breast-fed babies normally breathe better than bottle-fed babies because sucking on a breast is a more active process than sucking on a rubber nipple. Almost every one of my patients reported some disturbance of this vital function during early infancy. Their deprivations and frustrations in this area resulted in the rejection and denial of their impulses to suck. Very early in life, they choked off the longing for oral erotic gratification in order to survive in a deprived state. These infantile feelings and impulses are re-awakened when the patient attempts to breathe more deeply. He reacts by choking them off, as he did when he was a baby.

Opening the throat wide to breathe evoked feelings of drowning in several patients. One patient reported this sensation on a number of occasions. Yet the patient could not find any incident in his memory which could give rise to such an experience. The logical interpretation was that the feeling of drowning represented his reaction to a flood of tears and sadness which welled up in his throat when its tensions were relaxed. In the same way, the choking sensations commonly reported by patients could be interpreted as the "choking off" of these overwhelming feelings of sadness. But the feeling of drowning makes one wonder about a possible association with intrauterine existence, where the fætus floats in a sea of fluid. It is now known that the fetus makes respiratory movements in utero from about the seventh month onward. These are not functionally meaningful. However, if a uterine spasm were to cut off the flow of oxygenated blood to the placenta for a significant time, it is conceivable that these tentative respiratory movements could become real attempts to breathe. In this situation, the feeling of drowning would result from the flow of amniotic fluid into the fetal throat. This is pure speculation, but the possibility of such intrauterine experiences cannot be ruled out.

In the treatment of the schizoid disturbance, breathing exercises are of little help. When breathing is done mechanically, it does not evoke any feelings, and its effects are lost as soon as the exercise stops. A patient will not breathe deeply in a spontaneous manner until his tensions are relaxed and his feelings released. These feelings are sadness and crying, terror and screaming, hostility and anger. Release occurs when the sadness is expressed in crying, the fear in the scream of terror, and hostility by the expression of anger. All of these, crying, screaming, and anger, require vocal utterances that are handicapped by the inhibition of respiration. Thus, the schizoid patient is in another one of his vicious circles: the inhibition of respiration prevents the release of feeling, while the suppression of feeling creates an inhibition of respiration. The circle is broken by getting the patient to become conscious of his inhibition of breathing, that is, to sense the tensions which inhibit his breathing and to try consciously to relax them. He is also encouraged to breathe while making guttural sounds. Generally such procedures will allow some feeling to arise, which will develop spontaneously into crying if the patient is relaxed.

A patient's first crying often occurs without a feeling of sadness. As his breathing deepens to involve his belly, he begins to cry softly in a primitive reaction to the previous tension. This crying is a rebound phenomenon, like the crying of an infant, who reacts in this manner to a frustration without knowing the emotional significance of his response.

Crying is, primitively, a convulsive reaction to tension which mobilizes the respiratory muscles to effect the release. In this process, a sound is uttered. The use of the vocal cords to communicate a signal is a later development. The best example of this primitive reaction is the baby's first cry after the tension of birth is relaxed. This cry gets the breathing started, just as it does for the patient in therapy. In all forms of tension the organism freezes; in crying it thaws out.

The growth of the ego and the development of motor coordination make available the response of anger to feelings of frustration. Anger aims to remove the frustration, while crying merely serves to release the tension. When the frustration persists because the anger is blocked or ineffective, recourse to crying is available to release the tension. Even adults may cry when the frustration persists despite all efforts to overcome it through anger. The persistence of a frustration creates a sense of loss and leads to a feeling of sadness which then becomes associated with the crying. At this point the crying takes on an emotional significance. The patient who cries with a feeling of sadness is in touch with his feelings.

Similarly, screaming can also be dissociated from its conscious association with terror. This happened to a young man during therapy. His breathing had deepened, and at my direction, he let his jaw drop and opened his eyes wide as he lay on the couch. The expression he assumed was one of fright, but he was not aware of it. However, he uttered a loud scream without feeling any fear. His screaming stopped when he lowered his eyes but was repeated involuntarily when he opened them wide again. In the course of therapy this patient became aware that there was a latent fright deep within him which became manifest when he opened his eyes wide. He sensed that there was something he was afraid to see, some image in his retina which was still too nebulous to discern but which frightened him. Then one day the image came into focus. He saw his mother's eyes looking at him with hatred, and he screamed again—this time, with terror. He had the impression, he told me, that the vision was related to an incident that occurred when he was about nine months of age. He was lying in his carriage crying for his mother. She finally appeared, but her anger at being disturbed was expressed in the look of hatred he saw. Following this vision, the fright disappeared from his eyes.

The dissociation between the expression of a feeling and its perception indicates that a denial mechanism is operative. To cry without feeling sad, to scream without feeling frightened, or to rage without feeling angry is a sign that the ego is not identified with the body.

ENERGY METABOLISM

The production of body heat is a function that is intimately related to the total personality. We recognize this relationship in our speech. Personalities are described as "warm" or "cold." A warm person is one who has feelings, a cold person is devoid of feeling. Warmth is also used to describe humanity, as when we contrast human warmth with the coldness of the machine. Broadly speaking, the schizoid personality has turned cold to the world, and his feelings are minimal.

Certain emotional states increase the body heat, while others decrease it. One gets hot with anger, cold with fear. The body melts with love and freezes with terror. We all know from personal experience that these adjectives are more than a manner of speaking, that they truly reflect what goes on in our bodies. When a person becomes excited, as in anger or love, the metabolism of his body changes. Its tempo is increased. He breathes more deeply, moves more quickly, produces more energy. His body heat rises as a manifestation of his heightened metabolism. Feelings such as fear, despair, and terror have a depressing effect upon the body. Even when these feelings are repressed, the metabolism of the body reflects their influence. The coldness of the schizoid individual is directly related to the fear or terror in his personality.

There is some objective evidence that the actual skin temperature of schizophrenics is lower than normal. F. M. Shattock found that a significant percentage of psychotics had cyanotic extremities (blueness and coldness of hands and feet at room temperature).[43] Another investigator, D. I. Abramson, noted excessive vasoconstriction in the arterioles of schizophrenic patients exposed to cold. He observed an improvement in their condition after treatment.[44]

There is also evidence that a tendency to a lower basal metabolism is typical of schizophrenia. R. G. Hoskins, who made an extensive study of this function in schizophrenia, states, that,

> Altogether we were and are convinced that one of the characteristic features of the psychosis appearing in the metabolic level is a deficiency in the uptake of oxygen.[45]

The coldness of the schizophrenic and the schizoid reflects a disturbed energy metabolism. His lower skin temperature, his excessive vasoconstriction and his decreased basal metabolism suggest an infantile pattern of response to the stress of life. In his response to cold he is like a very young infant who cannot mobilize the extra energy to meet this stress. He has the same dependent needs as the young infant: to be held, to be protected, and to be warmed. In other words, the scizophrenic (and the schizoid to a lesser degree) is not fully prepared for an independent existence. His reluctance to breathe and his shallow breathing express a tendency to regress to an infantile level of existence.

The schizoid clings to the illusion that survival depends upon finding a mother figure who will satisfy his needs for warmth, protection, and security. Cutting the symbolic umbilical cord which ties him to this mother image is equivalent to casting him into a world which he regards as cold, hostile, and uncertain. This infantile dependence shocks parents when they see it in their supposedly grownup children. I have often heard parents complain that, "He acts as if the world owes him a living." But a parent will only be shocked if he has blindly dismissed the difficulties and problems which his child has presented during the period of growing up.

The corollary of this concept is that independence evokes in the schizoid a feeling of panic. To stand on his own feet is felt by him as an emergency calling for emergency measures. These measures consist of (1) costal respiration, (2) a tendency to anaerobic metabolism, (3) a reduction of motility.

1. The emergency nature of costal respiration was discussed in the first part of this chapter. Briefly, in the schizoid individual costal breathing replaces abdominal breathing and fails to yield an adequate supply of oxygen.

2. Under stress, this lack of oxygen may lead to anaerobic metabolism (the release of stored energy without the introduction of oxygen). This type of metabolism is a less efficient method of energy production and is called "the alarm reaction" by J. S. Gottlieb and associates, "since it appears to be called upon as an energy-producing reaction in emergency situations."[46] These investigators found that this type of metabolism was characteristic of chronic schizophrenics.

3. The reduction of motility is an emergency device to conserve energy. Normally, motility is decreased in states of alertness both to heighten sensitivity and to mobilize the energy for "fight or flight."

In the schizoid condition these emergency mechanisms tend to become the "normal" pattern of response, for the schizoid regards his daily living as a matter of survival. It follows, therefore, that in a real crisis the schizoid has no reserves to fall back on. Hoskins reaches this conclusion from his study of the biology of schizophrenia.

> It would seem that the prodigality of effort required for organic adaptation leaves the patient with but inadequate energy for successful adaptation to the social field.[47]

In Chapter 3, I pointed out that the schizoid individual uses all his energy to hold himself together. His muscular system is immobilized to maintain the integrity of his organism. He depends on his will to support a sense of self. The will, as we have seen, is an accessory mechanism usually reserved for emergency situations.

MOTILITY

One can also approach the physiology of schizoid behavior through the analysis of body movements. The term "motility" refers to the capacity of living organisms to move spontaneously. It embraces a broader range of motion than the term "mobility," which refers to the displacement of the organism in space. The motility of a living organism is an expression of the total living process. If this process is disturbed, as in the schizoid personality, certain distortions of motility become evident.

The schizoid individual shows either a reduced motility or a restless and exaggerated hyperactivity. Hypomotility is characteristic of the schizoid individual who tends to be detached and withdrawn. It is evident in his paucity of gesture and lack of spontaneity. It is implied in the term "masklike visage" that describes his facial expression. It is seen in the stillness of the schizoid's body when he talks. His arms and hands are rarely employed as means of communication. This lack of expressive body movement during a conversation is partly responsible for the feeling that the schizoid is "not with it."

Schizoid hypomotility may also be regarded as a state of partial shock. Depersonalization or the complete dissociation from the body has been compared to a state of shock by Paul Federn.[48] Everything we have said about schizoid physiology supports this view: lowered basal metabolism, shallow breathing, etc. The physical rigidity of the schizoid body is an attempt to counter the shock and maintain some degree of integrity and function. This attempt breaks down in the collapsed state, where the condition of shock is more evident in the loss of muscle tone. In both cases, however, the shock is not so severe as to paralyze the vital functions, but is limited to the surface of the body. And it is not an acute state of shock but a chronic condition.

Schizoid shock should be interpreted as a reaction to the feeling of rejection and abandonment. It represents an infantile response to an infantile experience and a fixation at this stage of development. Regardless of his age, the schizoid is both a mute infant and a wise old man who knows the experience of struggle, suffering, and closeness to death. I shall discuss the schizoid's fear of death in the next chapter. It is important here to point out the connection between the state of shock, the unconscious state of panic, and the conscious feeling of desperation.

The state of shock accounts for the quality of automatism often seen in the schizoid's body movements. In his way of moving he often looks like a robot. One of my patients noted this quality in himself. He remarked, "Walking down the street, I saw my reflection in a store window and I looked like a wooden soldier." By this remark the patient indicated that his rigidity reflected a state of shock. He was like a wooden soldier marching to his doom, oblivious to the panic within him.

Hypermotility is often seen in the schizoid individual with paranoid tendencies who impulsively "acts out" his feelings. The movements of these individuals are characterized by unevenness, inappropriateness, and rapidity. They are often accompanied by emotional outbursts the intensity of which bear little relation to the ideas expressed. Such movements represent an inability in this personality structure to contain and control the excitation. The following description by a patient of her behavior illustrates this restless hyperactivity:

I felt I was playing some kind of game. It was very quick and very charged and made people nervous when they were around me. They said I discharged such wild energy all over. I had to keep going. I had to keep talking, and my ideas became very abstruse. My conversation was high-strung and rapid, seemingly very intellectual on the surface. I realize now I acted this way so that nothing could touch me on the inside.

This particular patient impressed me during our first sessions with her apparent warmth. She spoke, seemingly, with much feeling. Her hands were warm and moist; her skin felt warm to the touch. I soon became aware, however, that this was a superficial phenomenon. Her body heat resulted from her hypermotility, which was a reaction to a deep sense of frustration in her personality. She reported that when she failed to reach a sexual climax the frustration almost drove her wild.

> Afterwards I would scream and shout. Then I would break down and sob for two or three hours, after which I felt released and at peace again. Or else I'd go for a very long walk or run up hills. I went horseback riding a lot. I'd take the fastest horse and make it go like mad. I didn't care if the horse threw me. I had the feeling that I had to go beyond something, something had to pop or let loose, and so I rode until I was exhausted.

As the patient gained insight into her personality, she attempted to control and direct her aggression, to restrain her rage, and to stop the "acting out." As a result, a change came over her body. Her hands became cold; even her face changed color. She remarked:

> My face was much warmer before. I don't recall having a pale face. People used to comment on my rosy cheeks. I noticed my hands have gotten thinner. I don't have much feeling in them now. I have become frightened finding out all these things about myself. I used to think I was just an emotional person.

These observations confirm the view that there is an underlying coldness in the paranoid patient that is masked by his hypermotility. It explains why objective measurements of the physiology of schizophrenia are often inconclusive. It points up the direct connection between motility and body heat.

The hypermotility of the paranoid individual is a "running away" from his body and its feelings. He is in constant flight or prepared for flight. His very strong tendency to fly (also, to fly off the handle) is manifested in certain physical attitudes. His raised shoulders, which seem to pull him off the ground, suggest the flight of a frightened bird. Most important, however, is his lack of contact with the ground. His impulsiveness and irresponsible behavior indicate that he doesn't have "his feet on the ground," in other words, he is not "well grounded."

In many ways the schizoid individual feels unprepared physically and emotionally to stand on his own feet. In my book, *Physical Dynamics of Character Structure*,[49] I used the analogy of the unripe fruit to illustrate his dilemma. The seed of a fruit that is prematurely detached from the tree does not root itself easily in the earth. A human being in a similar condition will strive to get back to the source of his strength, his mother. His unconscious tendency will be to reach upward to her in his desire to be picked up and held. His flight is upward, away from the ground and from independence. His conflict can be depicted diagrammatically.

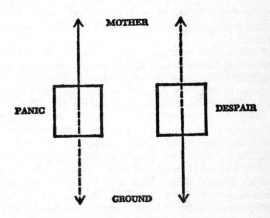

FIG. 14 The schizoid hang-up

The way upward is blocked by an unconscious feeling of despair. Having repressed the infant in his personality, he denies the longing to return to mother. This unfulfilled longing is then transformed into despair and creates the illusion that reunion with a loving mother will someday occur in adult life. This illusion transforms his mother image into that of a sexual partner. At the same time, demonic forces mock his illusion and compel him to face the necessity of independence.

The way downward, to an independent existence, is

blocked by an unconscious sense of panic. He lacks the inner conviction that his legs will hold him up. He relies on emergency mechanisms to sustain him. He is afraid of falling, since, in his despair, he feels that no loving arms will pick him up. Unable to reach up, unable to let himself down, the schizoid individual finds no respite and no peace. He is never free from the fear that he "can't make it, and no one will help."

The schizoid lives in limbo, suspended between reality and illusion, infancy and maturity, life and death. He rejects his past but feels unsure of the future. He has no present, no ground under his feet. Feeling dangers within and fearing dangers without, he is immobilized in fright or mobilized for flight. In both conditions, he is never far from a feeling of panic, and never sure which button can set it off.

Physiological functions are not fixed and immutable. The strong interaction between psyche and soma in the human organism negates such a view. Just as set muscular patterns of response can create a feeling of panic, the release of these muscular tensions can eliminate this feeling of panic. Most important in this respect are the tensions that restrict respiration. If one can breathe easily, the underlying feeling of panic disappears. Similarly, the physiological responses which are determined by an unconscious sense of despair change when an individual can face his despair. When he lets go of his illusions he will fall into despair, but surprisingly, he will find himself on solid ground, alone but not helpless. In this process he will lose the panic that his "hung-up" condition imposed. Alone, he will discover his identity with his body, and firmly planted on the ground, he can develop an independent adult life.

10

Eating and Sleeping

COMPULSION AND ILLUSION

EVERY psychiatrist is confronted with patients who struggle with their weight or cannot fall asleep. The patient who suffers from these problems feels desperate. He senses that he is in the grip of forces that act upon him against his will. He feels helpless in the face of his compulsive eating and compulsive rumination, and he relates his desperation to this feeling of helplessness. This explains why a person's mood changes for the better the moment he goes on a diet. Dieting seems to give him the feeling that he has gained control over his drives, achieved self-command, and restored his self-possession.

Unfortunately, in most cases the effort collapses after the goal has been reached. When the weight has been lost, the person relaxes his program of austerity and slowly slips back into his old eating patterns. This means another effort and another diet. I had a patient who was always starting a new diet but who never finished the old one. As soon as her weight went up several pounds, she went on a diet. This made her feel better, but then, when she lost several pounds, she resumed her compulsive eating. This went on for a number of years during her therapy, until she realized it was some kind of game. Then she remarked, "I know I won't stop eating between meals until I accept myself."

Compulsive eating and the inability to fall asleep are symptoms of an inner desperation that stems directly from a lack of self-acceptance. Therefore, when a person goes on a diet his desperation doesn't stop. It takes on a new form. He becomes compulsive in his dieting as he was compulsive in his eating. But he remains just as desperate as before.

The compulsive eater has the illusion that his next diet will be definite. He will then regain his youthful figure, which he will forever guard. Behind this illusion, he has another about perpetual youth. But what illusion does the insomniac have? Without being aware of it, he believes that nothing can happen to him if he stays alert. He holds on to consciousness as if it were his life. And nothing does happen: he doesn't fall asleep. But there is another illusion, of more recent date, connected with sleeping—the illusion of the sleeping pill. This illusion says that the person cannot possibly fall asleep without the pill. That dependence on the sleeping pill is an illusion can be demonstrated in many cases. Substitute a placebo for the pill, and the patient will go to sleep just as well as if he had the real thing. I tried this on several patients who were hung up on sleeping pills and it worked. The pill may be regarded as a substitute for the rag doll or teddy bear the patient clutched when he went to sleep as a child. Those objects in turn, were substitutes for the mother he desired to have close to him. A grain of reality is found at the core of every illusion.

A devil lurks behind every illusion, appearing in the cloak of reason and tempting the individual to give in to his immediate desires. "Go on," he says, "eat the chocolate. One little piece of chocolate can't harm you." Or, he may advise, "Take the pill tonight. You'll sleep better for it; then tomorrow you won't need one." His logic is hard to counter. One small piece of chocolate does no harm. One pill is not dangerous. The person believes that the pill does enable him to sleep better. The devil claims to speak for the body; this misleads the person, since his deepest instinct is to satisfy the body's desires. But the voice of the devil stems from repressed feelings which have become perverse in the course of the repression. The frustrated infantile desire for the breast cannot be satisfied by food or a pill. The illusion of oral gratification that overeating seems to fulfill adds a compulsive element to this activity.

There is, of course, a relation between overeating and sexual frustration. By frustration I mean the lack of a satisfactory sexual release in orgasm. For while inter-course brings a person into contact with his body, without an orgasm he is left in an unfulfilled state. This lack of fulfillment easily leads to overeating. Before the current popularity of dieting, it used to be said that one could tell when marital sex stopped. The wife became fat. Now, because of dieting, one can't tell. Not every person who is sexually frustrated overeats, but the reverse is true, every-one who compulsively overeats is sexually unfulfilled. The person who is sexually satisfied tends to be free of these neurotic drives. The individual who is in touch with his body senses its true needs and acts rationally to fulfill them.

EATING AND SEXUALITY

If the question of whether to eat or not to eat arises in a person's mind, it is a sure sign that the desire to eat stems from a feeling of desperation. The hungry person doesn't raise this question. The desperate person answers it in the affirmative. He may blame his continual eating on a feel-ing of boredom, but his boredom and passivity often re-flect a greater problem than he is willing to recognize. Food acts like a sedative on many people. It temporarily quiets their restlessness and allays their anxiety. Parents often use food for this purpose with children. The demand-ing child is commonly given something to eat to soothe his irritability. Food can therefore become charged with meanings other than the satisfaction of hunger.

One of my patients struggled with her compulsive eating for more than fifteen years without being able to overcome the tendency. Since her weight was a real handicap to her career as an actress, she gave this problem a lot of thought. The ideas she associated with "eating" reveal how deeply rooted in her personality this compulsion was.

1. "It means that I am taking care of myself. I always thought of myself as an orphan."

2. "Eating is an affirmation of the primary function in life."

3. "Eating is my only pleasure. I find no pleasure or meaning in life except eating."

4. "I am afraid of being hungry. I am afraid I am going to die if I am hungry."

5. "Eating is my answer to a feeling of loss—of my mother and my work."

6. "I realize eating is a negation of my sexuality."

Food is always a symbol of the mother, since the mother is the primary food giver. Mothers accept this symbolic relationship when they take the refusal of food as a personal rejection. By the same token, some mothers derive a personal satisfaction from a child's eating, as if the child's eating was an expression of love and respect for the mother. Very early in the life of most children food becomes identified with love. To eat becomes an expression of love; not to eat is an expression of rebellion. Very often the child realizes that not eating is one way to get back at an obsessive mother. This patient went through many experiences in which her personal likes and dislikes with respect to food were either completely ignored or treated as negative reactions. But her rebellion was crushed. She had to submit in order to survive. In her mind now, food still retained its original identification with love and the mother. For her, to reject food was to deny her need for her mother and to stand upon her own feet as a person.

This patient had never made a commitment to adulthood and maturity. She even expressed the thought that the very idea of such a commitment filled her with panic, the panic of the schizoid personality confronted with the necessity of leading an independent existence. Unable to establish roots and terrified of being cut off, she "acted out" her desperation by overeating.

The ideas she voiced about the meaning of food were distortions of her true feelings. Her compulsive eating was a self-destructive act, not a "taking care of" herself. Every time she ate more than she should, she felt guilt and despair. There was no real pleasure in this eating. It only felt good when it "assuaged the tension." She had never been hungry in her life, and I doubt very much if she was afraid of the feeling of hunger—at least for food. In a deeper sense she was hungry: hungry for love, hungry for pleasure, and hungry for life. She would gladly have restricted her eating if she believed she could satisfy these other needs. Her eating was a sign of her despair.

One day this patient remarked:

> I am paranoid. I wonder if people are hostile to me,
> if I am going to kill them or they me. But I am afraid
> to express or identify with these feelings. I carry my
> head in the air to pretend I am not paranoid. I have
> fears of being poisoned, fear of a knife being stuck into
> me. I am very aware of people talking about me.
>
> By being fat, no one would look at me and my hus-
> band would not be jealous and angry at me. I am
> petrified of his anger.

Her fear of being a sexual person was responsible for
her paranoid ideas. To understand these ideas, one must
interpret them with reference to the oedipal situation,
where the child is the apex of a sexual triangle involving
mother and father. There was an acknowledged sexual
attraction between the patient and her father. He used to
force the child to walk naked in front of their guests to
show that she wasn't ashamed of her body. It is not surprising, therefore, that she expressed the feeling, "I am very
aware of people talking about me." He used to examine
her panties every day to see if she was incontinent. The
fear of having a knife stuck into her betrays her fears of a
sexual assault by her father. Her father's sexual interest in
her had a hostile and sadistic quality which frightened
her.

The fear of being poisoned should, on the other hand,
be interpreted as a fear of her mother's hostility because of
the feelings between father and daughter. The mother is
seen by the child as the jealous and rejected woman who
would destroy her rival. The patient projected this image
of her mother upon her husband. But this doesn't explain
the panic she experienced watching her husband's recital.
The tension she felt in her belly on that occasion was the
result of a sexual feeling for him that arose when she
viewed him as a man instead of a mother figure. Her
suppression of this feeling produced the tension.

Being fat was a device this patient used to negate her
sexuality and avoid its associated dangers. And by carry-
ing her head high, she meant to show that she was above
such vulgar preoccupations as sex and the attention of
men. But her sexuality was not so easily denied. In many

movements and gestures she was flirtatious and seductive without being aware of it. As a result, she was always on the verge of a panic that her sexual feelings would arise at the wrong time.

PARANOID BEHAVIOR AND OVEREATING.

Compulsive eating is a form of paranoid behavior. The compulsive eater "acts out" his feelings of frustration, rage, and guilt by overeating. Overeating serves to reduce his feeling of frustration, to express his rage, and to focus his guilt. Eating and devouring are infantile modes of expressing aggression. Compulsive overeating is a literal doing away with or destruction of food, which is a symbol of the mother. The repressed rage against the mother finds an unconscious outlet in this activity. At the same time, however, the mother is incorporated symbolically into the individual, thereby temporarily relieving the feeling of frustration unconsciously associated with her. Finally, the guilt is transferred from the repressed hostility to the act of overeating, a maneuver that masks the true feelings and renders the guilt more acceptable.

The frustration that underlies compulsive eating stems from the mother's denial of the infant's need for oral erotic gratification. The rage arises because of the mother's seductive attitude. Expectations are aroused in the child that cannot be fulfilled. This mixture of desire and rage toward the love object produces an overwheming sense of guilt, a guilt so intolerable that it must be projected to others or displaced to food. Once this displacement occurs, the individual is trapped in a vicious circle. His guilt increases his frustration and augments his rage, which drives him to further compulsive eating and more guilt. Without a resolution of this guilt, the problem of overeating is often insurmountable.

In the unconscious, food is a representative of the mother's breast, primal source of nourishment. However, when the relation to the mother becomes charged with an unbearable guilt because of her pattern of seduction and denial, the longing for oral gratification is transferred to the father. His penis becomes a substitute nipple which also becomes identified with food. Compulsive eating is, therefore, a symbolic incorporation of the penis and, in a man, reflects the presence of latent homosexual tendencies in his personality. The homosexuality is sublimated in the overeating. As a final result, sexual satisfaction is transformed into the forbidden fruit, and the strong erotic feelings of childhood are repressed.

The connections between repressed sexual feelings, paranoid behavior, and overeating are illustrated in the following case of a compulsive eater who was treated by one of my colleagues.

This patient, whom I will call Aldo, was a young man of Greek origin whose parents had come to this country when he was two years old. Aldo was twenty-five years old, five feet five inches tall, and weighed 215 pounds. He was a waiter by profession, which added an occupational hazard to his problem of overeating. While his weight handicapped his work, Aldo was surprisingly light on his feet. His fat was located in his trunk, thighs, and upper arms. His face, hands, and feet were small and his neck was surprisingly thin. His chest was also narrow and thin. The fat in Aldo's body was especially pronounced about his waist and hips, which together with a pulled-back pelvis, gave these areas a womanish appearance. The conflicting elements in Aldo's body structure confused his identity. He was both thin and fat, masculine and feminine.

Aldo felt desperate and isolated by his fat body. He was embarrassed to approach girls and ashamed to engage in physical activities. He felt terribly guilty about overeating, but he was unable to control his appetite. He could lose weight by dieting, but when his will collapsed, he overate again.

Shortly before coming to therapy, Aldo had an experience that made him realize his need for help. His father had died six months earlier. Following this event he went on a strict diet that reduced his weight considerably. It was while attending an Easter party that his paranoid tendency manifested itself. He had been drinking and was feeling "high" when he began to have delusions of power. He thought he could predict events and even control them. I shall continue in his own words.

I saw a young woman in the corner of the room. A voice told me, "She is yours." So I approached her and said, "Come with me. You are mine." When she resisted, I took hold of her arm and started to pull her away. She called to her husband, who tried to stop me.

Things didn't make sense to me. She was mine and should have come with me. I held on to her arm while fending off her husband. Then one of the other men punched me and knocked me down. Everyone was looking at me in a hostile way.

I became panicky. I felt that my world was collapsing. I thought that if I didn't take my life in my hands I would be lost. I grabbed one of the men and with a superhuman strength I threw him across the room. At this point, all the men jumped on me and subdued me. They restrained me until I quieted down. Finally, several of the men drove me home. When I woke up the next morning I knew I must seek help.

Aldo believed that if he could understand what had brought on this episode he would gain some insight into his personality, including the problem of overeating. The experience of his strength was a revelation to him. He had always regarded himself as a submissive person, afraid of authority and unable to asert himself. His submission had obviously covered a repressed violence. Because of his submissive attitude, his aggression was unavailable in ordinary life. In the course of therapy it developed that the death of his father and his loss of weight were operative factors in the genesis of Aldo's paranoid outbreak.

During therapy Aldo recalled a childhood incident that shows the relation between his violence and his sexuality. He became aware of the incestuous relationship that had developed with his mother in his early years. "She treated me like her boy friend." Then he added, "I have the strong feeling that as a boy I caught my mother and father in bed and that I threw myself out of the window to break them up—to get my father out of bed."

Whether this really happened or whether he only imagined it is unimportant; what is important is the intensity of the oedipal situation. Aldo regarded his father as his enemy but he also identified with him. He felt that both he and his father were negated by the mother, who was the dominant figure in the home. He remarked that she constantly compared him to his father, implying that the father was a man but the son was nothing. The father, too, was unable to make his mother happy. Both men were objects of her contempt and ridicule.

Aldo's relation to his mother was a complex one. To the degree that his masculinity was negated, his eating was encouraged. Aldo's mother was preoccupied with the functions of the alimentary canal. The success of a day was measured by the amount of food he consumed and the regularity of his bowel movements. If he was constipated for a day, he received an enema. In effect, his body was violated at both ends by his mother, and he was forced into a submissive role with respect to her. At the same time she treated him like a "boy friend."

Consciously, Aldo feared and identified with his father. Unconsciously, he hated and identified with his mother. Each parent used him to get back at the other; for each he was the symbol of the other. It is understandable that Aldo grew up with an inadequate identity. He couldn't decide whether he was a thin boy or a fat one, and on a deeper level, man or woman.

To be fat meant to be feminine, submissive, and helpless. It denoted a lack of will, a vulnerability to sexual attack, and a sense of desperation. He remarked once, "The fear of being helpless, of having a penis shoved down my throat, or of being raped—these are the things that haunt me. The worst possible thing my mother could do is to expose her breasts to me. It's repulsive."

To be thin meant to be masculine, self-assertive, and in command of himself. But to become thin required an exaggerated use of his will (which also made him feel omnipotent and act overaggressively). Aldo remarked, "I would have to use all my will power, but I don't have the will at this time. I feel overwhelmed. I can't grit my teeth and say 'no' to food. If it was a matter of survival, I'm sure I could do anything. But I can't do it just to feel better."

The alternatives Aldo pictured, to live by one's will power or to resign, were impossible solutions. For him to use his will power as if every morsel of food was a matter of life and death would turn him into a monster. Once the will becomes omnipotent and the supreme value, schizophrenia beckons. A feeling of omnipotence had preceded his paranoid reaction. The other alternative was to feel helpless, resigned to his weight and fate.

Aldo lacked any conscious motivation toward pleasure. He remarked, "I don't deserve pleasure because I'm evil. There is too much hate in me." The self-denial of pleasure leads an individual to reject his body. The resultant loss of pleasurable physical activity reduces him to an infantile dependence on food as the only means of bodily satisfaction. This regressive behavior is never free from a sense of guilt. Aldo ate and suffered. The problem of the overeater is the loss of the feeling of a right to pleasure. Patients who suffer from compulsive eating invariably remark at one time or another. "I don't feel I have the right to pleasure." When the individual regains the right and the capacity to feel pleasure, his eating automatically becomes self-regulated. Eating that is governed by the pleasure principle becomes a pleasure and not a compulsion.

Aldo's body had become a source of humiliation to him and he dissociated himself from it. He lived, as he put it, "in his head." At the Easter party he experienced this living in the head physically. "Everything was whirling through my head. I felt it bulge. I felt it was going to explode." This kind of dissociation is different from that which occurs in the withdrawn state. In the latter, the depersonalization results from a marked reduction in body sensation and motility. The detached schizoid goes "dead." In the same circumstances, the paranoid individual goes "wild." As his energy goes into his head, his ego becomes overcharged, his will becomes a superhuman force, and his body becomes capable of actions that are normally impossible. At such times the paranoid individual seems possessed of a strength and force that is not only superhuman but monstrously inhuman. That strange forces are at work in this state was evidenced in Aldo's case by his feat of hurling the man across the room.

Further insight into his personality may be gained from the following figure drawings.

Figure 15 is the picture of a monster. In its facial ex-

FIG. 15

pression and body structure the figure has an inhuman quality. The mass of the body in the figure is concentrated above the waist, in contrast to Aldo's body in which the mass was below the waist. The figure also becomes sketchy below the waist, especially in the legs and feet, which indicates that he had no clear image in his mind of these areas. In a sense, the figure is a true picture of how Aldo sees and feels his own body in his unconscious: the upper half is exaggerated to compensate for the impotence of the lower half. His inability to draw the hand reveals his lack of contact with that organ.

Figure 16, the drawing of the female figure, is less sketchy—as if Aldo has a better conception of the female than of the male body. The face has a leering and hostile expression. With her finger pointing to the genital, the figure seems to be saying, "Look what I've got!" What she has looks like a phallic organ.

This figure introduces the concept of the phallic woman, or the mother with a penis. Many young boys picture mothers with a phallic organ not only because they are unacquainted with the female anatomy, but because their mothers act in a masculine way toward them. The phallic mother forces her son into a submissive position, "acts out" upon him the contempt she feels for her own sexuality, and, in effect, castrates him by treating his body as an object. While doing these drawings, Aldo remarked, "Castration is my violence button. I could go wild."

The male monster that Aldo drew represented the aspect of rage in his personality that was hidden and repressed behind the facade of the roly-poly fat boy. As such, it was a demonic monster, formless and inchoate, hateful and destructive. His demon had the strength of a monster. On the surface, Aldo was the submissive fat boy. He said, "As long as I am operating in my mother's valence I am going to have this big ass. That means that I must please my mother in order to survive." Pleasing the mother often takes the form of being submissive to the mother's demands that the child eat what she offers.

It became clear as therapy progressed that Aldo's paranoid episode at the party occurred when he unconsciously tried to free himself from his "slavery" by "acting out" his revenge on the female. His motivation in approaching the

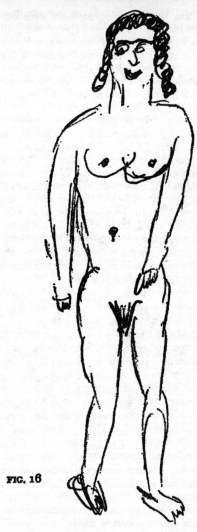

FIG. 16

young woman was the "desire to have sex with her plus a sadistic need to test my control and power over her." Had she been submissive, he would have made her perform lewd acts. He wanted to transform her into a "piece of ass," thus reversing the role of his relationship to his mother. He would assert his masculinity, necessarily in a perverse manner, since the "acting out" of repressed sexual feelings always takes the form of the perverse.

Aldo's difficulty lay in the unacceptability of the alternatives that his problem presented: to identify with his body with all its humiliating connotations or to deny the body and escape into paranoid thinking. The first was intolerable; the second was disastrous. The unpleasant feeling in his body and its unattractive appearance made him attempt to find his personal worth in his mind. As he saw it, the "nothingness" of his body could be countered by the omnipotence of the mind, the vulgarity of his body by the nobility of the mind, the contamination of his body by the purity of the mind. Through the will, his rejected and despised body became merely an instrument of action.

There are two ways of reacting to a situation in which the body is experienced as unacceptable. One way is to "deaden" the body, to withdraw inward behind a shell, and to reduce one's activities. The other way is to withdraw upward, to rise above the body through an overidentification with the ego and the will. The second way is the paranoid mechanism. It leads to delusions of grandeur (megalomania), ideas of reference (people are talking about me), and feelings of persecution (people are hostile). In megalomania, the feelings are withdrawn from the body and focused on the ego. Freud made the observation, "In paranoia, the liberated libido becomes fixed on the ego, and is used for the aggrandisement of the ego."[50] Freud's statement must be understood to mean that, in the paranoid individual, sexual energy (libido) is displaced (liberated) from the genitals to the ego, resulting in the deflation of the genitals and the inflation (aggrandisement) of the ego. Sex becomes an obsession from which ideas of reference and persecution derive.

Both tendencies—to go wild and to go dead—are present in all schizoid personalities in different degrees. To the extent that a person has been "acted upon" or used as a child, he will tend to "act out" or manipulate relationships as an adult. If his experience as a child is one of rejection or abandonment, he will tend as an adult to withdrawal and rigidity. Withdrawal produces the thin, narrow body structure of the asthenic individual. "Acting out" may include overeating if this is one of the ways the child was manipulated by the mother.

Aldo came to his therapist for treatment once a week for a period of two years. Treatment was directed to restoring his identification with his body. He was encouraged, in therapy, to be more self-assertive and aggressive by kicking with his legs or striking the couch. Relaxation of the diaphragmatic spasm opened the way for the release of the tension in his stomach. Because of his overeating, he suffered continually from heartburn and indigestion. His efforts to breathe deeply made him nauseous. The nausea forced him to throw up, which, at first, was difficult and distasteful to him. He learned, however, to do it easily, and it gave him considerable relief from his heartburn. But nothing was able to stop him from eating again right after the session. Aldo described the effect of the therapy as follows:

> For an hour a week you are accepted, understood and appreciated for who and what you are. Aside from these deep feelings which are very important to me, things happened to my body. It hasn't changed yet but I've gone through various exercises that have brought feelings into my body that I didn't feel before. I have sensations in my body all the time now, tense feelings, relaxed feelings, aches and pains. I am able to release my crying—under control. I have confidence that it won't get out of hand. I can feel my legs, my feet and my back. I am aware of a relationship between my body sensations and my behavior. It's like a whole new thing happened to me. I still live in my head but I can't get away from my body anymore.

On one occasion his doctor proposed a tug-of-war using a rolled bath towel. They tried it twice. Aldo, with his weight advantage, was able to pull the doctor into his corner, but not without considerable effort. When it was over he was breathing heavily. He remarked that he was surprised he had won. He had never been able to win a fight before. He would come close to winning, but when he was about to succeed, he would give up and let the other person win. This fear of success was interpreted as a fear of overcoming his father and possessing his mother.

The material presented in Aldo's case demonstrates the close connection between the lack of self-assertiveness and compulsive eating. When adult forms of aggression are unavailable, the paranoid individual will fall back on eating as the most primitive form of self-assertion, even though it proves to be self-destructive.

Aldo did not lose any weight in the course of therapy, but during the next year he was able to take off fifty pounds through dieting and exercise. He said it had not required a great effort of will because he was able to identify with his body and accept its needs. My associate saw Aldo four years later. His weight had remained down and overeating was no longer a problem.

I do not wish to give the impression that all fat people are paranoid. But overeating is one common way of "acting out" the frustration that results from a person's inability to find meaningful satisfaction on an adult level. There are other ways of "acting out" one's frustrations: rebellion, race prejudice, sexual promiscuity, drinking, etc. "Acting out" is a paranoid mechanism which is found to some degree in all schizoid individuals. I have described only the compulsive eater who can't say No to food, who lives in his head, and whose main connection with his body is through the digestive tract.

The opposite of the compulsive eater is the individual who is obsessed with the idea of slimness. It is currently fashionable to be slim. In part, this fashion can be explained as a reaction to the overeating which characterizes our "overweight society," and in part, it is explained by the intensity of the competitive struggle which makes life a race. In this race the fat ones are obviously handicapped. It reminds me of a rhyme children chant to taunt the overweight child.

Fat and skinny had a race
All around the pillow case;
Fat fell down and broke his face,
And skinny won the race.

The race of life is run against death, and here, too, the fat person seems to be at a disadvantage. The preoccupation with slimness is a manifestation of a desire for youthfulness and an expression of our fear of aging. Growing old is looked upon as a curse and a disaster. Since aging is a natural process of our bodies, a feeling of inevitable doom will hang over every desperate individual who tries to cling to youth. The desperation of our culture can be gauged by the fact that youthfulness has become its supreme value.

Slimness denotes other desirable attributes: the tall, thin body with its small head, long, narrow neck, and sloping shoulders seems to express elegance, refinement, and the aristocratic manner. In his play *Cat on a Hot Tin Roof*, Tennessee Williams has the leading lady speak disdainfully of her sister-in-law's children as "no-neck monsters." The thick neck is commonly associated with grossness, the coarse peasant type. The absence of a well-defined neck (see Aldo's figure drawing [Figure 15]) strikes people as monstrous. But the abnormally long neck also has something inhuman about it. Although it is admired in our society, it indicates that the person holds himself above his body and, indeed, rejects his body. Refinement can be carried to excess. Emotional health is never found in the extremes. A thin body can be as much a sign of a disturbed energy metabolism as a fat body. Between these extremes is the full-bodied person whose body is a source of pleasure to him.

In their efforts at dieting, people seek the trim look and the trim feeling. No one enjoys being heavy or feeling weighed down. When the body feels like a weight the average person's first thought is to diet. Reducing the weight of the body brings its mass into better balance with the available energy. The real problem, however, is not the extra pound of weight but the lack of energy. This lack of energy is responsible for the feelings of fatigue, depression, and passivity from which so many people suffer. It is also the problem of the schizoid personality.

On the psychological level, the discrepancy between mass and energy is reflected in the feeling that a youthful spirit is trapped in an alien and older body. The body feels heavy, bloated and out of proportion to the inner feeling of youthfulness. On the emotional level, the individual is like a child who feels his mature body as a burden. What is more natural than to reduce this burden by dieting? However, it doesn't work. The biological needs is to mobilize the body through pleasurable physical activity and adequate breathing. Psychologically, the person must identify with his body and mature emotionally.

The satisfaction that people derive from dieting may also be explained by the identification of food and the mother. The rejection of food is a rejection of the mother. Dieting thus provides an opportunity to "act out" one's supposed hostility against the mother in a symbolic way. Mother = food = body. The current wave of dieting not only expresses the wish to escape from the corporeality and the mortality of the body, it also reflects the antimomism of our day.

SLEEPING

The expressions "falling asleep" and "dropping off to sleep" suggest that the process of going to sleep involves a descent from one level to another. The two levels are, of course, consciousness and unconsciousness. One wonders why such verbs as "falling" and "dropping," which denote a downward displacement in space, became attached to the process of sleep. Are they vestiges of man's original arboreal existence? George Shallop points out in *The Year of the Gorilla* [51] that not infrequently the gorilla falls out of his nest during sleep. The gorilla nest is, however, only ten feet above ground, and the animal does not seem to suffer from the experience; but for other primates who live and nest in the treetops the threat of falling poses a greater danger. Falling anxiety in man may be an atavistic carryover from his primeval state. The human infant at birth retains the ability to hold himself suspended by his grip.

The loss of this reflex in a few days may be the biological basis for the fear of falling.

The ape protects himself from falling during sleep by the construction of a nest. Our beds may be the sublime transformations of arboreal nests. It seems that we have also transferred the fear of falling from the treetop to the bed. The dream of falling is, indeed, perhaps the most common type of anxiety dream. These reflections may suggest a phylogenetic basis for the association of sleep with the fear of falling. However, they do not explain why the actual process of going to sleep is described as "falling asleep." We return to the idea that the descent referred to is a physical displacement downward within the body.

In ancient philosophy, the body was divided into two zones. The region above the diaphragm was related to consciousness and the day; the region below belonged to the unconscious and the night. The ascent of the sun above the horizon which brings the light of day 'would correspond to an upward flow of feeling from the abdomen to the chest and head. This upward flow of feeling would then bring consciousness into being. The reverse occurs in sleep. The setting of the sun corresponds to the descent of feeling from the upper half of the body into the nether regions below the diaphragm. This concept could explain the use of the terms, "sinking into slumber" and "falling asleep." Waking is often experienced as an ascent, or rising, out of the depth.

Drowsiness is normally experienced as a feeling of heaviness in the eyes, in the head, and in the limbs. It requires an effort for the drowsy person to keep his eyes open or to hold his head up. He feels that his legs won't sustain him. He yawns. The yawn is generally interpreted as a need for oxygen, since it is accompanied by one or two deep breaths. But it is also an attempt by the body to release the normal tension of the jaw muscles to facilitate the relaxation of the whole body. Alertness diminishes when one is drowsy because feeling is withdrawn from the periphery of the body, that is, from the sense organs and the musculature. Where alertness is maintained because of a situation of alarm, drowsiness does not, of course, develop.

The transition from drowsiness to sleep is perceived as a

"sinking" from the head into the body. During the first stage of this transition, the person becomes conscious of his body. He feels its heaviness, that is, its substantiality and its mass. He feels his legs and feet, and very often, his aches and pains. His breathing deepens and becomes more unified. It becomes more like that of the infant or the animal.

In the second stage, there is a more or less gradual loss of consciousness of the body, starting with the surface and then extending to the whole body. The body image fades out. If sleep does not come quickly, one may become conscious of the internal organs, particularly of the heart, and sense the pulse in different parts of the body. These sensations may become vivid as feeling and attention recede from the surface of the body to the interior. At some point in this process the light of consciousness goes out, and all perception ceases.

The anxiety that prevents sleep frequently arises somewhere during this second stage. It seems related on the one hand, to the dimming of consciousness and the sensation of sinking, and on the other hand, to the perception of the interior organs. The sensation of sinking and the awareness of the heart beat or the pulse seem to be danger signals to many people, restoring their alertness. The alertness focuses attention upon these deep body sensations, which become magnified in the stillness of the night to an internal clamor. Sleep becomes impossible until the clamor subsides.

Not every insomniac experiences these perceptions in the course of his restless night. To avoid the anxiety that he has experienced on other occasions, he fights unconsciously against letting himself sink into his body. Without being aware of it, he holds on to consciousness, and his anxiety becomes transformed into the fear that he will not be able to fall asleep. Since every anxiety is a danger signal, this one, too, will maintain his bodily tension and his state of alertness.

The development of consciousness, as Erich Neumann[52] points out, creates the categories of day and night, light and darkness, the mind and the body. The ego, which arises from consciousness, associates itself with day, light, and consciousness, while the antithetical concepts of night, darkness, and the unconscious become attributes of the body. When the ego becomes dissociated from the body, it withdraws its identification with the body and sets itself up as the representative of the self. The body with its attributes of night and darkness becomes the nonself, or death. The descent into the unconsciousness of sleep becomes a symbolic descent into the tomb. The dimming of consciousness arouses the fear of death and activates the preoccupation with death which lies at the core of the schizoid disturbance.

One of my patients reported a dream in which, as she said,

> I vividly experienced the reality of death—what it means to be lowered into the ground and to be there until one disintegrates.

Then she added:

> I realized that it will happen to me, as it does to everyone. As a girl I couldn't fall asleep because of my anxiety that I would die during my sleep and wake up in a coffin. I would be trapped; no way out. In the dream, I became so anxious that I thought I would go out of my mind. Then I awoke.

Dreams of death or dying are not uncommon. Every human being carries with him the awareness of his eventual demise. But this knowledge of death does not create anxiety in the individual whose instinct or feeling for life is strong. Where impulse formation is reduced or weakened, as in the schizoid personality, the anxiety that develops from the suppression of feeling becomes attached to the idea of death. This is natural, since death is the loss of feeling. The schizoid individual compensates for his fear of death by an overemphasis on consciousness and the ego. Ego-consciousness or egotism, becomes a substitute for body feeling.

The dream has another interpretation, which complements its obvious meaning. Sleep is a symbolic return to the womb, a regression to the primal state of unconsciousness which also includes the idea of .death, so that tomb and womb are related images. The patient's dream image of waking up in a coffin can therefore be interpreted as being trapped in the womb with no way out during a uterine spasm which reduced the oxygen flow to the fetus. Lack of oxygen, as was pointed out earlier, is also the physiological basis of panic, which the adult pictures as "being trapped—with no way out." All organisms react to the feeling of being trapped with panic, and all panic reactions produce respiratory distress. This relationship explains why the schizoid individual who is close to panic because of an inability to breathe fully dreams of being trapped, why the trap is associated with the womb and the womb with a tomb.

The state of suspension between life and death is existence in limbo. It is the typical schizoid condition, neither "here" nor "there," neither infant nor adult, unrooted in reality but clinging desperately to consciousness. For the schizoid individual the day is a struggle for survival but night evokes the unconscious terrors. These often appear as nightmares when the censor that guards sanity relaxes its vigil, and the dark forces of the body take over. At times patients express fear of falling asleep because of the terrible dreams they experience. But more terrifying than the nightmare—the horror that can be visualized—is the descent into unconsciousness and the unknown.

The fear of the unknown derives from the ego's fear of the body and its mysterious processes. In the animal, where the ego is relatively undeveloped, fear of the unknown and fear of falling asleep are practically nonexistent. The animal lives the life of the body in the bliss of its ignorance of death. The human being who suffers from self-consciousness and the awareness of death equates the animal state with paradise in his unconscious mind. He longs to return to this blissful condition, at least in sleep, but his fear of the body and his panic at the loss of ego control bar the way. The more alienated a person is from his body, the greater is his longing for the sweet oblivion of deep slumber, but the more frightening is the transition from wakefulness to sleep.

Any activity which brings the individual into deeper contact with his body promotes the transfer of control from the ego to the body. A satisfying sexual experience is, of course, the most natural and the greatest soporific. In the healthy person sleep comes immediately after orgasm if the sexual activity takes place at night. And the sleep that follows satisfying sex is generally a deep and refreshing experience. Pleasurable sex has this result because it brings the person into more contact with the body and transfers feeling into the lower half of the body. Satisfactory masturbation acts in the same way, especially for young people. In infancy, nursing functions in similar fashion to lull the mind with the pleasurable feelings of the body. The nursing infant drops easily into sleep with his mouth still on the nipple, secure in his body and in his closeness to his mother.

In the adult, feelings of security and warmth, which the infant obtains from its closeness to its mother, are provided by pleasurable contact with his own body. Since physical activities promote this contact, they often facilitate the process of falling asleep. I have urged patients to do some simple physical exercises just before going to sleep as a means of overcoming their dependence on sleeping pills. In such exercises the important thing is to deepen and regularize the breathing, which relaxes the body and fills it with pleasurable sensations. In most cases, this simple procedure has enabled the patient to fall asleep easily. Very often breathing alone, while lying in bed, suffices. However, use of such breathing techniques in individuals whose identification with the body is limited and who may become panicky at the onset of body sensations is inadvisable. For these persons a moderate program of exercise is preferable. With the desperate individual, of course, these simple therapeutic techniques are insufficient.

The fear of falling, whether it is the fear of falling from high places or the fear of falling asleep, is related to the fear of falling in love. The common factor in all three is a feeling of anxiety about the loss of full control of the body and its sensations. In analysis it is frequently shown that the patient who presents one of these anxieties is susceptible to the others. In love, the ego surrenders its power to the love object and in sleep, the ego surrenders to the body. The healthy adult welcomes both experiences because they are pleasurable sensations. Fear of love, like the fear of sleep, stems from the anxiety which in the schizoid individual accompanies the surrender of the ego or the descent of the "self." In love the "self" descends from the head to the heart.

Such movements of feeling in the body, which the adult often experiences as sinking sensations, are the delight of little children, who seek these sensations on their swings, slides, and similar amusements. The healthy child loves to be thrown into the air and to be caught by the waiting arms of a parent.

11

Origin and Causes

REFERENCE to some feature of a patient's body often calls forth the remark that the feature in question is a familial trait. The patient may remark, "My mother and grandmother have the same short legs and heavy thighs. It must be hereditary." No doubt there are hereditary factors that determine to some extent the form and shape of a person's body. Children tend to resemble their parents. However, this resemblance may also be due, in part at least, to an identification with the parent. Sometimes the son is an exact image of his father, or the daughter the image of her mother. Such cases seem to be strong evidence of some hereditary basis for personality. One notes, however, that these look-alikes share common ways of thinking and have similar patterns of behavior, which cannot be explained by present-day concepts of heredity.

The role of heredity in determining body structure is difficult to assess. The structure of the body is not fixed and immutable. The body is subject in the course of its development to innumerable external influences which act upon and modify its features, its expression, and its motility. Just as the nature of the soil, the quantity of rainfall, and the amount of sunshine condition the growth of a tree, so the quality of nurture a child receives will affect his total development. His experiences during the formative years when he is fully dependent on his parents will condition his responses as an adult.

Conditioning results in fixed patterns of neuromuscular reaction to given stimuli. Learning how to act or how not to react is a process of gaining muscular control and coordination. In time these controls become automatic. The conditioned response becomes an unconscious reaction and develops into characterological attitudes of behavior. Character in the sense of a fixed pattern of behavior is therefore determined by the quantity and quality of the controls imposed upon muscular activity. The muscles that are subject to these unconscious controls are "chronically tense, chronically contracted, and removed from perception."[53] W. Reich[54] used the term "armor" to describe the function and effect of these spastic muscles upon the personality. Muscular armoring is a defense against the external environment, but it is also a means of keeping dangerous impulses in repression. Character, then, is functionally identical with the muscular armor.

Biology tells us that the shape of bones is influenced by the pull of the muscles that insert into them. Bone formation is a constant process in the living body, more active during the early years, but never entirely quiescent. Thus the structure of the body is constantly being modified as a reflection of the muscular tensions to which it is subject. This fact justifies the use of the body's structure in the analysis of personality. It also provides a basis for the attempt to modify body structure through the release of chronic muscular tension.

If heredity is not responsible for muscle tension, it cannot be blamed for those disturbances that are created by chronically tense muscles. The origin and causes of the diminished respiration, the reduced motility, and the bodily rigidity of the schizoid personality must be sought in the conditions of his early existence. How far back in the life of a person should we go in search of the constitutional factors that predispose an individual to this disturbance? We have to go back to the womb, for the effect of prenatal influences cannot be ignored if we are to understand the etiology of the schizoid structure. The constitution of an individual, that is, the basic make-up of his body, is already present at birth.

CONSTITUTIONAL FACTORS

The schizoid body type has been described earlier as asthenic, *i.e.*, of slender build and slight muscular development. The word "asthenia," from which "asthenic" derives, means weak and debilitated. There is a fundamental weakness in the schizoid personality which is present in every schizoid individual, regardless of his body type. This weakness is an inability to mobilize his energy and feelings and direct them to the satisfaction of his needs. Regardless of his apparent strength, the schizoid lacks the energy to sustain an aggressive attitude toward the world.

The lack of aggression in the schizoid structure is caused by the "freezing" of feeling and motility. I have made many references to the fact that the schizoid body structure is "frozen." This word describes the constitutional factor in the schizoid structure more accurately than Kretschmer's term "linear" and more fully than the word "weak." What is frozen is the natural motility of the organism. This is true even in those cases where the "acting out" of negative and destructive tendencies is the dominant mode of behavior. These tendencies should be understood as a desperate effort to break free from the inner tension and constraint imposed by an earlier "freeze," one that took place while the organism was still in the womb.

In Chapter 3, I ascribed the frozen condition of the schizoid body to an inner terror. It is significant that this terror is nameless, shapeless, and associated with the dark. In my analysis of many schizoid individuals, I have been unable to discover any single experience that could inspire such terror. This leads me to suspect that this terror has its roots in intrauterine experiences that are "nameless and shapeless."

Current research into the etiology of schizophrenia is largely focused on familial background. The personalities of the mother and father and the interaction between them have been extensively studied. Clausen and Kohn note that early writers on the subject described the mothers of schizophrenic children as "cold, perfectionistic, anxious, overcontrolling and restrictive—to connote a type of person unable to give spontaneous love and acceptance to the child."[55] Hill finds the mothers of schizophrenics ambivalent and tending to freeze whenever anything unpleasant is mentioned.[56]

It seems that the subject which is most unpleasant and most often causes these mothers to freeze is sex. In my professional encounters with them I have found them to be sexually immature and hostile to the male, although these attitudes are often covered up by a façade of sexual sophistication. Hill found in most cases "that the mother was frigid or was an immature person without capacity and tolerance for mature psychosexual intimacy with another person."[57] Hill also notes that they were dominated by their own mothers, "who were opposed to sex and men."[58] Two other investigators of this problem, M. J. Boatman and S. A. Szurek, describe these mothers as sexually apathetic or unresponsive and state that they are "extremely fearful and inhibited" about acknowledging any sexual desire to their husbands.[59] Many of them are alcoholics, while others are addicted to tranquilizers or sleeping pills.

The basic fault in the personalities of these mothers is the avoidance of reality. They are caught up in their own conflicts, which they cannot resolve. Preoccupied with their own desperation, they react to the child as an image or an object. I have had many occasions to interview both the mother and the child, and occasionally both were in treatment at the same time. It was always a surprise to me to see how little the mother understood the difficulties of her child. Invariably the child complained about the lack of understanding and reacted negatively to the mother because of it. Hill observed the same phenomenon and concluded that "they [the mothers] have no awareness of the reality of their children."[60]

One word the schizoid invariably applies to his mother is "cold." This doesn't mean that the mother doesn't care, but that her caring is selfish, indifferent to the patient's needs, and without an emphatic understanding of the patient's feelings. My own experience with this kind of mother is that she lacks a feeling of warmth for her child. I have seen her act overtly cold and hostile at one moment, then guilty, anxious and solicitous at another. She is overinvolved on the one hand, but rejecting on the other. These reactions stem from an emotional coldness in the mother's personality, to which the child is constantly exposed. There is good reason to believe that since the coldness is part of her personality, the child is subject to this "coldness" while it is in the womb.

The schizoid personality has its origin in a "cold" womb. A "cold" womb is one from which feeling has been withdrawn as part of the overall dissociation from the lower half of the body. The withdrawal of feeling from the lower half of the body is the somatic counterpart of a negative sexual attitude. The woman who is afraid of sex and hostile to men deadens her pelvis to reduce the anxiety connected with sexual feeling. This is the mechanism of sexual repression, and the result is a state of tension in the pelvis and abdomen which adversely affects the uterus. Patients who suffer from this disturbance frequently report a feeling of emptiness in the belly which disappears when they become pregnant. The fetus serves to fill this emptiness, but it receives little in return. It has to develop in relatively barren soil upon which the glow of sexual excitement shines infrequently.

The effect of this condition upon the fetus is a withdrawal of energy from the surface of its own body. In the *Physical Dynamics of Character Structure*,[61] I suggested that this process can be compared to the freezing of a solution of brown sugar. If the solution is gradually frozen, one notes that the brown color becomes concentrated in the center, while the periphery of the solution is clear ice. The center also retains its fluidity to the last, since the cold penetrates from the outside inward. A similar phenomenon occurs to an embryo in a "cold" womb. The free energy of the organism retreats to the center, while the skin and peripheral structures contract. The musculature which is close to the surface and one of the last organ systems to develop is particularly vulnerable. What becomes frozen, then, is the motility of the organism.

Unfortunately, our birth records make no provision for a description of the physical appearance and motility of the baby at birth. Without such records it would be impossible to prove the theory advanced above. As a medical student and intern, I assisted at quite a number of births. The difference among newborn babies is sometimes enormous. Some are full-bodied, lusty in their cry, and have firm, clear skins. Others are small and wizened and look like old men. They have to be stimulated to breathe. Of course, these latter fill out later with proper care, but one wonders how their personalities will evolve. On the basis of such observations, it can be said that many constitutional attributes are evident at birth.

A number of writers have called attention lately to the importance of prenatal factors in the development of the organism. L. W. Sontag states, "Yet if constitution turns out to be an etiologic factor in schizophrenia, it is not unthinkable that such modifications of constitutional characteristics . . . may in some instances be influenced adversely by fetal environment."[62]

Ashley Montagu says, "On the whole, evidence generally supports the hypothesis that stressful emotions in the pre-pregnant and pregnant woman are capable of affecting the conceptus in various ways. . . .

"Maternal attitudes, whether of acceptance, rejection, or indifference to their pregnancy, may well spell the difference, in some cases, between adequate and inadequate development of the foetus."[63]

A. A. Honig writes that on the basis of his work with regressed patients, he is "inclined to add that even stimuli felt while being carried in the mother's womb are traumatic. Perhaps the mother's psychosomatic tensions may affect the infant in utero."[64]

The proposition that the predisposition to the schizoid disturbance has a prenatal origin throws light upon several important elements in this illness. (1) It supports the theory of a constitutional factor without appealing to heredity to justify this hypothesis. (2) It explains the "commitment to the womb" which is often found at the center of this disturbance. The term "commitment to the womb" describes the schizoid individual's endeavor to reestablish a parasitic type of relationship in adult life and his reluctance to "cut the umbilical cord" that ties him to his mother. This tendency is more evident in the schizophrenic patient, but it exists to some degree in all schizoid individuals. It indicates a fixation at the prenatal stage because the needs of the organism at that stage were not fulfilled. It suggests that the difficulties the schizoid person has with such basic functions as sucking and breathing stem from inadequate development in prenatal life. (3) It provides a firmer base for the view that the schizoid disturbance is, in part, a deficiency disease. The deficiency is the lack of warmth, on the physical level in the womb, and on the emotional level in postnatal life. (4) This extension of the origin of the schizoid problem to the period of gestation enables one to venture some interpretations of patients' feelings that would not otherwise be logical. For example, the following remark by a patient may refer to this period: "I'm afraid. They want me to die, but I won't let them. [*They* is a vague reference to unknown forces.] I feel on guard—waiting for something to happen. Something to do with the dark."

The schizoid often expresses his strong conviction that his problem has its origin in intrauterine experiences. One can ignore such references as fantasies, but to do so is to deny the patient's inner feelings, which he is struggling to accept. In the absence of evidence to the contrary, I believe that such observations by patients merit serious consideration.

One of my patients made a series of interesting remarks in this regard. First, she mentioned her relationship to her mother: "I've always had weird feelings about my mother —that her attachment to me was incestuous." Then she added: "My mother told me that she couldn't stand my father sexually but continued to live with him until I was twelve." She continued:

I believe that we have prenatal memories, and I have always felt that my mother tried to abort me. When there is a prenatal thing like this, it must affect the fetus. The blood supply was probably cut off. When you want to abort a child, it is emotionally aborted even if you don't do it.

During the discussion that followed this recital the patient expressed her feeling that a child who has gone through such an experience is marked for life. She believed that some deep wound is inflicted upon the organism that leaves a naked scar. I could neither agree nor disagree. We have no way of knowing how the fetus reacts in utero to such a procedure or what effect it may have on the future personality of the child. In this case, however, one thing was certain. This patient was deeply hurt, her personality split into an alert mind sharpened to the point where it could confront any danger, and a lifeless body that she experienced as a burden. She was an intelligent, sophisticated woman with the emotional development of a child. When I saw her, the difficulties of her life had overwhelmed her. Her despair had reached the point where she thought of death as the only way out.

It is hard to conceive that an attempted abortion could have such a far-reaching effect. But in this case, as in others, the attempt to abort the child stemmed from personal difficulties of the mother. The mother was an immature person who resented the intrusion of the child into the idyllic relationship between husband and wife. The child was not wanted, and this fact more than any actual attempt at abortion helps explain the patient's disturbance. When a child is not wanted, a mother will be unable to extend to the newborn infant the love and acceptance it requires. As her statement indicates, the patient was somewhat aware all her life of this lack of acceptance. It is manifest in countless small gestures, looks, and intonations, to which the child is extremely sensitive. Thus, while the rejection of the child may begin in the mother's body, it continues long after the birth of the child. Once a mother has turned cold to a child, this attitude rarely changes in the course of the child's life.

The unwanted child becomes the recipient of the mother's guilt. In her attempt to unburden herself, the mother burdens the child with her guilt. Most commonly, she makes the child feel responsible for her own problems and unhappiness. How often does one hear a mother exclaim to her child, "You have been nothing but trouble for me!" The unwanted child is particularly vulnerable to this guilt. Since a mother's motives cannot be questioned by a child, the unloved child believes that this state of affairs is his fault.

The schizoid problem has its origin in the mother's ambivalence about the child. She wants it and doesn't want it. Her attitude to the child varies with the stresses of her personal life. Her feelings of hostility and rejection at one moment are followed by a seemingly strong desire for the child at another. This desire, however, is generally motivated by the image of motherhood and has its roots in the mother's illusion that she will be fulfilled in this role. Where a woman's uncertainty about her pregnancy is limited to the conscious layer of her personality it does no harm to the developing organism. On the other hand, when the conflict extends to the depth of the personality, that is, when it stems from the woman's rejection of her body and its sexuality, the fetus in her womb will feel its effects.

A woman responds to her pregnancy with the feelings she has for her own body. As far as her sensations go, the fetus is a part of her body. As an expression of her womanhood, it belongs to the lower half of her body. Fetus, womb, and sexuality form an inseparable unity. In the majority of cases, pregnancy serves, at first, to dignify the sexual aspect of the woman's personality. She experiences an initial sense of well-being which derives from a new-found self-acceptance. However, if the underlying conflict has not been resolved, it intrudes itself into this idyllic state. Her good feelings disappear, and the period of gestation becomes a literal confinement. If the commitment to the child is not wholehearted, the woman cannot avoid some feeling of being trapped and the child some feeling of being unwanted.

PSYCHOLOGICAL FACTORS

The constitutional predisposition to the schizoid body structure develops in the womb, but the forces that maintain that disposition into adulthood arise from the psychology of the parents. The child is a sexual symbol to its parents, and their reaction to it will be determined by conscious and unconscious feelings and attitudes about their own sexuality. For each parent the child is also the representative of the other partner. It is not uncommon to hear parents refer to a child as "your" child rather than "our" child. To appreciate the psychological factors that can arise in disturbed homes, it is necessary to bear in mind the following equations:

$$\text{Man} = \text{penis} = \text{sperm cells} \searrow$$
$$\text{Child}$$
$$\text{Woman} = \text{vagina} = \text{egg cells} \nearrow$$

A child is the visible evidence to a parent of the sexuality that led to its conception. It will become the target, therefore, of all the feelings that surround this function in the minds of the parents. These feelings will vary with the state of the relationship between the parents and, of course, with the sex of the child. Thus, the feelings which attach to a boy are not identical with those which become focused upon a girl. The difference between the two attitudes is often expressed in the reaction which greets the announcement that the newborn is a boy or a girl. Similarly, a first child meets with a reception different from the second, third, or fourth. If allowance is made for these different responses, one can understand why one child will show a more severe disturbance than another child of the same family.

Parents are often at a loss to comprehend their role in this disturbance. They believe that they respond to all their children with the same feelings. This isn't true, of course, and the effect of this belief is to make the child feel responsible for the failure of a good relationship to develop. Parents believe that since they do the same things for all their children, they should get the same results. They overlook the fact that it is not what they do but how they do it that spells the difference between acceptance and rejection. Most parents are unwilling or unable to see the importance of unconscious attitudes to which the child is sensitive.

It has become evident to investigators studying the background of schizophrenics that the family situations from which they come are full of overt conflict or charged with unexpressed hostility. T. Lidz and S. Fleck found not a single well-integrated family in their study of schizophrenic homes. They remarked that the "extent and pervasiveness of the family pathology were unexpected."[65] Sexual problems were common in these families, particularly that of incest. Lidz and Fleck note further that "At times a patient was clearly justified, and not delusional, in fearing that if he lost control incest could well occur."[66]

While some overt sexual behavior on the part of a parent toward a child is not rare in the families of schizoid or schizophrenic patients, the causative psychological factor in this disturbance is the unconscious sexual identification with the child. In these families, the mother sees her child in the image of her own sexuality. In the attempt to free herself from a deep sense of humiliation about her female sexuality, which she views as submissive, dependent, and inferior, she projects these qualities upon her child, hoping thereby to reverse her own infantile experience and gain an ascendency which was denied her.

This projection is relatively easy if the child is a girl. The similarity of sex creates an unconscious identification which facilitates the transfer of feeling. The daughter thus becomes the embodiment of her mother's rejected sexuality. The mother may be in awe of her child or despise it, deny it or subvert it for her own satisfaction. She will react to her daughter exactly as she reacts to her own sexuality, with confused and ambivalent feelings. In this process, daughter and mother become identified, and a bond is established between them which neither can sunder without, in principle at least, destroying the other.

A mother subverts the child (boy or girl) when she becomes openly seductive, creating an incestuous relationship between herself and the child. Generally, this seduction begins when the child is young. The mother gets an erotic thrill from touching and handling his body. An extreme example of this kind of behavior on the part of the mother is shown in the following statement a patient made:

> I was so attracted by the baby. I could touch his penis. I could take his penis in my mouth. I could kiss his behind, even crawl into his anus. Of course, I don't do it. The smells of him! His body is so beautifully built.

Such feelings express the mother's unconscious identification with the child. He is what she wanted to be, and she would like either to swallow him so he becomes part of her or to enter his body and be part of him. This is not only an incestuous desire on the part of the mother, it is also a homosexual fantasy in which she takes possession of the child as if it were her property and makes it submissive to her needs.

When a mother is aloof, withdrawn, and cold to her child, this can be interpreted as a defense against her unconscious incestuous and homosexual feelings toward it.

Hill makes the same observation about these mothers: "She rejects the boy, the boy's genitality—perhaps through envy and the incestuous threat—and she rejects her daughter through disappointment and fear of rivalry."[67] On some deep level, however, the child is aware of the reason for the rejection. Unconsciously, he senses the homosexual and incestuous bond that ties him to his mother. He is sexually involved with her at the same time that he hates her and feels sorry for her. He is caught in the same ambivalence that characterizes her attitude.

We can understand the child's dilemma if we realize that these two processes are at work simultaneously. Withdrawal from the seductive mother risks arousing her fury; reaching out to the rejecting mother risks provoking her anxiety and hostility. The child is forced either into an outward submission that covers an inner defiance or an overt rebellion that masks an inner passivity. In these relationships one can anticipate outbreaks of rage and violence. The child meets his mother's hostility with his own murderous impulses. However, he is caught in such conflicts of hatred and dependency, denial and identification, that eventually he is frozen into immobility.

THE TRAUMA OF IDENTIFICATION

Many of the problems discussed above are illustrated in the following case history. This patient, whom I will call Helen, was a young woman about thirty years old. She came into therapy because she was unable to establish a stable relationship with a man. She had been sexually involved with one man after another, but each affair broke up when the man would not fulfill her excessive demands. Helen was deeply confused about her role as a woman and suffered from severe anxiety. She had the typical schizoid facial appearance; her eyes lacked focus, and her jaw was defiantly set. Her body was well developed although poorly coordinated in movement. There were many paranoid features in her personality: she was hyperactive, loquacious, and volatile.

In the course of therapy, I asked Helen to soften her jaw, to allow her chin to recede. As she did this, she began to cry softly and deeply. She remarked, "The pain in my heart is unendurable." When the crying subsided, I suggested that she reach out with her mouth as if for the breast. "What's the use?" she exclaimed. "I begged for love but all I got was humiliation."

To enable Helen to release more feeling, I had her mobilize her facial muscles in an expression of fright. She dropped her jaw, raised her brows, and opened her eyes wide. This expression dispelled the mask. When Helen assumed it, she became frightened. Her head seemed to freeze. She was unable to move it for a moment and couldn't scream. When she relaxed her face she remarked:

> What am I afraid of? Something I would see? Her eyes? I can't look into my mother's eyes even now. There is something hateful and murderous in them. And she's insane. You can't look into insane eyes without being frightened. Yet, she loved me, too.

After making these observations Helen began to tremble. Her fingers and wrists became cold and stiff. She continued:

> I remember how I begged her and screamed and cried. I guess I wanted her more than anything else in the world. We played together and she made many things for me. She could make magic. But she was so sad. I couldn't stand her sadness. I couldn't help her. She was too frightened herself. Her eyes were far away, too. She frightened me terribly.
>
> I don't know why I feel so funny. Does one die of a broken heart? Schizophrenia is death. You kill the part that hurts so you can survive.

Helen was caught in a whirlwind of emotion that tossed her about wildly. Her mother's affection for her was mixed with a sadness the child could not endure. It was a relationship that swung from love to hate, from pity to terror, from hope to despair. The confusion, ambivalence, and strangeness which the child senses in its mother disturbs its own integrity. It is not possible for a child's mind to integrate such contradictory feelings as fright and sympathy.

Helen related to me some time earlier that her mother had had several abortions prior to her own birth. She said:

My mother was afraid in her belly when she carried me. She told me that she prayed to God I wouldn't be punished for her sins. She was afraid I would be born crippled or deformed. She yearned for me. She had a great tenderness, but it couldn't come through her touch.

Such intense guilt indicates the severity of the sexual disturbance from which her mother suffered. Unable to accept her own sexuality, she projected it upon her daughter and identified with her. Helen stated that when she was six or seven her mother put her in silk panties and curled her hair despite her protests. "She made things for me by hand," Helen commented, "to give me the best." But at a later session Helen said:

Sitting at the dinner table with my family, I realized that they were selfish to the point of disgust. Sometimes they gave you everything, then nothing. It was as if I knew it all along but I denied it. She gave me things, but I was a tool for her. I was given nice clothes to be attractive to men. She used me to make a good catch; then she would be able to sponge on them.

The mother's identification with her daughter's sexuality is clearly expressed in Helen's remarks. Parents live through their children in many ways, but when a parent identifies with a child on a sexual level, the result is a schizoid disturbance. In turn, the child is forced to identify with the mother whose repressed sexual feelings are projected upon it. This identification compels the child to live in the service of the mother's sexual needs. The trauma of identification resides in the rejection of a child's individuality—to fit a parental image; the subversion of its sexuality—to fit a parental need; and the possession of its psyche—to make it submissive to the parent.

Helen's relationship to her mother had a latent homosexual element, which emerged only in Helen's dreams and associations. She related a dream that revealed this element.

All my life I have been scared. I often dreamed that my mother had a penis. Lately, I had the same dream again. This time she had a penis with pus running out. It made me want to vomit.

Helen's association to the dream was the feeling that her mother had always tried to seduce her, especially in breast feeding. The penis with pus is a translation of the nipple with milk leaking out. If a mother forces her nipple upon the child, it becomes like a penis which is intruded into an opening. The mother who assumes an aggressive role toward the child acts out upon the child her repressed masculine identification. This attitude forces a child into a passive homosexual relationship with the mother. Helen also recalled that her mother used to crawl into bed with her, which Helen resented. The normal pattern is for the child to crawl into bed with the mother. When this pattern is reversed, it becomes a seductive action, as described in Chapter 5.

Helen's sexual involvements paralleled her relationship with her mother. Each of her affairs was marked by the ambivalences of love and hate, submission and defiance, fear and sympathy which characterized her feelings for her mother. She "screamed" for love but was never fulfilled. She identified with the man as she had identified with her mother; she was not an independent individual. This attitude introduced a homosexual element into these relationships. No wonder she was confused! No wonder her liaisons broke up! She related to men as if they were her mother, while in her fantasy she was looking for her father, who would save her from destruction.

In my analysis of the schizoid personality I find that every patient at an early stage of life turned from the mother to the father in search of warmth and support. The child turns away from the mother because of her unconscious anxiety and hostility. As a result, the father becomes a substitute mother figure for the child. But this creates a real problem when it occurs at an early age. Every one of my patients had an oral fixation upon the penis for which I could find no other explanation than that the penis had become a substitute nipple. The biological reasons which promote the identification of the penis with the nipple are set forth in my book *Love and Orgasm*. Once this identification takes place in the child's mind, it becomes easy to picture the mother with a penis.

When the phallus represents both nipple and penis, the individual is caught in an insoluble conflict. The function of the phallus as a genital organ is hindered by its symbolic significance as a nipple. Its role as a breast is impeded by its obvious function. The unity of the personality is split by the excitation of two antithetical levels of functioning, oral and genital. Adult ego organization, which depends upon the primacy of genital excitation, is weakened. The woman who suffers from this split sees the male both as a mother and a man. He is expected to provide support and understanding as well as genital excitation and fulfillment.

Unfortunately, fathers are generally as emotionally disturbed as mothers. Lidz and Fleck remark that "The fathers, just like the mothers, are so caught up in their own unresolved problems that they can rarely fill the essentials of a parental role adequately."[68] Actually, many of the fathers in disturbed families show marked feminine tendencies which facilitate the transfer of oral desires from mother to father. Helen noted of her father, "He could not be a man against my mother. My father was like a woman, even to his pendulous breasts."

The relationship that developed between Helen and her father was also an incestuous one. She described it as follows:

> My father let me get away with almost anything I wanted. We took long walks at night. I was with him almost constantly, and of course, I slept with him. I remember things like tying my nightgown to his pajamas so he wouldn't leave me in the middle of the night. This went on until I had my first crush; then I couldn't bear it.

Helen said that her mother had not approved of this arrangement. However, it became the practice in the family for Helen to sleep with her father, while her brother slept with her mother. I asked Helen if she had any sexual feelings for her father. "I don't think I had," she answered.

"Were you aware of any sexual feeling on his part?" I asked her.

"No. I feel he just cuddled me like he would a cat—there was just an animal warmth between us. I just liked the feeling of being held by him." When Helen said this a sly smile appeared on her face. I observed this smile many times in the course of her therapy. It gave me the impression that she had a secret. At this point I interpreted it as an expression of her deep awareness of men, of what they want, and how she can control them. One week after I made this interpretation, she told me:

> You were right last week when you said I wanted a man to love me for myself not just for my bottom. Because this is all they wanted me for. After a while I gave that without their asking because I thought that then they would love me and take care of me. This should have been done for me by my mother. Since it wasn't, I made the bargain with my father. In my deepest feelings, I always felt used by men.

The smile also revealed Helen's preoccupation with sex, which dominated her personality. She was driven in circles: from orality to genitality and back again, from submission to defiance and back again, from a mother figure to a father figure and back again. Helen reported a recurrent dream which portrayed her dilemma:

> I dreamed that I saw my dentist as God. He said, "You came into the dentist's office very peacefully, very unaware, and I caught you. I caught you because you were taken so unawares. You are not going to die like other people. You won't even have the peace of death. You're going to go around and around and around. You won't know peace."
>
> I knew I was tied to a barber pole. I could see the stripes up and down and I kept whirling around in circles. I remember crying—I even begged, "Please just let me die." I recall waking up screaming and striking out.

The barber pole is an obvious phallic symbol. Helen is tied to sex in a way that allows neither escape nor fulfillment. This kind of sexuality describes her relation to her mother-father, a child-adult sexuality that was stimulating and exciting, but that provided no opportunity for orgastic release. This formula of excitation without fulfillment became the pattern of her adult sexual activities. Helen was tormented, and in her torment, death seemed to offer the only peace. The dream also indicates that Helen did not really understand what was going on with her father. She was "taken unawares," so that in a part of her she still felt herself to be pure and innocent. She was a little girl looking for warmth and support but responding biologically to adult sexuality. Her body picked up the sexual excitement of her father but lacked the ability to focus this excitement into a genital striving.

Two opposite tendencies were at work in Helen's personality. She was the innocent little girl seeking love, and she was also the harlot who knew what men wanted and who would use sex in the attempt to gain her ends. This is the typical schizoid split so often seen in the combination of naïveté and sophistication, innocence and perversity, prudery and lasciviousness. Helen was caught in another antithetical situation: she desired the breast but was excited by the penis. In effect, she needed both at the same time: the breast to satisfy her infantile longing, the penis to release her sexual excitation. She was in an impossible situation, in which she could only go around in circles.

SEX AND PARANOIA

In the split personality, sexual feeling is experienced as alien, compulsive, and "bad." The schizoid individual cannot identify with his sexual feelings because they were not his feelings in the first place. They were the feelings of his parents which he incorporated emphatically. The incorporation of feeling is not an active procedure; it is more like an infectious process. Exposure to the feeling is often all that is required. For example, a person exposed to another individual's sadness for some time will frequently begin to feel sad himself. It is as if the sadness permeates or takes possession of him. He has to shake it off to free himself from it. However, it is not easy for a child to shake off an emotional atmosphere to which it is constantly exposed in the early years of its life. The schizoid child has only one recourse: to deny the feelings, to cut off body sensations, and to dissociate from sexuality. By this maneuver the child retains a purity of spirit and mind, while its body is surrendered to the father or mother.

A male child, in a similar situation, will also turn to the father for warmth and acceptance in his attempt to escape his mother's ambivalence and projection. If the father can accept the mother role without weakening his masculinity, if he can give the child security and love without negating the value of the female, he may be able to prevent the development of a schizoid personality in the child. Generally, however, the child is rejected by the father or only tentatively accepted. He may reject the male child as a competitor and threat to his own insecure position, or he may include the child in his passive acceptance of the situation. In most family situations, the father will hestitate to show affection to a child that the mother has rejected, out of fear of antagonizing the mother. In severely disturbed homes, the parents have a symbiotic relationship which excludes the child and forces it into isolation.

The disturbed mother does not accept the child until she has formed an image of it which satisfies her ego needs; her acceptance, then, is of her image, not her child. However, in order to gain the acceptance and love he needs, the child will attempt to conform to her image. Thus, a secondary libidinal investment can be made in the child through the image which is superimposed upon the original rejection. The relationship which develops in this way is strongly colored with incestuous and homosexual feelings, through identification and mutual "servicing." In this situation, the boy risks the hostility of his father by becoming a "mama's boy." This will not deter him, since this kind of relationship to his mother seems to satisfy both oral and genital striving at the same time. He is caught in the same dilemma as the girl who becomes sexually involved with her father. This development lays the basis for paranoid tendencies in a personality.

Paranoid behavior can be described as a going around in circles. At the center of the circle is the phallic symbol, the nipple or the penis (mother or father). The paranoid individual dare not make an aggressive move toward the desired and forbidden object. His maneuver, then, is to circle the object hypnotically and to manipulate the situation to compel the object to come toward him. This means that he tries to make the other person responsible for the action of satisfying his needs. At the same time, he also identifies with the phallic symbol and reverses his role by assuming the dominant position of father or mother. This maneuver is the basis for the paranoid ideas of omnipotence, reference, and persecution. He is now in the center of the circle, the object of desire and envy, the fountainhead of life about which the world revolves. The paranoid individual oscillates between feelings of helplessness and impotence, worthlessness and megalomania, envy and persecution. At some moments he feels himself to be on the periphery of the circle, an outsider; at others, he is the kingpin, the cynosure of all eyes.

The paranoid is obsessed with his sexual potency, which is the source of his feeling of indispensability. He is acting out his infantile situation, in which he felt his power to excite his mother erotically. The female, as in Helen's case, who has experienced with her father the lure of her sexual appeal, acts this out in her relation to men.

The effect of this complex interplay of forces on the child's personality is to heighten his ego consciousness and sensitivity. This is a natural response to a situation of danger. In this case, the danger resides in the ambivalent and confused parental feelings. The child becomes aware of the hostility and guilt which emanate from his parents and develops a heightened sensitivity to emotional nuances as his first line of defense. In acquiring this sensitivity, he also becomes very keenly aware, on a nonverbal level, of the frustrated sexual feelings and perverse tendencies of his parents. This awareness of adult sexuality is repressed at about the age of seven, when the child withdraws from the sexual triangle. He retains, however, an exaggerated sensitivity to emotional undertones. The schizoid illness can be compared to an allergic disease in that the child has become sensitized to the unconsciousness of others. Children who are secure in their relationship to their parents are *self-contained*, less conscious of adult sexuality and free from the identifications that usurp their individuality.

12

Reclaiming the
Body

A BODY is forsaken when it becomes a source of pain and
humiliation instead of pleasure and pride. Under these
conditions the person refuses to accept or identify with his
body. He turns against it. He may ignore it or he may
attempt to transform it into a more desirable object by
dieting, weight lifting, etc. However, as long as the body
remains an object to the ego, it may fulfill the ego's pride,
but it will never provide the joy and satisfaction that the
"alive" body offers.

The alive body is characterized by a life of its own. It
has a motility independent of ego control which is manifested by the spontaneity of its gestures and the vivacity of
its expression. It hums, it vibrates, it glows. It is charged
with feeling. The first difficulty that one encounters with
patients in search of identity is that they are not aware of
the lack of aliveness in their bodies. People are so ac-
customed to thinking of the body as an instrument or a
tool of the mind that they accept its relative deadness as a
normal state. They measure bodies in pounds and inches
and compare their shape with idealized forms, completely
ignoring the fact that what is important is how the body
feels.

I have repeatedly stressed how afraid people are to feel
their bodies. On some level they are aware that the body is
a repository of their repressed feelings, and while they
would very much like to know about these repressed feelings, they are loathe to encounter them in the flesh. Yet, in
their desperate search for an identity, they must eventually

confront the state of their bodies. They must accept the relevance of their physical condition to their mental functioning, despite the doubt with which they approach this proposition. To overcome this doubt, they must experience their physical tension as a limitation of personality, and the release of this tension as a liberation of the personality. The discovery that the body has a life of its own and the capacity to heal itself is a revelation of hope. The realization that the body has its own wisdom and logic inspires a new respect for the instinctive forces of life.

The issue every patient faces is: can he trust his feelings to guide his behavior or must these feelings be suppressed in favor of a rational approach? By their very nature, feelings have an irrational quality—which doesn't mean, however, that they are necessarily inappropriate or irrelevant. The irrational stems from sources in the personality that lie deeper than the roots of reason. The irrational is always opposed to the reasonable because the irrational speaks for the body, while the reasonable speaks for society. The distinction between these two can be illustrated by the behavior of an infant. His demands are always irrational. It would seem that if a mother holds her baby for two hours, this would provide a reasonable amount of body contact, considering that she has other chores. But baby doesn't reason. If it feels like being held longer and cries when it is put down, its behavior is irrational because unreasonable, yet perfectly natural considering its feeling. Were the baby to suppress its crying or its desire, mother could describe it as a reasonable and good child. The psychiatrist, however, would recognize the beginning of an emotional problem.

The person who rejects the irrational negates the infant within him. He has learned, unfortunately, that it's no use crying, mother never comes anyway! He makes few demands on life because he has been taught early that his demands were unreasonable. He doesn't become angry because anger had always provoked retaliation. He has become a "reasonable man," but in the process he has lost the motivation of pleasure and the aliveness of his body. He has, in this process, developed a schizoid tendency. Yet the irrational breaks through in perverse form: he finds himself subject to violent rages, depressions, and strange compulsions. He feels withdrawn and detached or overwhelmed and embroiled.

In a healthy person the irrational is not suppressed in favor of the reasonable. The healthy person accepts his feelings even when they run counter to the apparent logic of the situation. The schizoid denies his feelings, while the neurotic distrusts them. The body is abandoned when the irrational is denied and feeling is repressed. To reclaim the body, an individual must accept the irrational within himself.

The awesomeness of the irrational is that it has the power to move us. It is the source of creativity and the fountain of joy. All great experiences have this irrational quality, which enables them to move us from within. As everyone knows, love and orgasm are *the* irrational experiences we *all* seek. Thus, the person who is afraid of the irrational is afraid of love and orgasm. He is also afraid to let his body go, to let his tears flow and to let his voice break. He is afraid to breathe and afraid to move. When the irrational is repressed it becomes a demonic force that may lead a sick person to destructive actions. In normal living, the irrational manifests itself by involuntary movements—the spontaneous gesture, the sudden laugh, even the twitching of the body before one falls asleep.

In this day of wonder drugs it is generally overlooked that the body has a natural capacity to heal itself. We are familiar with this property of the body when it comes to minor wounds and illnesses. Doctors count upon this property in major illnesses and operations. In most cases, medicine aims to remove the obstacles that impede this natural function of the body. Emotional illness is not an exception to this principle. The therapeutic task is to remove the obstacles that prevent the body from spontaneously releasing its tensions. This principle underlies the psychoanalytic process. The technique of free association is a device that enables a person to bring to consciousness the repressed irrational elements in his personality. It is hoped that if a person can consciously accept the irrational in his personality, he will be free to respond naturally and spontaneously to life situations. The weakness in this concept is that the conscious acceptance of a feeling does not lead, necessarily, to the ability to express this feeling. It is one thing to recognize that one is sad, it is another to be able to cry. To know that one is angry is not the same thing as to feel angry. To know that one was incestuously involved with a parent does little to release the repressed sexual feeling locked in the body.

When I was a small boy I was terrified of dogs. To help me overcome this fear my parents bought me fuzzy toy dogs, which they encouraged me to pet and stroke. I remember them saying, "See, it doesn't bite. It won't hurt you." It may have helped reduce my terror, but I was still frightened of any dog that made a sudden move at me. I didn't fully overcome this fear until, as a grown man, I took a dog into my home. Living with the animal I learned to trust him.

The fear of the dog is the fear of the irrational. To many people, as to my mother, the animal is not to be trusted because he is an unreasoning beast. He is guided by his feelings and moved by his passions, and is therefore unpredictable. On the body level, the human being is an animal whose behavior is unpredictable from a rational point of view. This doesn't mean that the body or the animal is dangerous, destructive, and uncontrollable. The body and the animal obey certain laws, which are not the laws of logic. The animal lover finds the animal perfectly comprehensible. To the person in touch with his body, the feelings of the body make complete sense.

I recently treated a young high school student who suffered from chronic asthma and who carried an atomizer with him constantly. At the slightest sign of any respiratory difficulty he reached for his atomizer. This happened as often as twenty times a day and occasionally at night. When I first saw him his breathing was extremely shallow and limited to the upper part of his thorax. His abdomen was extremely tight, and his chest severely constricted. With these tensions, just going from one classroom to another produced a feeling of distress. Whether this tension produced the asthma or whether the asthma produced the tension was unimportant; the fact was that as long as the tension persisted he was vulnerable to respiratory difficulty in a situation of stress.

To release the tension, the patient had to be encouraged to breathe more deeply, especially abdominally. In the therapy sessions I placed him in a number of positions which forced him to breathe abdominally. In addition, lying on the couch, he was directed to kick his legs rhythmically into the couch. At the beginning, these activities produced a minor asthmatic reaction, which the patient countered by using his atomizer. Soon, however, the patient became aware that his recourse to the atomizer was based on anxiety rather than need. If he didn't use the atomizer, his difficulty disappeared spontaneously after a minute or two. He became aware, then, that underlying his respiratory problem was a feeling of panic associated with breathing.

The superficial picture the patient presented was that of a person who was afraid that he would be unable to breathe under stress. However, the real picture was that of a person who was afraid to breathe because of the feelings it would evoke. He also suffered from severe sexual anxiety relating to his guilt about masturbation. The tightness and contraction of his abdomen were the means he used to suppress his sexual feeling and avoid the guilt and anxiety. The result of this maneuver was that his anxiety was displaced to his chest. Abdominal breathing made him conscious of his original anxiety and guilt, and the release of his anxiety made it possible for him to let his belly out and to breathe down into his abdomen. Step by step the patient's breathing improved to the point where he had no further need of an atomizer.

The first obstacle to the process of natural healing is the patient's unawareness of the tensions in his body. In the absence of specific symptoms such as headaches or lower back pain, the average person doesn't feel and doesn't know what tensions exist in his body. His posture has become so much a part of him that he takes it for granted. The first step in therapy is to help the patient gain some contact with specific areas of tension. Patients begin to experience their inadequacies, their disabilities, and their weaknesses when they are put in positions of stress. The positions of stress that I use are designed to test the integration and coordination of the body. For example, the patient is asked to stand with his feet about thirty inches apart, toes turned inward, knees bent as much as possible, the back arched, and hands upon the hips. An illustration of this position is shown in Figure 17.

The well-integrated and coordinated body can assume

FIG. 17

this position easily; the knees are fully flexed, the feet are flat on the ground, the line of the body from the heels to the back of the head forms a perfect arc, the head and trunk are centered, the breathing is abdominal and relaxed, and the person is not uncomfortable.

In the emotionally disturbed person a number of signs indicate the nature and location of his tensions. If his body is too rigid, it cannot be arched properly and full flexion of the knees is impossible. When an attempt is made to flex the knees further, the pelvis is pulled backward and the upper part of the body leans forward. On the other hand, when the body lacks tone there is an exaggerated break in the arch of the back. In both cases abdominal respiration is difficult and the breathing is strained. In many schizoid bodies the tension is unequal on the two sides, and one observes that the trunk becomes twisted one way, while the head is twisted the other. Persons with lower back problems may complain of pain in that region. Often the heels turn inward when the person assumes this position because of spasticities in the muscles of the buttocks which rotate the thighs outward. If the feet are not properly grounded, the individual becomes aware of a lack of balance. The legs may tremble, sometimes violently, if their muscles are too tense.

The use of this position is based on the principle that the body functions like a bow in many activities. The pitcher throwing a ball, the woodcutter swinging an ax, the fighter throwing a long punch, and the tennis player serving a ball show how the body arches backward like a bow to gain the impetus for the forward thrust. However, it is in the sexual function that this principle has its greatest importance. The sexual movements, as I pointed out in *Love and Orgasm*, are also based on this principle. Any disturbance which hinders the body from moving according to this principle will decrease the ability of the person to achieve full orgastic satisfaction. This is particularly true of the body that is split between its upper and lower halves. Since many aggressive movements of the body depend on this principle for their power, the effect of these disturbances is to reduce the individual's capacity for aggressive action.

A bow functions well only if its ends are secure. In the

body, the corresponding points are the feet and the head. When the body functions like a bow, its lower end is anchored to the ground through the feet, while the upper end is stabilized by the muscles of the back of the neck which hold the head firm. In effect, an individual is moored to reality at both ends of his body, below through his contact with the ground, and above through his ego. The schizoid individual is weak at both points. When he hits the couch with both fists from a backward arch, his feet often leave the ground at the moment of impact. It is necessary in the treatment of the schizoid problem to help the patient gain a better sense of contact with the ground. The position shown in Figure 17 serves to increase the patient's feeling of his legs and perception of their tensions. This position is reversed, as shown in Figure 18, to bring the patient closer to the ground and to develop more feeling in his legs.

In Figure 18 the patient is shown bent forward. All her weight is upon her feet, which are approximately fifteen inches apart, with the toes turned slightly inward. Her fingers touch the floor lightly for balance. The knees are always flexed in this position, although the degree of flexion may vary according to the amount of stress one wishes to place upon the leg muscles. In this position, the diaphragmatic block is generally released and breathing becomes abdominal. The patient feels his legs and feet vividly and becomes acutely aware of tension in the calf muscles and in the hamstrings. He senses the quality of his contact with the ground. He may remark, for example, that he does not feel his heels touching the ground. He may perceive that his feet are not flat on the ground because of an exaggerated tension in the arch of the feet. By pressing down on his feet and spreading his toes slightly, his contact with the ground can be increased.

All persons who assume this position develop a tremor of the legs sooner or later. When this happens, sensation increases sharply. The tremor may be fine or gross; it may be limited to the legs or extend upward to the pelvis. It is always experienced pleasurably as a sign of life. Sometimes the vibration is accompanied by a tingling sensation in the feet and legs. When the tremor first occurs, the patient will invariably ask, "What causes my legs to vibrate so?" Since

FIG. 18

vibration develops in all patients, in the younger more quickly than in the older, I explain that it is due to the natural elasticity of the body and is its normal reaction to stress. The vibration of the body can be compared to what happens in an automobile when the motor is turned on. A lack of vibration indicates a dead motor. A fine steady purr denotes a smoothly operating machine. Coarse or jerky vibrations tell us that something is amiss. The same thing holds true for the human body. Vibration is a sign of life. We use the expression "a vibrant personality" to express our awareness of this relationship.

It can be observed that as feeling in the legs and feet increases, respiration deepens spontaneously. Breathing is an aggressive function which depends, in the adult, upon contact with the lower half of the body. Once his legs become charged and alive, the schizoid patient experiences his body differently. He feels grounded. Formerly, he moved on his legs; now they move him. This is how one patient described the difference:

> After last session I felt so good. I wasn't frightened. My legs felt so alive. The most remarkable thing was that my head wasn't telling my legs what to do. I had the sense of security that my legs were under me and knew what to do. But they also felt numb after so many years of nonfeeling. I was convinced that as soon as I get my legs back, I will be able to function.

It is important to emphasize that these positions are not exercises. If done mechanically, they lead nowhere. If one uses them to gain feeling in the body, they are simple and effective. Therefore, no time limits are involved. A patient exploits a position for as long as it produces meaningful sensations in his body. When a position becomes too painful or too uncomfortable the patient changes it. These positions were developed by my associates and myself in the course of many years of work with the problems of breathing and muscular tension. One that we have found particularly helpful is to have a patient arch his back over a stool as shown in Figure 19. This position was adopted from the natural tendency people have to arch across the back of a chair when they have been sitting too long. This arch stretches the muscles of the back, releases the tensions about the diaphragm, and promotes deeper breathing. I always follow this position with that of Figure 18, as this reverses the stretch and returns the patient to the ground.

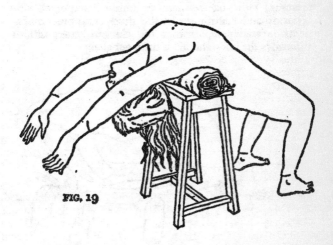

FIG. 19

Figure 20 shows a patient in a position of hyperextension. This position is particularly effective in stretching the muscles of the front thighs, which are often found to be quite spastic. Since the pelvis is freely suspended in this position, it will often develop a spontaneous movement if the patient is relaxed. These involuntary movements of the body are important in releasing tension. They also give the patient a feeling of aliveness in his body. When sensations flow through the body and into the legs and feet as a result of breathing, the patient feels unified. At such moments a patient may remark, "I feel all in one piece."

The passive positions described above are used to bring a patient into contact with his body, to increase body sensation, and to produce some release of tension through tremor and involuntary movement. Since they deepen breathing and excite the body, they are used almost routinely at the beginning of most sessions. They are followed by a number of active movements which I shall describe below. The repetitive use of these passive positions has a cumulative effect on the body. Each time they are used, it becomes easier for the patient to breathe freely. As a result, more sensations arise in the body. Most patients find these positions so helpful that they do them at home each morning. This practice increases a patient's contact with his body and contributes to the therapeutic process. Patients invariably report that the use of these positions stimulates the body and helps them get going.

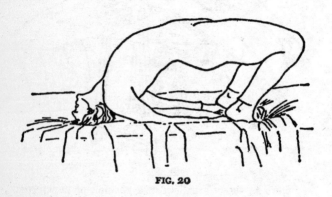

FIG. 20

In addition to the passive positions, many active movements are used to help a patient sense and express his feelings more directly. Figure 21 for example, shows a patient prepared to strike the couch with a tennis racquet. This movement serves both to release aggression and to develop coordination and control. Male patients strike the couch with their bare fists.

At first, patients' movements, when striking or kicking the couch, are fragmented and uncoordinated. In striking the couch from a standing position they tend to flail their arms while their backs and legs are relatively uninvolved. In kicking the couch while lying on it, they use their legs aggressively but the head and upper part of their bodies are held rigid and do not join in the motion. As a result, these activities seem like exercises and patients often com-

FIG. 21

plain that they derive no feeling of release or satisfaction from them. Their lack of coordination is a sign that they have not committed themselves fully to the activity, that is, the activity does not embrace the whole body. As coordination develops, the expressive movement takes on a unitary quality and becomes an emotional experience.

A patient's inability to commit his body totally to an activity should be treated in two ways. His unconscious resistance should be analyzed psychologically while his coordination must be developed physically. Typically, a patient will rationalize his inability to put himself fully into these activities, saying that he has no reason to be angry, etc. This is an example of the schizoid defensive maneuver. Every patient has something to be angry about, otherwise he would not be in therapy. It can be shown that he was always afraid to express his anger. It can be pointed out to him that a healthy person is capable of identifying with a feeling of anger sufficiently to permit him to execute the movements of hitting or kicking in a coordinated and integrated manner. When the patient realizes that his incoordination reflects his inability to express feeling, he accepts the physical procedures outlined earlier as necessary to his improvement.

The capacity for emotional expression is proportionate to the degree of muscular coordination. A well coordinated person moves and acts gracefully. His whole body participates actively in every gesture and movement. Thus, his every movement has an emotional quality, and the individual can be described as emotionally alive. The disturbed person doesn't move in this way. His normal movements are stiff and awkward or ataxic and gauche. Yet such an individual may manifest an unusual grace and coordination in some special activity in which he has trained and to which he *can* give himself fully. Many actors, dancers, and athletes may show this grace and coordination in their special fields despite the fact that they suffer from severe emotional problems. However, off stage and in ordinary everyday situations one can observe that their body movements reflect their lack of ease and security.

As patients learn to relax or let go in such activities as striking the couch or kicking their legs, their general muscular coordination increases spontaneously. It is not a matter of learning how to hit or kick. Coordination that develops through the conscious mastery of a skill is limited to the specific skill. In such activities as hitting the couch or kicking, the patient confronts his fear of letting go in movements that have an emotional expression. By letting go in such activities, he overcomes his fear of the irrational. Through such experiences the body heals itself. Children's play serves the same purpose. Though a play situation is unreal, children take it seriously and become quite emotional in their responses. The adult who has suppressed the child in his personality has to rationalize all his actions.

Kicking the couch while lying on it is an excellent opportunity to regain this infantile capacity. Kicking while lying on one's back introduces an infantile element into the activity and permits the patient to abandon himself more freely to the movement. The patient may kick the couch with legs bent or extended. I have already observed that the schizoid patient tenses his abdomen and restricts his breathing when doing these movements. In addition, he stiffens his neck, which prevents his head from participating. He has to be encouraged to "let go" of his head so that it moves together with the rest of the body. In rapid and intense kicking with the legs loosely outstretched, the head is whipped up and down with each kick. In most patients this creates a feeling of being "carried away" by the movement and the patient often becomes quite frightened. Since this activity is supervised and there is no danger, the patient soon learns to give in to the feeling and enjoy the release.

Since almost everyone has something to "kick about," all patients sense the validity of this activity. Kicking also provides an opportunity for the lower half of the body to take over the hegemony of the organism. When the kicking becomes intense, the ego temporarily surrenders its control over the body, allowing the body to respond freely to its impulses. This capacity to surrender ego control is especially important in the sexual function, where orgastic satisfaction depends upon the ability of the individual to "give in" to the overwhelming sexual excitation. Kicking also enables a patient to identify with his infantile feelings.

Babies lying on their backs kick their feet freely and spontaneously in the natural joy of living or in anger and frustration. Kicking up one's heels is a sign of exuberance. Finally, kicking, even more than walking, promotes the flow of blood and thus improves the circulation.

Kicking with bent knees may also be combined with a rhythmic flailing of the arms against the couch in a movement which resembles a childish temper tantrum. In this activity, the two sides of the body should move alternately so that the right arm and the right leg move together and synchronously, followed by a similar movement of the left arm and leg. In this coordinated movement, the head rotates left and right as the corresponding arm and leg strike the couch. (In patients where the two halves of the body are dissociated, this coordination breaks down and the right arm moves together with the left leg. Moreover, when this movement involves two opposite sides at the same time, the head is immobilized.) In the course of this physical therapy, the patient is directed to sense his body, to understand and identify with its feelings and sensations, and to interpret them in the context of his history and life.

It should be pointed out that the mobilization of the patient's body is a slow procedure. Since he has abandoned his body because of pain, this pain will return as he reestablishes contact with it. After several months of therapy one patient remarked, "I have to take it slow. My body is just feeling the pain. I have pain all over my body. I never knew I was so afraid of pain." Pain in the schizoid body can assume frightening proportions if it is associated with inner feelings of despair and terror. On the other hand, when a patient realizes that the pain stems from the struggle of the body to come alive and is not an expression of a destructive process, he can accept the pain as a positive sign. To help a patient understand the role of pain in the healing process, I use a familiar example. When a finger is frostbitten, it is not painful. The person may not even be aware of the condition. However, when the finger begins to thaw out, the pain often is very severe. The thawing out must be done very slowly. This illustration is particularly appropriate to the schizoid problem, for in many respects the schizoid body is frozen, and the therapy can be compared to a thawing out.

THE THERAPY OF A SCHIZOID PATIENT

This patient, whom I will call Sally, was a dance teacher. She complained about her relations to people, about her frustration and despair, and about her fears.

Sally's therapy extended over a period of several years, with sessions once a week except during the summer. Despite the fact that she was a dancer, the muscles of her body were extremely tense. She had very little sensation in her legs. Her breathing was very shallow. Her eyes had a wild, frightened look and were out of focus much of the time. She was extremely anxious.

The early part of her therapy consisted mostly in getting her to breathe and feel her body through the use of the passive positions described above. At first, she could tolerate these positions for only a very short time. Gradually, her tolerance increased. At times, I kneaded her tense muscles with my hands. This released some of their spasticity and gave the patient a feeling of body contact and self-awareness. In the first part of her therapy she cried frequently and expressed her deep despair. She said:

> I don't know what love is. I don't know what a woman is or what a man is. They are shadows in my mind. Only my mother is not a shadow. She's a hawk [the patient made her hands into claws] who killed my father and made a wreck out of me. All I feel is pain, and because of the work here, it's like you can put your hands in it. It's like looking into a deep, empty well, which hurts. I feel it will never be filled up.

The release of these feelings of pain, sadness, and despair opened the way for more positive feelings to flow into her body. She alternated for a while between feeling alive and happy, then frightened and lost. She observed:

> Stretching my body gives me strong sexual feelings. When these feelings are absent, I feel the pain. There is a pressure in my stomach. I have a feeling of "lostness" and blackness, as if there is no meaning in life. Up to now, my body has been an instrument for me.

Therapy was a series of crises, from each of which Sally emerged with more self-contact and greater strength. Any aggressive movement terrified her, and she reacted with a feeling of despair and hopelessness. The assertion of a negative attitude was especially frightening. One such crisis was provoked by the simple maneuver of striking her fists into the couch while lying on it and saying, "I won't. I won't. I won't." Immediately after asserting herself in this manner, Sally jumped off the couch and ran to a corner of the room, where she cowered, crying. Her terror was such that, at first, she resisted my attempt to console her, but then she allowed me to sit next to her and put my arms around her. She said there was no one she could turn to in her fear and misery. She distrusted me as much as she needed me.

In her next session Sally remarked, "I realize that I never gave in to my mother. As a result, I was unable to function. I was paralyzed, and all my life was a kind of waiting for something to release me." What Sally meant was that she had passed her life in an attitude of unspoken defiance, afraid to say No, unable to say Yes. This negative layer in her personality, which was functionally identical with the state of contraction of her muscles, paralyzed all aggressive movements. During this session Sally repeated the procedure of hitting the couch saying, "No, I won't." This time there was less panic, but she became alternately hot and cold, as waves of feeling swept over her and receded.

The following week Sally returned to the idea of her paralysis. She said:

> All my life I moved with inhibitions. I cannot be myself. I felt freer after the crisis when I cried so much, but there comes a point where I cannot go on.

During the succeeding two months I concentrated on the physical aspect of Sally's problem. Despite her work as a dancer, she complained of stiffness and pain in her body. Now she became aware that her choice of dancing as a profession was motivated by the need to make her body come alive through movement. I have found this to be true of many professional dancers. While the dance helps keep the body alive, it does nothing to release its chronic tensions. Now, using the positions and movements described above, she stretched her body, breathed, and moved. Her tolerance for body feeling was very limited. She became panicky if any involuntary movements developed. Many times she drew away, frightened, and wanted to leave. I restrained her gently, and she allowed me to lead her back. At the end of each session, I could see in the softening of her body outline, in the brightness of her skin, and in the expression of her eyes that she felt better, more alive and more in touch with herself. The improvement did not last until the next session, one week later; however, it was easier each time to bring the feeling back.

Several weeks later I noticed that Sally was beginning to thaw out. She came in looking sad and complained of a feeling of congestion in her chest, which up to this moment had been a "dead" area, without feeling. She also mentioned a feeling of fullness and pain in her pelvis. As we talked she began to cry deeply. "I have never been a child," she said. "I had to be grown-up to get away from my mother." We did no physical work at this hour, and Sally allowed the sadness to envelop her. In the course of her crying, she remarked that she was aware of a feeling deep in her vagina. She said that she had the sensation of a bud within her that could open up like a flower. Every schizoid person carries within his body a lost infant whom he hides from himself and protects against the world. The dilemma of the schizoid individual is that he dare not accept the infant within him and cannot, in consequence, accept the reality of his body or the world.

The suppression of the infant prevents the spontaneous reaching out and touching that characterizes an infant's response to a love object. Sally admitted that she was afraid of any physical contact with me. She dared not reach out with her hands to touch me. When I encouraged her to do so, her movements were hesitant and awkward. When I moved to touch her she recoiled. I could comfort her only when, under the stress of fear and anxiety, she regressed to the position of a helpless and frightened child.

Sally's eventual acceptance of the infant within her made it possible for her to begin to reach out and to touch me. This time, instead of the rejection she experienced as an infant, she met with a positive response from her "substitute mother," the therapist. She slowly learned that she could make demands on life, and the fixation that had arrested her emotional growth began to dissolve.

After a summer recess, therapy was resumed with an

attempt to mobilize stronger aggressive feelings in the patient. I noticed that her jaw had relaxed considerably. At times it still appeared to be grim and hard, but at other times it looked soft. Sally remarked that she was afraid of making an angry face, since it would look like her mother's—full of malice and hatred. This was the first session in which she allowed herself to scream while lying on the couch and hitting it with her fists. She screamed, "I won't," and then said of her action, "It's good, but not real yet."

In the succeeding session she spoke about feeling a lack of reality in her behavior. She expressed the idea that she was special, that she wasn't a part of the world of people. Her relationships, she said, were a mask to hide the fact of nonexistence, of aloneness. This brought her to speak of her father. She recounted a scene in which he lay dying in an oxygen tent. She had stood frozen beside his bed unable to reach out or say anything to him. There were no tears in her eyes as she related this incident. Sally felt that she could not touch life and that life didn't touch her.

To help Sally gain a feeling of power from aggressive actions, I suggested that she strike the couch from a standing position with a tennis racquet. Her reaction to my suggestion was surprising. She picked up the racquet gingerly, made a tentative gesture of hitting the couch with it, then dropped it precipitously, as if it were a loaded gun or a live snake. She began to shake and to jump all over the room. It was several minutes before she could bring herself to pick up the racquet again. She struck another blow, dropped the racquet, and went jumping away, waving her arms like a bird.

In the course of several sessions, Sally used the racquet repeatedly to strike the couch. Each time, she could hit more effectively and was less frightened. On several occasions, after striking a few blows, she would drop the racquet, move away, and begin to cry. She was struggling with her fear of violence. Some time later, I asked her to voice an expression of anger—like "Damn!" or "I hate you!"—while striking the couch. But she could say nothing. Her expression while using the racquet was one of fright; her eyes and mouth were wide open, and she was speechless. Watching her, I became aware of another reason why Sally became a dancer. She was so frightened in emotional situations that words did not form, and she relied upon her body movements to express her feelings. Later, as she gained increasing strength and courage from the therapy, she struck the couch with some vehemence and said, over and over again, "Stupid! You stupid!" She felt it was directed at her mother. She was returning the castigation she had suffered as a child from her mother.

Sally's problem with the expression of anger took considerable time to overcome. After she was able to express some anger in the therapy session, she still faced the necessity of allowing her anger to come out in real life situations. This was more difficult. When she failed, the result was a setback. One day she related the following incident:

> Something happened to me in my lecture class. The teacher made a remark to me like, "Just sit back." I became very angry. I thought, What nerve! I felt myself get hot with anger, like flashes of lightning inside me, but I didn't let it out. I felt my body go tight and become very tense muscularly. Then I became numb. Since then, all my neurotic anxieties have returned, and all my easiness is gone.
>
> The anger seemed to swim inside me, like a fish that couldn't get out. Then it became frozen—like stuck in the ice. It gets stuck because I am to rational. Why does someone always have to tell me what I feel? Why can't I feel what is inside me?

The therapy progressed rapidly after this for a number of weeks. Sally continued to improve, and her personal life ran more smoothly. Each session, we went through all the exercise positions, and she used the tennis racquet regularly. She was able to express her anger toward her mother. She hit the couch steadily and angrily, calling her mother "Stupid, stupid, stupid!" Her breathing had deepened perceptibly. "You know," she said to me, "I am not as cold as I used to be. In the past I always used a feather quilt in winter; now all I need is a little cover. My hands are warmer too, but my feet are still a mess."

Therapy has its ups and downs. Following the release of her aggression, Sally experienced an exhaustion which frightened her greatly. She didn't know how she could go on, and the idea that she might not be able to carry on terrified her. Sally felt she would go out of her mind with worry.

It was her body that saved her. Its need for sleep overpowered the torment of her mind. In sleep she found the answer to her anxiety. When she could carry on no longer, she found renewal in sleep.

All schizoid patients go through a phase of deep exhaustion on their road to recovery. After having held on so tightly for many years, they experience the letting down as a relief, and this brings to consciousness the weariness and fatigue which had previously been blocked off from perception. The feeling of exhaustion represents a fuller contact with the body. I regard it as a sign that the body is able to assert its needs against the neurotic ego. If the patient gives in to this feeling of exhaustion, it stops all his compulsive activity and thereby decreases his feeling of desperation. This feeling of exhaustion may last for weeks or even months. From it the person learns that he can survive nicely without his compulsions.

Emphasis in this account upon the use of a tennis racquet to bring out the feeling of anger should not be taken to suggest that other means or other forms of expression are unimportant. The approach must be total, and the physical therapy must involve the whole body. One further incident from this case will illustrate another procedure.

Some time after her return from Europe, Sally remarked, "In the last two months I've had dreams that my teeth crumbled the moment I attempted to bite down with them." Such a dream should be interpreted to mean that the patient is afraid to bite, literally and figuratively. Sally's inability to get a "good bite on things" or to "sink her teeth" into life described her difficulty. But the dream also had a literal significance. Her jaw was so tight that she could not open her mouth fully. Forward and backward movements of the jaw were limited. To meet this situation, Sally did an exercise in which she extended her jaw forward, showed her teeth, and made an attempt to growl or snarl. This was difficult for her, and the gesture was made without any feeling. In time, however, she began to enjoy this activity and could make a growl or snarl that sounded real. To help her feel her teeth and gain confidence in them, I had her bite on one end of a towel while lying on the couch. Holding the other end, I raised her head and torso above the bed while she arched her back. Her weight was supported by her feet below and by her teeth above. At first, she was frightened by this exercise, but she was able to hold on for longer than one minute. The experience made her teeth feel alive and gave her a sense of strength and security in them and in her jaw.

As I bring this case history to a close I would like to point out that the feelings a patient expresses in therapy are relative. In contrast to his lack of feeling before, the experience of pleasure in his body seems like heaven. But, what seems at first to be a great feeling may not appear so satisfactory as the therapy progresses and the patient's demands on life increase. For the man just released from an institution, freedom is everything. Soon, however, he will want more: a place to stay, someone with whom to share his bed, a way of making a living, etc. Sally's progress should be viewed in this light. Therapy initiates a continuing growth process.

To reclaim the body, its pain must be replaced by pleasure and its despair by positive feelings. However, for the schizoid patient the way to pleasure is through pain, the path to joy leads through despair, or to put it differently, the road to heaven passes through hell. The schizoid individual, whose life has been lived in limbo, empty and meaningless, undertakes this odyssey because it promises hope. Apart from the body, life is an illusion. In the body, one will encounter pain, sadness, anxiety, and terror, but these are at least real feelings, which can be experienced and expressed. The ability to feel pain is also the capacity to feel pleasure. To give in to tiredness is to find the peace of rest. Every bodily feeling implies its opposite. To be without feeling is to exist in a vacuum, cold and lifeless. No one knows this more than the schizoid person, but he has lost the way back to his body. Once the patient finds the way back, he will reclaim his forsaken body with all the fervor of the lost child who finds its loving mother.

13

The Achievement
of Identity

THE FEELING of identity is not present at birth. An individual develops his identity as his ego grows and matures. For most patients, therefore, the problem is not to recover a lost identity, since they never had a real identity in the first place, but rather to achieve a sense of identity by developing a stable and well-functioning ego.

The feeling of identity is based on the awareness of desire, the recognition of need, and the perception of body sensation. When a patient says, "I don't know who I am," he is in effect saying, "I don't know what I feel, what I want, or what I need." He knows that he needs help, but beyond this, his self-awareness is limited and his identity is vague. He is not aware that he is sad or angry, that his body is constricted by muscular tensions, and that he is unable to love and to feel pleasure. Dimly, on some deeper level of consciousness, he may recognize these facts, but he is unable to state them as personal experiences.

The feeling of identity is inchoate in the baby's first cry at birth. By this cry, the infant asserts its first feeling and its first desire and need. The feeling is one of discomfort; the desire and need is to be close to the mother's body. If the infant is immediately put to the breast and nursed, the crying ceases, which tells us that the discomfort has ended and the need has been met. The cry is an assertion of the infant's existence and identity as a sentient being. Of this, however, the child is unaware, since the functions of perception, awareness, and recognition are undeveloped. As the infant grows, these functions become active. With increasing maturity, body sensations become more intense, needs and desires more extensive, consciousness more acute, and the expression of feeling more specific. The child develops a feeling of identity.

The ego grows through the perception and integration of body sensation on the one hand, and the expression of feeling on the other. If a child is inhibited in the expression of feeling or made to feel ashamed of his body sensations, his ego will not mature. If he is prevented from taking the measure of himself, from exploring his strength and discovering his weaknesses, his ego will have a precarious foothold in reality and his identity will be nebulous. If, moreover, he is indoctrinated with "shoulds" and "shouldn'ts" and brought up to fulfill a parental image, his ego will become devious and his identity confused. Such a child will subvert his body and manipulate the environment to maintain the image. He will adopt a role based on this image, and he will equate his identity with this role.

An identity based upon a role disintegrates when the role collapses under the stress of real life situations. The person who plays a role is performing, and he requires a receptive audience if the performance is to provide him with any satisfaction. The original audience was mother and father, who fostered the role and encouraged the performance. In adult life the role player seeks another person who is attracted by the projected image and responds to the role. But an audience of one, who is always the same person, soon loses its power to excite, and a performance that is constantly repeated becomes tedious. The two parties finally become bored by such a relationship and drift apart, the performer to find a new audience, and the audience to find a new performer. The realization that something is amiss may not occur to these people until after several disappointments, but in many such individuals there is an underlying feeling of emptiness and despair. In the intimacy of sex relationships particularly, role playing becomes farcical, yet the individual who plays a role knows no other way of being.

The role creates a distortion in self-perception. The person confined to a role sees himself and all situations in terms of the role. Role playing colors all perceptions and narrows all responses. It constitutes the major obstacle to the recovery of identity, since role playing is generally unconscious.

The patient who lacks an identity is usually unaware that he plays a role. In most cases he is even unaware of his lack of identity; his complaints of misery and failure stem from a feeling of frustration in his role playing. Having adopted a role to please his parents, he cannot understand why the rest of the world is not equally pleased with his behavior. He comes to the psychiatrist to find out how to make his role playing more successful.

The role which a patient adopts as a child becomes part of his character structure. It is manifested in his manner of speaking, his carriage, his gestures, his expressions, and his movements. It is evident in his bodily attitude if one can correctly interpret this attitude. This, however, the patient cannot do, since he is unaware of the pattern of rigidity in his body. He takes his body for granted. To unmask the role it is necessary to analyze the patient's total character structure.

Therapy involves a confrontation between patient and therapist. In this confrontation, the patient will learn about his transference, namely, that he sees the "other person" as the image of his father or mother. He will discover the roots of this transference in his need for approval and his fear of self-assertion. He will find that he feels guilty about his sexual feelings and is inhibited in the expression of negative feelings. If he can accept these feelings, he can reclaim his body and his identity.

UNMASKING THE ROLE

Mary, the child-woman whose case I discussed in Chapter 5, played the role of the "kissy doll." At the beginning of her therapy, she was seeing a specialist for a breast condition, which she said he treated by massaging her breast. She described him as an older man and said that she was disturbed by the treatment, not so much by what he did but by the way he touched her. She felt his touch was too caressing.

Can it be assumed that Mary's perception of the doctor's feeling toward her was valid? The child-woman or the "Lolita personality" has a strong fascination for certain males, who feel insecure and inadequate in relation to a sexually mature woman. It may even be hypothesized that

Mary's personality had the unconscious function of exciting such men. Her passive submission to the treatment by the specialist supports this idea; her helplessness can be viewed both as a defense against her own sexual feelings and as a lure to the male. That Mary regarded her special child-woman personality as a lure became apparent when she complained one day that a man in whom she was interested had not made a pass at her while they were alone. He could not have been much of a man, she remarked with contempt, since he didn't respond to her.

The child-woman personality permits a female to enter into a sexual situation and enjoy its excitement without assuming the responsibility for her actions. She seduces a man with the feeling of a child, that is, her dominant feeling is a desire for affection and warmth. If she is seduced, her submission is to a father figure who, she feels, will take care of her and protect her. In both situations, the feeling of guilt for the underlying sexual desire is avoided. The childlike quality in a woman is the result of the repression of sexual feelings in the oedipal situation. It should be interpreted as a defense against the danger of a sexual involvement with the father.

This female personality places a man in a dilemma. If he treats such a woman as a child, he reinforces her justification for this defense, and confirms her immaturity. If he treats her as a woman, he overlooks her infantile needs for understanding and support. To respond to her as a child who needs support, and at the same time, as an equal sexual partner is impossible. My patient complained, for example, that her husband didn't have intercourse with her frequently enough, and that at other times he was unresponsive to her need to be cuddled. Since a man will fail to satisfy this child-woman no matter which course he takes, the effect of this bind is to make him feel guilty and responsible for her unhappiness.

To unmask the role, the patient's physical appearance must be interpreted as a facet of her personality. The immaturity of Mary's body made her appear very innocent and naive, yet in her discussions with me she revealed a sophisticated understanding of sex and life. When a patient's physical appearance presents an exaggerated picture, one frequently finds that it conceals the opposite attitude. One learns to expect that sadness will be found under the mask of a clown, fear behind the seeming strength of the bully, and rage under the façade of rationality. A bewildered or frightened expression in the eyes, a determined set of the jaw, and a physical rigidity of the body betray the insecurity that is associated with playing a role.

While I was aware of Mary's obvious fears and helplessness, I also sensed her unconscious attempt to use sex as a trap. My knowledge of her role playing convinced her that I could not be seduced into a relationship that would prove disastrous for the therapy. I was able, therefore, to analyze the contradictory aspects of her personality. As the child, she felt inferior and helpless, but as the woman, she regarded herself as superior and controlling. Her helplessness and childishness could be interpreted as a device to humiliate the male. If she seduced him, she could hold him in contempt. He could not be much of a man if he responded sexually to the child in her personality. By this maneuver, the man was reduced to the image of her father, who was completely under the domination of her mother.

Mary and her mother achieved the same dominance over the male, using completely opposite approaches. The mother subdued her husband by her forceful aggression; the daughter rendered hers impotent by her helplessness and passivity. Both homes were dominated by the female. It may be said that mother and daughter were one, in that each was an aspect of the other. Mary's passivity contrasted with her mother's aggression, Mary's helplessness with her mother's strength, Mary's smallness with her mother's bigness, and Mary's femininity with her mother's masculinity. It was as if the personality of the mother was split, the passive feminine component being projected into the daughter as an inferior quality, while the masculine, aggressive component was retained by the mother. Psychologically, mother and daughter complemented each other, and together they formed a demonic unity. This unconscious identification between mother and daughter accounted for Mary's feeling that she was attached to her mother by an umbilical cord.

Mary and her mother had a symbiotic relationship in

which each was dependent upon the other. They telephoned each other regularly, and much as Mary resented her mother's comments and criticism, she felt helpless to prevent them. She was afraid of her mother, yet she didn't want to hurt her. She felt that her mother lived off her and through her.

In these symbiotic relationships, when a mother is dominant and aggressive, a child is reduced to a passive and submissive position. Its independence is denied, its motility is restricted and its security is undermined. Its legs are weakened, and its breathing is reduced. The mother refuses to free the child, whom she unconsciously regards as a part of her being. Gisela Pankow comments that "she [the schizoid child] cannot come down to earth in order to be born because the tie between mother and daughter has never been cut."[69]

To give up the role, Mary had to become aware of her identification with her mother and what it meant. I asked her if she realized that in some respects she was like her mother, whom she consciously rejected. Mary conceded that she had allied herself with her mother against men, but she also recognized her submissiveness to her mother. The combination of identification and submission forced Mary into the role of a "kissy doll." This role provided her with a solution to her complex relationships to both of her parents, for, as we shall see, it was also encouraged by her father.

Mary's role served her in three ways: (1) The role of a "kissy doll" represented a passive sexual attitude which contrasted with her mother's unfeminine sexual aggressiveness. In this way Mary repudiated her mother. (2) By being a "kissy doll" rather than a sexual person, Mary also expressed her contempt for men, which allied mother and daughter. (3) The roll of "kissy doll" also stemmed from the unconscious homosexual relationship between mother and daughter, in which Mary participated submissively as the plaything of her mother.

The underlying identification with her mother is revealed in the following statement:

There are times when I feel that I am my mother. Last night as I was going to bed, I had the same expression on my face as my mother. Her face in repose is ugly, common, vulgar; her mouth sags. I feel sometimes that if I am not careful, if I let myself go, my face will fall into the same ugliness as hers.

She looks full of hate when she is off guard. Her eyes turn to ice. She's a tiger—a man-eating tiger.

Mary identified with her mother, yet was afraid of her. In relation to herself she saw her mother as a cat with claws; in relation to men she saw her as a man-eating tiger. To avoid the "cat," Mary turned to her father for understanding and love. But Mary's father was a passive male who was afraid to assert himself against his wife. Thus, he could neither protect his daughter nor encourage her to adopt a more independent attitude. In his weakness, he was vulnerable to the sexual temptation of a girl child, and so he kissed her with open mouth and caressed her body in the mistaken belief that it was love. Mary could not reject this perverted expression of paternal feeling, since it was preferable to her mother's claws. She felt sorry for her father, and identified with him, since both daughter and father were tyrannized by the mother. As a "kissy doll," Mary did not threaten his masculinity, and in this role, she could obtain some measure of body contact and warmth. Mary exploited this relationship as, later, she was to exploit all relationships with men.

Who was Mary? She was the seducer and the seduced, the victim and the victimizer. Like a $+1$ and a -1, her identity added up to zero. One half of her personality was identified with her mother's aggressiveness, while the other half was identified with her father's passivity. All that Mary could claim as her own was a repugnance to her body and a defiance of life. In her desperation, she lived on the illusion that someone would respond to the doll without exploiting it. The only person who could react to her in this way would be a therapist.

When this analysis of her role playing was completed, I noticed that Mary looked at me differently. There was an expression of affection in her eyes. Up to this moment, she had regarded me as the uncle in Sophocles' play *Antigone*, who demanded that she accept an intolerable reality.

The reality that Mary found intolerable was the necessity for an independent existence. As a "kissy doll" she would be supported and exploited, and while she resented the exploitation, she was unprepared to surrender the support. Through the analysis of her role, Mary learned that she could not have one without the other. To be free from the danger of exploitation, she had to stand on her own feet, assume the responsibility for her life, and find pleasure and satisfaction in the functions of her body. She had to discover her identity, which means that she had to recover her feelings and gain the ability to express them.

In the process of unmasking the role, a patient first learns how he distorts his perception of other people into the images of his mother and father—how, in fact, he distorts reality. Second, the patient becomes aware of his negative feelings, which were previously projected onto other persons (therapist, husband, children, etc.). Third, he becomes conscious of a defiant attitude which sets him apart and forces him into isolation. Finally, the patient feels what it means to live for himself, to know his feelings, and to be able to express them. Every step of this process involves an interaction with the therapist, who is in turn an object of manipulation, a reason for negativity, a cause of defiance, and finally another human being, whom the patient can accept and respect since he has become able to accept and respect himself.

The role is a set pattern of behavior developed during infancy and childhood in the course of a child's adaptation to the family situation. It is a product of the interaction between the child's personality and needs on one side and the parents' personalities and demands on the other. When parents insist that a child be or behave in a certain way, they are setting its future role in life. More important, however, in determining that role are the parents' unconscious attitudes and expectations, which are communicated to the child through look, touch, gesture, and mood. Generally, the role is pretty well determined by the time the child reaches the age of seven.

Since each child is different, and since no two family situations are identical, the role becomes the unique and individual mode of existence of the desperate person. The child who is fortunate enough to grow up with the freedom to live for himself and the security that his needs and desires will meet with a generous response doesn't develop a role. The role represents the best possible adjustment a child can make to an ambivalent or hostile family situation.

In the course of his adjustment the child forms the identifications with his parents that shape his personality. An unconscious identification permits no choice of response. Children are natural imitators, and they will spontaneously pattern themselves on parental behavior and attitudes. Imitation describes a natural process, whereas identification refers to a pathological phenomenon. The child who imitates broadens his personality by learning through copying. The child who identifies narrows his personality by restricting his possible responses.

Identification is an unconscious process. Wilhelm Reich made the point that the major identification is always with the threatening parent.[70] There is a saying that one can only fight the devil with the devil's weapons. Yet when a person adopts the tactics of the enemy, he becomes like the enemy. Whoever uses the devil's weapons becomes a devil. Identification occurs when a child incorporates into his feeling and thinking a parental attitude in order to cope with the hostility underlying this attitude. In this process, the attitude becomes part of his own personality. As long as the identification remains unconscious neither the child nor the adult has a choice in his manner of responding to situations. To the extent of his identifications, he is his mother or his father, often both, and he behaves as they would.

Broadly speaking, the roles people play may be classified as dominant or submissive. In every neurotic relationship, one person takes the dominant role, while the other takes a submissive role. Individuals who play roles have to find an appropriate counterpart to their role to make a relationship feasible. For example, a woman with masculine aggressive tendencies will team up with a man who has passive feminine tendencies. Similarly, the man who holds himself out as a hero is unconsciously looking for someone to worship him. These relationships rarely work out satisfactorily, since behind the roles there are real people whose real needs are unfulfilled by role playing. The person who takes the submissive role resents being submissive, while the individual with the dominant role constantly feels frustrated. Dominance is meaningless if the other person is submissive.

All role playing involves mutual support and exploitation. The masculine aggressive woman who dominates her home finds support for her insecure ego in the passive acquiescence of her husband. The passive husband gains the support of his aggressive wife in making decisions and coping with the world. She exploits his weakness by reducing his masculinity to explain her failure as a woman. In the same way, by being submissive, the husband can blame his weakness upon his wife's hostility. Underlying all role playing is the fear of self-assertion and the guilt for sexual and negative feelings.

SELF-ASSERTION

A conscious sense of self, or identity, develops when the expression of feeling becomes ego directed. Behavior takes on a volitional quality. The child is aware of what it is doing and has some idea of how its behavior affects others. Its actions or utterances are no longer purely discharge phenomena which release tension, they also serve now as means of communication. At this point, one can speak of self-assertion. This means that a sense of self has arisen in consciousness, or as R. A. Spitz states, that the subject is aware of himself as "a sentient and acting entity."[71] According to Spitz, this first occurs at about eighteen months of age.

The specific behavior which indicates that this development has occurred is the expression of No, either by word or by the gesture of shaking the head. Spitz writes, "The acquisition of the 'no' is the indicator of a new level of autonomy, of the awareness of the 'other,' and of the awareness of the self."[72] The expression of Yes, either by gesture or word, is a later development. Prior to this event, a child can indicate acceptance or refusal by appropriate body movements. It can open its mouth to receive the food its mother offers or turn away as a sign of rejection. But this behavior is semiautomatic, it is not the result of a judgment which is communicated to the parent. By saying No or Yes, the child substitutes communication for direct action, and in this process, senses itself as an active agent able to make choices.

The concept of No embraces the idea of opposition in addition to rejection. The child's refusal of food is not directed against the mother but against the proffered object, whereas the expression of No is a communication that is personally directed. The No opposes the child to its parent and thus sets the child apart as an autonomous force. Aware of the parent's will, it is also aware of its own rejection of this will.

The discovery of the self through opposition intrigues the child. It explores this new avenue of self-expression, often saying No even when it is offered a desired object. I recall an incident which occurred when my son was about two years old. I offered him a cooky of the kind that he liked, but he shook his head in refusal before he saw what it was. When he recognized the cooky, he reached out for it. A patient told me an interesting story in this respect. She said that she remembered how she became aware of herself as an independent personality. In response to a question by her parents, she deliberately told them a lie. As she spoke the lie, she realized that she didn't have to tell the truth and she became aware that she could choose how to answer. It made me wonder whether children sometimes deliberately lie to test and affirm the sense of self.

The assertion of the negative is conditioned upon the previous expression of affirmative attitudes. Before the development of the concept of No in a child's mind, its behavior can be viewed as an expression of the affirmative. The striving for pleasure and the avoidance of pain are instinctual responses, and as Spitz states, "Affirmation is the essential attribute of instinct."[73] Par contra, the negative is an attribute of the ego and arises through the awareness of opposition. Just as the ego derives its strength from the body, so the expression of No gains its strength from the prior fulfillment of desire and need.

Clinical experience shows that the person who doesn't know what he wants can't say No. If he says the word, it is expressed without conviction and lacks a tone of determination. The logical explanation is that the negative is meaningless without some feeling of affirmation. In most logical systems the negative arises in opposition to a preceding affirmation. The psychological explanation is that the self rests upon the perception of feeling; when feeling disappears, therefore, the basis for self-assertion is lost and the expression of No is weakened. The self is like a mountain whose base is shrouded in clouds, while only its peak is visible to remind us of its existence. Similarly, the conscious self is the peak of a psychological structure whose base rests in the body and its sensations.

Broadly speaking, self-assertion takes two forms: the conscious reaching out for what one wants and the conscious rejection of what one doesn't want. The expression of these impulses may be by word or deed. Both forms of self-assertion and both modalities of expression are blocked in the schizoid individual. His illness limits his ability to make demands and express his resistance to the demands of others. Faced with this difficulty, he may withdraw from relationships, or if he enters into them, he is submissive and rebellious at the same time.

Schizoid withdrawal denotes a mute negation; schizoid rigidity a mute resistance. In effect, the schizoid is saying, I won't reach out. But he is unconscious of this attitude because he is unaware of his body. In this situation, any attempt to elicit an affirmative expression will fail. In therapy, the approach to the affirmative is through the negative. The logic of therapy is that one proceeds from the outside to the center, whereas growth and development occur in the opposite direction.

The release of repressed negative feelings allows the positive feelings of desire and affection to flow spontaneously. When the frozen exterior of the body is thawed out, the longing for contact and warmth erupts in crying that has an infantile quality. Many patients remark about how much this crying sounds like a baby's. It is the voice of the repressed infant buried under the façade of sophistication and the mask of death.

In the preceding chapter I described some of the physical techniques used to bring a patient into contact with his body. These techniques make him aware of his muscular rigidities. Many of these exercises release tension and increase breathing, but the major task of freeing the patient from his rigidity is accomplished through the use of expressive movements. For example, kicking the bed is an expressive movement because to kick is to protest. On the other hand, if it is done mechanically without an awareness of its meaning, it is purely an exercise. Hitting the couch with the fists or a tennis racquet is another expressive movement. A number of other expressive activities can be used to increase a patient's self-assertiveness.

In one such activity, the patient lies on the couch, head back and knees bent, and strikes the couch with his fists saying, "No!" with each blow. Both the intensity of the sound and the strength of the blow indicate the degree to which the patient can express a negative feeling. In most cases, the voice is weak and the blows are hesitant and tentative. These patients have to be encouraged to make their assertion more emphatic. But even with this encouragement, it is almost impossible to get a full commitment to this activity. One hears such rationalizations as, "I have no reason to say No," or "To whom shall I say No?" This behavior contrasts sharply with the enthusiasm most children show for this activity. It is soon discovered that these patients were unable to oppose their parents.

Occasionally, this expressive activity meets with a positive response from patients. I recall one woman about forty years old who remarked after this activity, "This is the first time that I have been really able to say No. It feels so good." In other cases, patients spontaneously burst into tears from this simple release. Generally, however, the ability to say No with conviction is built up through constant repetition.

Many words can be coupled with this movement. "I won't!", "I hate you!", and "Why?" are natural components of this gesture, but others are available. Sometimes I oppose the patient's assertion by saying, "You will," and clasping the patient's wrist. My action stops most patients cold. They don't know what to do. Again, there is the occasional patient who will resist and attempt to continue his assertion in the face of my opposition. Resistance and defiance is typical of children who find pleasure in confrontation and opposition when they are not afraid of their parents. Most patients, however, are afraid to oppose my authority. They are submissive in therapy as they are in life, while their rebellion and resistance is locked within.

If the patient continues to develop his ability to express negative feelings openly, he will sooner or later turn against the therapist. He will bring his rebellion into the open. He will assert himself against the therapist as a symbol of all authority. This is illustrated in the following case. The patient came late to his session and remarked:

> I had the fantasy that I wouldn't come. You would ask me, "Why?" I would say, "Screw you." I would get back at you.
>
> I feel that I'm stupid, and it's all your fault. As long as I accept your values, I can't think for myself. To hell with you and all you approve of.

In discussing these feelings, the patient said that when he was in the schizoid state and withdrawn, he was imaginative. He had no dearth of ideas. He liked to read. Now he felt stupid. My values, as he interpreted them, meant to be manly, to be aggressive, to be in the world. He felt that this was asking too much, but he also realized that to remain schizoid had become intolerable. Further analysis showed that he associated intelligence, imagination, and sensitivity with his mother. My values, as he termed them, were aspects of his father, with whom he had never developed a close relationship.

Under stress, schizoid individuals will often express negative feelings, but in a form that does not promote the sense of identity. They become hysterical and scream or shout all manner of hostile remarks. Hysterical reactions should be distinguished from emotional expression. The hysterical reaction is like an explosion which overwhelms the ego's restraint, whereas a true emotion is expressed with the approval and support of the ego. An emotion is a unified and total response of the person, the hysterical reaction is split, with the body acting out, while the ego is helpless to stem the flood. Hysterical reactions are common in the schizoid personality, but their effect is to further the dissociation of the ego from the body.

Another expressive movement which is particularly effective in releasing tension also involves the expression of No. With his head back and knees bent as in the preceding example, the patient tightens the back of his neck, thrusts his jaw forward, showing his teeth, and shakes his head in very quick movements from side to side. During the movement, the patient says, "No," softly or loudly. The pitch of the voice rises as the movement continues, and in some cases it may reach a scream. This movement is an exaggeration of the normal head-shaking No, for it mobilizes the feeling of obstinacy associated with the tightening of the back of the neck. It is a movement the schizoid individual finds difficult to execute properly. The tension in the muscles at the junction of head and neck is so severe that his head shaking becomes irregular and ataxic. His obstinacy is unconscious and therefore beyond the control of his ego. With continued practice, however, the neck tensions release and the assertion of No becomes more forceful.

Shaking the head in rapid movements also has the effect of shaking the whole body if the breath is expelled at the same time. Voicing the No permits this to happen. It can be said that the schizoid individual needs to be shaken up, but it is preferable that he do it to himself. Hans Selye, writing about the effectiveness of shock therapy in the treatment of mental illness, says, "Nobody really knew how these shock therapies worked. . . . It seemed as though the patient was somehow 'shaken out of his disease,' very much as a child can be made to snap out of a tantrum if you suddenly splash a glass of cold water into its face."[74] Shaking the head consciously does not have the effect of electric shock treatment, but it is effective in jarring the muscular rigidity of the schizoid individual who, fortunately, does not need the stronger treatment.

The principle behind these movements is that the negativity locked in spastic muscles can be released if the tense muscles can be activated by appropriate movements. Shaking the head is one way to mobilize the tense muscles at the base of the skull, and thrusting the jaw forward mobilizes the tense jaw muscles. I pointed out in Chapter 4 that the schizoid individual has a rigid jaw which expresses an attitude of defiance. He is not consciously defiant; in fact, he is not conscious of the rigidity of the jaw. By exaggerating the defiance, however, he will become conscious of this rigidity. He will complain of pain from the stretch placed on these muscles. And when the defiance is openly expressed, the tension in his jaw muscles will diminish.

The rigid, defiant schizoid jaw prevents the normal reaching out with the mouth to suck. Since this is the primary mode of reaching out to the world, and the first aggressive movement an infant makes, the inhibition of this action sets the stage for the inhibition of all other movements of reaching out to the world. In an infant or normal adult, the mouth can be extended softly and fully. When the schizoid patient attempts this movement, he thrusts the jaw forward together with his lips. As a result, the feeling of reaching out is absent. The schizoid movement is an ambivalent gesture. The forward movement of the jaw is an expression of opposition (negative) while the lips try to reach out in an affirmative expression. Both feelings are cancelled out. The inability of the schizoid patient to reach out with his mouth without thrusting out his jaw dramatizes how repressed negative feelings block the expression of positive or affirmative feelings.

Another expressive movement which can be used to release negation is head banging. This is done, of course, against a foam-rubber mattress. It is the opposite of nodding the head. Children use it in extreme states of frustration to release the tensions in the back of the neck and at the base of the skull. Hitting the head rhythmically against the bed jars the body of a tense individual. On the other hand, it is not unpleasant if one is fully relaxed. It shakes up the body and deepens the respiration. Quite often, it produces a feeling of nausea by its effect on the diaphragm. If the patient can throw up by gagging, this maneuver produces a considerable release of diaphragmatic tension.

Every expressive movement of the body can be used to relieve tension and develop the capacity for emotional expression. I have emphasized those movements which express negative feelings, but it is important also to use gestures of affirmation. Reaching up with the arms and saying, "Mama" often opens a wealth of feeling if the patient allows himself to experience the gesture. I have seen many men cry when they made this gesture.

Therapy is a process of self-discovery. It takes place, however, in relation to another person, the therapist, whose interaction with the patient parallels the patient's early experiences with his mother and father. The phenomena involved in this interaction are called transference, resistance, and countertransference.

TRANSFERENCE, RESISTANCE, AND
COUNTERTRANSFERENCE

The role a patient plays becomes the basis of his relationship to the therapist. This is the meaning of the term "transference." A patient transfers to the therapist the feelings and attitudes developed in his relations with his parents. He sees the therapist as a substitute mother figure or a substitute father figure, and he plays his role faithfully, with the expectation of gaining love and approval and thereby overcoming his fears and anxieties. If the patient plays the role of the good, obedient child, he will try to impress the therapist with his effort and sincerity. If his role is that of the business tycoon, he will try to take over the therapy to show his power and sense of command. Should this continue, therapy will fail. Role playing is the main psychological resistance to the therapeutic undertaking.

A patient, and this is particularly true of the schizoid patient, also comes to therapy seeking the acceptance and warmth that he lacked as a child. He needs to gain contact with the infant within him whose existence he has denied over the years. To gain this contact and achieve his identity he must have the positive support of the therapist. This need places the therapist in the position of a mother figure. The more seriously disturbed the patient is the more he requires the kind of support of which he was deprived as an infant. John Rosen, writing of the therapeutic role in the treatment of the schizophrenic patient, says, "He must be the idealized mother who now has the responsibility of bringing up the patient all over again."[75] A. A. Honig states that when "I asked each of my recovered patients what role I had played which enabled them to get well, they invariably answered, 'Mother.' "[76]

Being a benevolent mother involves more than a verbal expression of interest. The therapist must come into contact with the patient the same way a mother does with a child, that is, via the body. If the therapist touches the patient with hands that are warm and tender, he establishes a deeper contact than words or looks could achieve. The therapist who pays little attention to the physical needs of the patient's body (to breathe and to move) confirms the schizoid dissociation of body and mind. The validity of the analytic approach should not blind one to the patient's need to ground his existence in his physical being. A patient must be encouraged to express his feelings in appropriate physical activity under controlled conditions.

The "benevolent mother" approach, however, is inadequate to resolve the schizoid dilemma. In the schizoid condition, oral and genital needs are so inextricably mixed that the patient is confused and often unaware of the meaning of his actions. The desire for body contact and closeness frequently masks a longing for genital gratification. Genital feelings are often displaced oral desires for contact. This confusion stems from the early incestuous and homosexual relationships of the schizoid child. Further, "benevolent mothering" creates a resistance in the schizoid patient who uses it to justify his continued role playing. In a patient's mind a benevolent mother is one who will accept him and approve of him as he is. Any demand that the patient come to grips with reality is interpreted by him as a lack of support. Thus, a transference based on a mother-child relationship becomes a resistance to the working through of the patient's problem.

It may be objected that a therapist has no right to make "demands" on a patient. Certainly, he has no right to dictate or control a patient's behavior or responses. Such action would justify the patient's resistance to the therapy. But to deny the therapist the right to express an opinion and to insist upon a passive attitude is to weaken therapeutic interaction. A patient cannot develop an identity in a vacuum. He must learn to assert himself against authority with the assurance that it will not lead to his rejection. He must see the therapist as a human being before he can accept his own humanity. He must gain the ability to cope with the personality of the therapist if he is to be able to cope with other personalities in the world. Effective therapeutic interaction does not take place if the therapist hides his personality behind a role.

A therapist responds to a patient's needs. He calms the anxious patient, reassures the frightened one, and sustains the faltering one. It can be said that in his supportive capacity he functions like a mother. However, he doesn't have the personal feeling for a patient that a mother has for her child. His response to the patient is realistic. He can reassure the frightened patient because in reality the fear is groundless. Should there be a real cause for fear, such reassurance would be disastrous. A mother, on the other hand, takes the burden of reality upon her own shoulders and spares her child. Similarly, a mother does not undermine a child's beliefs (Santa Claus, the goodness of people, the reward of honesty), whereas the therapist aims to remove the patient's illusions. Reality demands that one cannot treat a grown person as a child. The therapist can respond to the child in an adult if he bears in mind that he is, of course, dealing with an adult.

To eliminate the underlying confusion of the schizoid state is a problem that demands skill, knowledge, and objectivity on the part of the therapist. These qualities are ordinarily assigned to the ideal father, who is wise and strong, counseling, and setting an example. The traditional analyst was commonly regarded as having played this role. As an ideal father, the therapist is the representative of outer reality, the reality of the world. In this capacity, he has to interpret the world for the patient, as a true father does for his own children. On the other hand, an ideal mother is the representative of inner reality, the reality of the body and its feelings. The therapist, whether man or woman, must be familiar with both realities so that he can help the patient reconcile his conflicts. He must know when to be supportive and when to be critical.

A therapist represents reality as opposed to the emotional illness that denies or distorts reality. But reality seems to have different meanings to different people. The proof of this statement is the great number of books on the subject of psychology, each of which deals with reality in its own terms. What a therapist offers, therefore, is the reality of his own being and his own existence, an existence broad enough to comprehend the confusion and anxiety of the patient without sharing it. The patient's assurance of help lies in the therapist's dedication to truth, the truth of his own personal being, the truth of the patient's struggle, and the truth of the body.

In *Love and Orgasm* I described the truth of the body as "an awareness of the expression, attitude, and state of the body."[77] The patient has lost this truth, for he is unaware of his tensions and limitations. He sees himself in terms of his ego image. The therapist, however, sees the patient as another human being, sitting opposite him. He can observe his expression and sense the attitude and state of his body. The therapist is in a unique position to help the patient gain this truth if he knows the truth of his own body.

On the level of body expression, the therapist reveals as much to the patient (by his physical appearance, his gestures, and the quality of his movements) as the patient does to the therapist. On this level there is no barrier of silence behind which the therapist can hide. If he ignores the truth of his own body, he will be loathe to face the truth of the patient's body.

"Countertransference" denotes the role which the therapist may come unconsciously to play and which he expects the patient to uphold. It denotes his illusions, which the patient must not shatter. It reflects his involvement with his own ego image and his denial of the truth of the body. To whatever degree this countertransference exists, it will constitute an obstacle to the patient's recovery.

It has been my thesis that emotional illness arises when image replaces reality, when projection and identification prevent an individual from being himself. These have no place in the therapeutic situation. The guarantee of truth is the patient's ability to express his negative feelings about the therapist and the latter's willingness to listen. For no therapist is a perfect human being. Perfection is not a quality of the human condition. But the therapist must be a real human being who has the courage to face the despair of the schizoid personality, the fortitude to cope with the patient's "devil," and the humility to realize that the patient's gains are the results of his own efforts. If a therapist has these qualities, his patients will imitate him, not identify with him, and through their experiences in the therapeutic relationship, achieve their identity.

14

The Ego
and the Body

BEWITCHMENT

An emotional illness is in many respects like a bewitchment. We often say of an emotionally disturbed person
that he is not himself, and the person himself may even
remark, "I don't know what has gotten into me!" The
implication behind such statements is that an emotionally
ill person is under the influence of an alien force or power
which seems to have taken possession of him.

In primitive societies, loss of self-possession is widely
regarded as a sign that a person is under a spell. The
primitive believes that all disturbances in his feeling of
well-being, including sensations of anxiety, are caused by
witchcraft or sorcery. He feels bewitched when his sense
of harmony with his body and his community is disrupted.
It is inconceivable to him that this could be due to anything but supernatural causes.

This view of illness as the result of an alien, malevolent
influence is also found in children. When my son was a
child he invariably asked about an illness, "When will it go
away?" I have heard other children use similar expressions, such as "Mummy, make it go away!" This childish
attitude toward illness is not significantly different from
that of the primitive who feels bewitched. The similarity in
all three cases (the emotionally disturbed person, the bewitched primitive, and the sick child) is shown by their
common tendency to turn to a superior figure, who is
assumed to possess the power to counter the disturbance

or malevolent influence. In this respect psychiatrist, witch doctor, and mother fulfill a common function.

If loss of self-possession can be equated with bewitchment, then any individual in whom there is a split between ego and body can be described as "bewitched." The bewitched person cannot distinguish between illusion and reality, image and body, word and deed. He is capable, therefore, of committing acts of destruction against himself and others which are incomprehensible to the rational mind. The Nazi holocaust can best be explained in terms of the "bewitchment" of the German people by Hitler. The question then is, What makes people vulnerable to the words of the demagogue?

Before we answer this question let us look at a classic case of bewitchment, as reported by R. J. W. Burrell in *Medical World News*. "I saw an old woman cast a spell on a man. 'You will die before sunset,' she said. And he did." Burrell explains that "the man believed he was going to die and he died. At autopsy no cause of death could be found."[78]

The man was receptive to the woman's curse because he believed in her occult powers. The old woman had spoken as if she could control the forces of life and death, and the man's undeveloped ego was incapable of testing the reality of her assertion. The terror she evoked in him split the unity of his personality, destroyed his feeling of identity, and made him susceptible to the bewitchment and curse. The primitive believes in the supernatural because he lacks the knowledge to explain the operation of natural forces in nature. In his helplessness he is terrified, and in his terror he is vulnerable.

The child who becomes schizoid is in the same position as the man in the above case. The hostile mother is like the old woman who placed a curse upon the man. Since the mother holds the power of life or death over her child, he is helpless and terrified in the face of her rejection. His undeveloped ego is incapable of coping with an attitude that denies him the right to the pleasure of his body and that dooms him to death in life.

The bewitchment reported by Burrell also suggests a parallel with the hypnotic process. It can be said that the man was hypnotized by the old woman. In hypnosis, the subject surrenders his ego to the hypnotist, who then takes command of the subject's body. It is well known that there are people who go into the hypnotic trance at the slightest suggestion. I have seen persons in an audience go into a trance state while merely listening to the hypnotist discuss his technique. On the other hand, an individual with a strong ego is resistant to the hypnotic attempt. The degree of suggestibility is directly proportionate to the weakness of the ego. While this weakness in children and in primitives represents a lack of ego development, in the civilized and adult state it is due to the dissociation of the ego from the body. A dissociated ego, like an undeveloped one, is incapable of testing reality objectively.

It is commonly assumed that education is the answer to the irrational in the human being. Within certain limits this is true. The primitive who lacks knowledge of the processes of life and death is vulnerable to witchcraft and sorcery. The child who cannot understand the complex forces operative in a disturbed family becomes schizoid. His emotional improvement is dependent upon this understanding, which he acquires in the course of an analytic therapy. Experience has shown, however, that education and knowledge are no certain bars to prejudice. Many very educated Germans were bewitched by Hitler's words. Intellectual fanatics are found on both sides of every issue and use similar words to justify their position. My thesis is that the ego rests upon two foundations; if either one of these is missing, it is vulnerable to bewitchment. These two foundations are: (1) its identification with the body (feeling), and (2) its identification with the mind (knowledge).

Without knowledge, the ego has no way to test reality. It depends, then, upon magic to influence natural processes. Lacking a firm grounding in the body, the ego has no feeling of reality. Its knowledge then degenerates into abstractions which are impotent to influence attitudes or behavior. Contact with the body provides the ego with an understanding of internal reality; knowledge gives it a grasp of external reality. These two realities often conflict. When they cannot be harmonized, the individual is in trouble. When they become antagonistic, a schizoid condition results. Because these two realities obey different laws, we are often confused in our understanding of life.

COMMUNITY VERSUS CAUSALITY

Reality as seen from the inside, that is, from the point of view of the body, is a continuum in which ego, body, and nature are linked by similar processes. What one thinks, how one feels, and the phenomena of nature form more or less of a unity in which an event in one realm of experience influences all others. This view of reality characterizes the primitive's and the child's attitudes to life. The relationship between these three realms of experience can be depicted by three circles intertwined with each other to form a continuum, as shown in Figure 22 below.

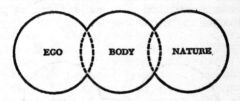

FIG. 22 The Ego-Body-Nature Continuum

This view of reality provides the primitive and the child with a total outlook. Since what happens in nature influences the body directly, the primitive looks for omens and auguries as directives to action. Conversely, he believes that he can influence nature through his bodily activities. Rain dances are believed to assure rainfall, sexual activity to promote the fertility of the fields. This inner reality, regardless of its distortions, gives the primitive and the child an immediate sense of identity based upon the feeling of the body. The primitive feels that he belongs to his family, his tribe, and nature, and the healthy child has a similar feeling of belonging. Because the continuum is an on-going whole, any disruption in the feeling of relatedness between the different realms of experience is attributed to an outside malevolent power.

The acquisition of knowledge transformed this primitive view of reality. Civilized man discarded the idea of the supernatural; he overcame the awe with which the primitive viewed the unknown and, therefore, mysterious processes of the body and nature; and he replaced the primitive belief in spirits by a faith in the mind and reason. Through its identification with the mind, the ego proclaimed its domination over the body. "I think, therefore I am" replaced the primitive's sense of identity based on "I feel, therefore I am." Finally, man became egoistic, objective, and detached, and lost the feeling of unity with nature.

Knowledge furnishes man with a view of nature and external reality in which events are related to one another by demonstrable causes. In this view of reality, the three realms of experience form discontinuous spheres which interact in direct causal relationships. Figure 23 portrays this objective, scientific view of reality.

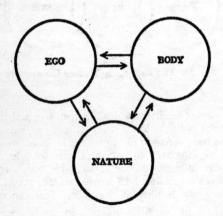

FIG. 23 The discontinuity of reality as seen by the objective mind

In the continuum of the primitive state no provision is made for the unexpected. When the unexpected occurs, it is regarded as a manifestation of the supernatural and beyond man's comprehension or control. Discontinuity, however, does allow for the unexpected experience, which becomes transmuted into knowledge through repeated observations by an objective ego. Knowledge, as opposed to magic, is dependable power, the consistent ability to act upon and control natural processes. Through his ego, man becomes the central actor in the drama of life, a maker of history. Civilized culture is a dynamic process marked by an ever-increasing knowledge and an ever-widening separation of the realms of experience.

These two views of reality may be described as community and causality. The communal view relates one realm of experience to another in terms of the all-embracing continuum. Causality discards the universal and explains relationships in terms of demonstrable actions. Each of these views has its respective advantages and disadvantages. The primitive (and the child) has a spontaneous feeling of belonging and a strong identification with the body and its pleasure function. He is, however, relatively defenseless against the vicissitudes of nature and therefore more exposed to calamity or illness. Modern man has achieved a relatively high degree of external security, but often at the expense of the feeling of harmony and unity with his body and nature.

This distinction between primitive and civilized ways of thinking and behaving is not absolute. Some knowledge of cause and effect relationships exists in primitive cultures. And some sense of relationship on the child-primitive level of continuum and unity exists in the normal individual of today. A healthy person identifies with his body and feels the closeness of his ties to nature. At the same time, on the ego level, he is aware of the operation of cause and effect relationships. His rational functioning is superimposed upon the sense of unity he experienced as a child; his ego does not negate this unity. The man grows out of the child; he does not deny the child. His ego is nourished by two springs, the subjective world of inner reality and the objective world of outer reality. He stands on two feet, one planted in each aspect of reality.

However, such individuals are the exception rather than the rule in our time. The schizoid problem has become so widespread that a more critical evaluation of the ego's role is required if we are to comprehend this disturbance. The conflict between the ego and the body, between knowledge and feeling, must be understood if the split that robs the person of his identity and destroys his pleasure in life is to be resolved.

It is not generally appreciated that the ego creates the discontinuities which it then attempts to bridge with knowledge and words. It gives rise to the categories of the "I" versus the "me," the "self" as opposed to the "other," man as subject acting upon nature as object. In this development, the body also becomes an object to the ego and is reduced to the role of an instrument of the will. The ego becomes an object of worship, a ruler instead of the counselor whose function is to mediate between inner and outer reality. Men, organizations, and even nations become concerned with their image, to the detriment of their basic functions.

The function of the ego is to test reality. However, the ego subverts this function if it begins to dictate the nature of reality instead of merely testing it. This happens when the ego denies its subservience to the body and asserts its supremacy. It is then like the hero who, after liberating the populace from one form of tyranny, becomes a dictator and subjects it to another. The ego originally functioned to protect the personality against witchcraft and sorcery. Now it beguiles the personality with words and images.

When the ego dominates the personality, the individual becomes a psychopath. The psychopath is deprived of feeling, sees himself only in terms of his image, and is wholly involved in the struggle for power. This is an extreme exaggeration of the normal tendencies of the ego, which are to develop an adequate self-image, to deny the irrational in the name of reason and logic, and to establish control over the motility of the body. In the normal person these ego functions are held in balance by the opposing force of the body and its feelings. Analytic writers speak of a system of checks and balances between the ego and the id. The id opposes the ego's image with the reality of the body, the ego's knowledge with the feelings of the body, and the ego's striving for power with the id's striving for the pleasure of the body. This system of checks and balances fails in a culture which values knowledge above feeling, power above pleasure, and the mind above the body.

As long as the ego dominates the individual, he cannot have the oceanic or transcendental experiences that make life meaningful. Since the ego recognizes only direct causes, it cannot admit the existence of forces beyond its comprehension. Thus, not until the ego bows down to a higher power (as in prayer, for instance) can an individual have a truly religious experience. Not until the ego surrenders to the body in sex can a person have an orgastic experience. And only when the ego abdicates before the majesty of nature will a person have a mystical experience. In each case, the dissolution of the ego returns the individual to the state of unity and continuum in which "moving" experiences are possible.

Falling in love is the best example of the power of enchantment inherent in the nonrational world of the body. In love, the ego surrenders its hegemony over the body, and the heart of the person is free to respond in some mysterious way to the heart of another person. The lover experiences a oneness not only with the beloved but with all of life. What rational explanation can be given for this unique experience? The lover, at least, needs none.

It is not generally appreciated that knowledge has an inhibiting effect upon spontaneity and feeling. The story is told about the centipede who became paralyzed when he tried to think about which leg to move first. Whenever one has to think about how to act, the action is stiff and awkward. The overtrained child behaves like an automaton and loses his charming naturalness of manner. There are two important areas where knowledge shows its harmful effects. In sex, the partner who performs on the basis of knowledge destroys the meaning of the act. Even if the knowledge is presumably correct, it turns the act of love into a mechanical gesture. This is the great danger of sex manuals. The other area is child raising. The mother who attempts to raise a child on the basis of what she has learned about child psychology will invariably go wrong. She will misinterpret the child's needs according to her preconceived ideas. She will fail to respond to the child's bodily expressions because these can only be understood with feeling. She will be confused when her feelings conflict with her precepts.

It has been said that a little knowledge is a dangerous thing, but all knowledge is "little" when it deals with life or personal relationships. The knowledge of the ego must be tempered with the wisdom of the body if behavior is to retain a human quality. I would rather see an ignorant woman raise a child with feeling than an educated woman raise it without feeling. Of the two ingredients in behavior, feeling is more important than knowledge. But our whole educational system is geared to knowledge and the denial of feeling. A. S. Neill, the author of *Summerhill*, wrote a charming book entitled *Hearts, Not Heads in the School*.[79] Unfortunately, hearts are not directly educable; it is the body of the child, and particularly, the child's need for pleasure in its body, that deserves more attention in the schools.

It is not my intention to attack the ego or negate the value of knowledge. My argument is that an ego dissociated from the body is weak and vulnerable, and knowledge divorced from feeling is empty and meaningless. These principles must have a direct application to education and therapy if the schizoid problem is to be overcome. An education that is to be effective in preparing a child for life must take into account his emotional as well as his mental development. It must concern itself with his body as well as with his mind, with feelings as much as with knowledge. It must provide a place in its curricula for the understanding of reality as a continuum as well as for the causal view of reality. The school should recognize that spontaneity and pleasure are as important as productivity and achievement.

THE CONCEPTUAL EMOTIONS

Causality is responsible for such emotions as guilt and shame, which lie at the core of all emotional disturbances. Guilt implies a knowledge of wrongdoing and an awareness of how one's actions affect others. It carries a connotation of blame which rests upon the assumption that a person can choose between right and wrong. This assumption, known as the doctrine of free will, stems from the belief in the power of the ego to dictate behavior. I am not prepared to argue the question of whether free will exists or not. In the treatment of emotional illness it is important to remove guilt, and this can be done by getting a patient to see that he acted in the only way possible for him to act under the circumstances of his life. His destructive activities are explained by the weakness of his ego and the presence of demonic forces beyond his control. When a patient has reclaimed his body and achieved an identity, his ego is in a position to exercise an effective control over his actions.

The healthy ego, however, does not act upon abstract principles of right and wrong. It is guided internally by the feelings of the body and externally by the environmental situation. It attempts to reconcile the one reality with the other, but since the healthy ego makes no pretense to omniscience, it accepts the possibility of conflict and failure.

Guilt destroys the integrity of relationships and distorts the behavior of a person. A normal relationship is maintained by the pleasure and satisfaction it provides. When guilt enters the relationship, pleasure and satisfaction disappear. The person who acts out of guilt resents the person toward whom he feels guilty, while the other person resents the guilty individual. These resentments, often repressed, slowly smolder into hatreds, until the relationship has completely disintegrated. The devastating effects of guilt are usually seen in relationships between parents and children or husband and wife. The parent who acts out of guilt toward a child resents the child, who in turn resents the parent and feels guilty about it. Antagonisms develop which increase the guilt on both sides. Psychiatrists' offices are full of patients who hate their parents and feel bound to them through guilt. Similarly, guilt between a husband and wife leads to ill-concealed hostilities.

Parents want to love their children, but a guilty parent seduces the child instead of loving it. The aim of seduction is to gain closeness, but its result is alienation. It is motivated by love but distorted by guilt. Eliminate the guilt, and whatever love is felt will come through honestly and directly, uncontaminated by negative feelings. Whenever negative feelings arise, they should also be expressed honestly and directly. One can cope with such negative feelings, since they are open and aboveboard.

Guilt is a conceptual emotion because it develops when a feeling is subject to a moral judgment. If the judgment is negative, the feeling becomes associated with guilt. If the judgment is positive, the feeling becomes associated with righteousness. Moral judgments arise in the ego through the incorporation of knowledge. A child is taught how to behave and he is made aware of the effect his actions will have on others. He is taught, for example, that his parents will feel hurt if he doesn't love them, that they will be upset if he doesn't respect them. However, a child cannot be taught how to feel. He will love his parents if their attitude toward him inspires this feeling and he will respect them if their behavior evokes his admiration. If his feelings are criticized, it can lead only to guilt. The child is made to feel by this teaching that he has a role in the drama of life, that he is a force for good and evil, depending on how he fulfills his role. He is made to feel responsible for his feelings. Social living would be impossible without a sense of responsibility. The problem is, therefore, how can we retain the sense of responsibility but avoid the feeling of guilt?

My answer is that a person is responsible for his actions and not his feelings. A feeling is a biological reaction of the body which is beyond the dictates of the ego. The ego's role is to perceive feeling, not to judge or to control it. What is within its control is action. A healthy person who feels angry or sexually excited is able to contain his feelings until an appropriate occasion arises for their expression. This produces responsible behavior. A healthy ego is not helpless in its relation to the body. If the expression of a feeling in word or deed would be harmful, the ego can restrain this expression through its control of the voluntary musculature without at the same time denying or repressing the feeling. Harm is thereby avoided without creating an inner conflict.

However, when an individual judges his feeling as "bad" he will suppress the feeling and condemn himself for experiencing it. His resulting action will no longer correspond to his original feeling but will reflect his guilt or self-condemnation. The suppression and eventual repression of feeling leads to a loss of self-perception which weakens the ego and undermines the individual's ability to act responsibly.

Sadness, anger, and fear (in contrast to guilt and shame) may be called perceptual emotions, since these feelings are directly perceived by the ego and are uncolored by judgment values. When a directly perceived feeling is judged by the ego as good or bad it loses its biological value and acquires a moral or conceptual value. This produces a confused situation in which self-acceptance becomes difficult if not impossible.

I am frequently asked by patients whether their feelings of sadness or anger are good or bad. How can I judge them? Feelings do not obey the rational laws of cause and effect. For this reason, they are ordinarily excluded from scientific study. They belong to the realm of community, not that of causality. Feelings are influenced by other feelings, without the necessity for action. A happy person raises the spirits of everyone around him without doing anything to produce this effect. A gloomy person is depressing even when he says nothing. Feelings are infectious; they permeate the continuum and affect all persons within their range.

When the idea of causality is applied to relationships which function in the realm of community, the result is confusion and guilt. In the communal relationship between parent and child, the child is affected by his parents' feelings far more than he is by their actions. He is distressed by his mother's unhappiness, disturbed by her anxieties, and relaxed by her contentment, quite apart from any actions she may take. Parents who do not understand this principle are confused by their children's responses. They often complain, "I cannot understand my child's reaction. I didn't do anything to him." The child reacts with his body to the body of his mother and not with his mind to her words or deeds.

The parent who thinks only in terms of causality cannot accept his negative feelings. Since he assumes a responsibility for the way he feels, he will attempt to deny or repress his negative feelings. Unaware, therefore, of his own feelings, he will punish the child for its hostile behavior without sensing the role his own repressed feelings played in this development. The idea of punishing children is alien to the primitive. In their reality, feelings are accepted and spontaneously expressed. It is permissible to strike a child in anger but not in punishment. If we moderns could learn to accept our feelings without moral judgment, our lives would be less burdened.

A distinction should be made between the concept of guilt and the feeling of guilt. In courts of law the guilt or innocence of a person is judged with respect to his actions. He may be guilty of breaking a law, for which he will be punished, but he is not guilty for feelings which do not result in actions. In daily living, however, guilt is made to attach to feelings even more than to deeds, and the result is emotional illness. I am constantly confronted with patients who labor under an enormous burden of guilt but who cannot say why they feel guilty. In depth analysis of these cases I have not been able to uncover any action which would explain the guilt. Invariably, I find that these patients have judged their feelings of hostility and sexuality as morally bad and have therefore repressed them. When these feelings are released, the guilt disappears.

On the level of the body there is neither guilt nor shame. But only the animal and the infant live fully in the body. Concepts of guilt and shame appear among primitives and children as a result of the development of the ego and the acquisition of knowledge. However, the guilt which a primitive or a normal child experiences is related to the commission of a deed, the violation of a taboo, or the infringement of an injunction. Both the primitive and the child are sufficiently identified with the body to accept its feelings as natural. Feelings of guilt and shame arise in modern man when this identification is broken.

Shame is a conceptual emotion because it arises when bodily functions are judged by social values rather than biological ones. Mental activities rate higher in the social scale than physical activities. Eating is socially acceptable, whereas defecation takes place in private. In our culture the face can be exposed with pride, while exposure of the buttocks is shameful. One may touch the nose in public, but not the genitals. These distinctions have a rational explanation. We admire those bodily activities that manifest the power of the mind or the ego. Bodily functions not subject to ego control and unavailable, therefore, for ego display are confined to the home or toilet. Broadly speaking, the functions of the upper half of the body have a higher social value than those of the lower half. Functions closer to the head are more egosyntonic than those farther removed.

Shame attaches to those functions of the body that are performed on an animal level. Man's effort to rise above the animal is clearly shown in the function of eating. If a person eats greedily, he is said to be a pig. Yet, if he accumulates money the same way, he gains prestige. We must not gulp our food as animals do or tear it with our hands. We eat with restraint to prove that we can curb our passions and are, therefore, superior to animals. But if this desire to rise above the animal level makes us ashamed of our bodily appetites, the pleasure of the body is sacrificed.

Obviously, a child must be taught how to behave among people; he has to learn table manners, forms of address, and the proper manner of dress. This training is necessary if people are to live in communities. Social living would be impossible without the concepts of guilt and shame. But when guilt and shame are extended to cover feelings as well as actions, the base for a joyful life is eroded.

The schizoid individual is ashamed of his body. This feeling of shame may be conscious, expressed in such remarks as "I don't like my body," or "My body is ugly," or it may be unconscious. When the shame of the body is unconscious, the person's behavior is often exhibitionistic. He exposes himself to deny the feeling of shame. In both cases, however, the ego's identification with the body is weakened. Feelings of shame and guilt are symptoms of this loss of identification. To restore the unity of the personality, the feeling of shame about the body must be overcome.

There are other conceptual emotions, such as conceit and vanity, which distort the personality. Conceit and vanity reflect the ego's awareness of the impression that one's physical appearance makes on others. The conceited person is preoccupied with his appearance; the vain person is obsessed by his appearance. This overemphasis upon appearance is an ego device to negate the importance of feeling.

KNOWLEDGE AND UNDERSTANDING

The dominance of the ego and its images in our culture is seen in the plethora of words that surround the modern individual. Words are used by desperate people to establish an identity, to fill the gaps between realms of experience, and to bridge the differences that separate one person from another. In their desperate search for meaning, people turn to words when their real need is for feeling. But words move us only when they are imbued with feeling.

Words become deceptive when they are divorced from feeling and substituted for actions. Parents talk of their love for children, but such statements are not the equivalent of an act of love. Love is expressed in action by a caress, a kiss, or some other form of physical contact of an affectionate nature. The verbal statement "I love you" denotes a desire for closeness and implies the promise of physical closeness. Theoretically, this statement expresses a feeling which will be translated into action at a later time. In practice, however, the statement is often used to replace the action. One of my patients described the deception she experienced through "words":

> "Words, words, words." They fill you with words, but you don't feel anything. My father called me his brown-eyed Susan, but I never could turn to him when I needed him.

In Chapter 2, it was pointed out that the schizoid individual substitutes pseudo-contacts for real feeling contact with people. Words are one form of this substitution when they replace feelings and actions.

The therapist is in a unique position to evaluate the treacherous aspect of language. Hour after hour he treats human beings who have been damaged and bewitched by words. He sees, in his schizoid patients particularly, the almost insurmountable gap between feeling and words. He sees the desperation with which patients try to bridge this gap by means of more words. He sees in this a reflection of their childhood exposure to ambivalent parents whose words belied their feelings—parents who used beguiling and seductive phrases that covered hostility, high sounding phrases that masked rejection, accusing phrases made in the name of love.

Identification with the body enables one to avoid the deception of words. It provides the ego with a foundation in reality. The treachery of language lies in its ability to bewitch the unwary. Who are the unwary? To be unwary is to be unaware; to be unaware is to be out of contact with the body. Areas of feeling are missing in the unwary person—a condition that disposes him to anxiety, beclouds his judgment, and renders him susceptible to the treachery of words.

Flattery is a simple example of the use of words to deceive. A person is vulnerable to flattery when he is out of touch with his body and impressed with his ego image. Because his ego does not rest upon the firm foundation of body feeling, it needs reassurance and support from the outside. He is, in this respect, like a deprived child desperate for his mother's approval. The flatterer is a clever seducer who senses this desperation in his victim. A person in touch with his body is less vulnerable to this seduction and more able to detect the falseness in the flatterer's manner.

The gullibility of people reflects their denial of the body. The gullible person is unwilling to confront the reality of his life. He ignores the reality of his own body and cannot, therefore, see the demagogue for what he really is. He does not observe the grimaces, the angry gestures, the hollow tones, the cold eyes, and the distorted body of the speaker. He has closed his mind's eyes to these physical signs as indications of personality, and his ego, dissociated from the body, is vulnerable to the bewitchment of words.

Knowledge can be deceptive when it is not coupled with understanding. Like the ego of which it is a part, it must be rooted in the body if it is to help an individual achieve a richer life. Where knowledge is grounded in the feelings of the body, it becomes understanding. To know, for example, that one had an incestuous attachment to his mother is to have information; to feel how this persists in the fear of aggression, in the inability to stand on one's own feet, and in pelvic tensions that decrease sexual feeling is to have understanding.

The literal meaning of the word "understanding" was emphasized by a patient during a group therapy session. She observed another patient standing on legs that were shaky and insecure, and she remarked, "You lack understanding." The ego with its knowledge is shaky and insecure if it does not stand firmly upon the reality of the body and its feelings. When the ego roots itself in the body, the individual gains insight into himself. The deéper the roots, the deeper the insight.

The bias against the body stems from its identification with man's animal nature. Civilization has been a progressive effort to raise man above the animal level. This effort has produced man's incomparable ego; it has liberated his radiant spirit; it has enlarged and expanded his consciousness. Man's body has become refined; its sensitivities have become sharper; and its versatility has increased. However, in this very process, the body as the representative of the animal has been denigrated. But the realm of the animal includes the passions and lusts, the joys and pains upon which the healthy, spontaneous motility of the organism depends. The infant is born an animal. If in the process of becoming civilized and acquiring knowledge, he rejects the animal aspect of his being, he becomes a desperate individual with a schizoid personality. Ego and body form a unity. We cannot reject one in favor of the other. We cannot be human and not animal too.

Man is primarily an animal by virtue of birth. He is fundamentally an animal by virtue of his dependence upon the animal functions of his body. In his normal relations, however, he finds it extremely difficult to bear in mind that primarily and fundamentally he is an animal. This is understandable in a culture dominated by ego values and organized on the basis of cause-and-effect relationships. Yet if he loses sight of his animal nature, he becomes an automaton. If he denies his animal nature, he becomes a disembodied spirit. If he subverts his animal nature, he becomes a demon.

The roots of a man go deep into the animal kingdom. To understand him, we must relate his present to his past, his ego to his body, and his body to his animal nature. He does not function only on the basis of causality. The community of the primitive and the unity of the animal are also part of his personality. He can deny these realities only at the peril of his sanity. If his ego is uprooted from its base in his body, he becomes a schizoid individual. He will feel ashamed of his body and guilty about its feelings. He will lose the feeling of identity.

There are indications that a new evaluation of the body as the basis of personality is emerging. We are becoming more aware of the role of chronic muscular tensions in emotional illness. A deeper understanding of animal nature has brought a new respect for the animal. We are rediscovering the importance of the body after its long dethronement and exile by the ego. But bias against the body as a symbol of the animal still exists in both high and low places.

Notes

CHAPTER 1

1. May, Rollo, *Existence: A New Dimension in Psychiatry and Psychology* New York Basic Books. 1958, p. 56.
2. Lilly, J. C., *Mental Effects of Reduction of Ordinary Levels of Physical Stimuli on Intact, Healthy Persons: A Symposium.* Psychiat. Assoc. Psychiat. Research Report No. 5, June 1956.
3. Friedan, B., *The Feminine Mystique*, New York, Norton, 1963, p. 181.

CHAPTER 2

4. Moyes, A. P., *Modern Clinical Psychiatry*, 3rd ed., Philadelphia W. B. Saunders. 1948. pp. 207–71.
5. Kretschmer, E., *Physique and Character*, New York, Humanities Press. 1951, p. 169.
6. Euglish H. B., and English, A. C., *A Comprehensive Dictionary of Psychological and Psychoanalytical Terms*, New York, Longmans, Green, 1958.
7. Polatin P., and Hock, P., "Diagnostic Evaluation of Early Schizophrenia." in *J. Nervous and Mental Disease*, March 1947 Vol. 105, 3, pp. 221–30.
8. Nannarello, J. P., "Schizoid," *J. of Nervous and Mental Disease* July-December 1953, Vol. 118, 3, p. 237–247.
9. Weiner H. "Diagnosis and Symptomatology," in *Schizophrenia* L. Bellak ed., New York, Logos Press, 1958, p. 120.
10. Fenichel O., *The Psychoanalytic Theory of Neurosis*, New York Norton, 1945, p. 445.
11. Weiner, H., *op. cit.*, pp. 119–120.
12. Rado. S., "Schizotypal Organization," in *Changing Concepts in Psychoanalytical Medicine.* S. Rado and G. E. Daniels, eds., New York, Grune & Stratton, 1956, p. 226.

13. Rado, S., *Psychoanalysis of Behavior*, New York, Grune & Stratton, 1956, pp. 270–84.
14. Sheldon, W. H., *The Varieties of Human Physique*, New York, Harper, 1950, pp. 239–40.
15. Arieti, S., *Interpretations of Schizophrenia*, New York, Robert Brunner, 1955, p. 43.
16. *Ibid.*, p. 405.

CHAPTER 3

17. Bellak, L., *Schizophrenia: A Review of the Syndrome*, New York, Logos Press, 1950, p. 24.
18. Federn, P., *Ego Psychology and the Psychoses*, New York, Basic Books, 1952, p. 175.

CHAPTER 4

19. Reich, W., *Character Analysis*, 3rd ed., New York, Orgone Institute Press, 1949, p. 481.
20. Arieti S., *Interpretation of Schizophrenia*, New York, Robert Brunner, 1955, p. 406.
21. Ortega y Gasset, "Point of View in the Arts," in *The Dehumanization of Art and Other Writings on Art and Culture*, Garden City, Doubleday, 1956, p. 103.
22. Cleckley, H., *The Mask of Sanity*, St. Louis, C. V. Mosby, 1955, pp. 423–25.
23. Kretschmer, E., *Physique and Character*, New York, Humanities Press, 1951, pp. 150–51.
24. Bleuler, E., *Dementia Praecox, or the Group of Schizophrenias*, New York, Int. Univ. Press, 1950, p. 42.
25. Wells, Grace, *How to Unsnarl Our Snarling Mechanism*, unpublished monograph, Copyright, October 1955.
26. *Op. cit.*, p. 191.
27. *Op. cit.*, p. 157.
28. *Ibid.*, p. 65.
29. *Ibid.*, p. 65.

CHAPTER 5

30. Fisher, S., and Cleveland, S. E., *Body Image and Personality*, Princeton, New Jersey, Van Nostrand, 1958, p. 238.
31. Bleuler, E., *Dementia Praecox, or The Group of Schizophrenias*, New York, Int. Univ. Press, 1950, p. 101.
32. Pankow, G., "Dynamic Structurization in Schizophrenia," in *Psychotherapy of the Psychoses*, A. Burton, ed., New York, Basic Books, 1961, p. 168.

CHAPTER 6

33. Reich, W., *Character Analysis*, 3rd ed., New York, Orgone Institute Press, 1949, pp. 218–45.

CHAPTER 7

34. Silverberg, W. V., "The Schizoid Maneuver," *Journal of the Biology and Pathology of Interpersonal Relations*, November, 1947, Vol. 10, No. 4, p. 383.

CHAPTER 8

35. Reich, W., *Character Analysis*, 3rd ed., New York, Orgone Institute Press, 1949, p. 472.
36. Rado, S., "Schizotypal Organization," in *Changing Concepts of Psychoanalytical Medicine*, Rado, S., and Daniels, G. E., eds., New York, Grune & Stratton, 1956, p. 226.

CHAPTER 9

37. Federn, P., *Ego Psychology and the Psychoses*, New York, Basic Books, 1952, p. 177.
38. Christiansen, B., *Thus Speaks the Body*, monograph, Institute for Social Research, Oslo, Norway, 1963, p. 47.
39. Reich, W., *Character Analysis*, 3rd ed., New York, Orgone Institute Press, 1949, p. 406, ftn.
40. Malmo, Robert B., Shagas, Charles, and Smith, Arthur A., "Responsiveness in Chronic Schizophrenia," *J. Person.*, June, 1951, 19:4, p. 368.
41. Hoskins, R. G., *The Biology of Schizophrenia*, New York, Norton, 1946, pp. 132–33.
42. Ribble, Margaret, *The Rights of Infants*, New York, Columbia Univ. Press, 1948, pp. 18, 28.
43. Shattock, F. M., "The Somatic Manifestations of Schizophrenia," *J. Ment. Sci.*, January, 1950, 96:402, pp. 32–142.
44. Abramson, D. I., *Vascular Responses in the Extremities of Man in Health and Disease*, Chicago, Univ. of Chicago Press, 1944, pp. 28–29.
45. Hoskins, R. G., *op. cit.*, pp. 135–36.
46. Gottlieb, J. S., Frohman, C. E., Beckett, P. C. S., Tourney, G., and Sent, R., "Production of the High Energy Bonds in Schizophrenia," *A.M.A. Arch. Gen. Psychiat.*, September, 1959, I, pp. 243–49.
47. Hoskins, *op. cit.*, p. 159.
48. Federn, P., *op. cit.*, p. 46.
49. Lowen, A., *Physical Dynamics of Character Structure*, New York, Grune & Stratton, 1958, p. 106.

CHAPTER 10

50. Freud, S., *Psychoanalytic Notes upon an Autobiographical Account of a Case of Paranoia*, Collected Papers, Vol. 3, London, Hogarth Press, 1953, p. 459.
51. Shallop, George, *The Year of the Gorilla*, Chicago, Univ. of Chicago Press, 1964, pp. 195–96.
52. Neumann, Erich, *The Origin and History of Consciousness*, New York, The Bollingen Foundation, Pantheon Books, 1954, pp. 105–09.

CHAPTER 11

53. Lowen, A., *Physical Dynamics of Character Structure*, New York, Grune & Stratton, 1958, p. 30.
54. Reich, W., *Character Analysis*, 3rd ed., New York, Orgone Institute Press, 1949, pp. 370–90.
55. Clausen, J. A., and Kohn, M. L., "Social Relations and Schizophrenia; A Research Report and a Perspective," in *The Etiology of Schizophrenia*, Don D. Jackson, ed., New York, Basic Books, 1960, p. 305.
56. Hill, L. B., *Psychotherapeutic Intervention in Schizophrenia*, Chicago, Univ. of Chicago Press, 1955, p. 112.
57. *Ibid.*, p. 118.
58. *Ibid.*
59. Boatman, M. J., and Szurek, S. A., "A Clinical Study of Childhood Schizophrenia," in Jackson, D. D., ed., *op. cit.*, p. 413.
60. Hill, *op. cit.*, p. 116.
61. Lowen, A., *op. cit.*, p. 344.
62. Sontag., L. W., "The Possible Relationship of Prenatal Environment to Schizophrenia," in Jackson, D. D. (ed.), *op. cit.*, p. 185.
63. Montagu, M. F. A., *Prenatal Influences*, Springfield, Ill., Charles C. Thomas, 1962, p. 215.
64. Honig, A. A., "Anxiety in Schizophrenia," *Psychoanalysis and The Psychoanalytic Rev.*, 1960, 47:3, p. 89.
65. Lidz, T., and Fleck, S. "Schizophrenia, Human Integration and the Role of the Family," in Jackson, D. D. (ed.), *op. cit.*, p. 332.
66. *Ibid.*, p. 341.
67. Hill, *op. cit.*, p. 121.
68. Lidz and Fleck, *op. cit.*, p. 335.

CHAPTER 13

69. Pankow, G., "Dynamic Structurization in Schizophrenia," in *Psychotherapy of the Psychoses*, A. Burton, ed., New York, Basic Books, 1961, p. 159.

70. Reich, W., *Character Analysis*, 3rd ed., New York, Orgone Institute Press, 1949, p. 147.
71. Spitz, R. A., *No and Yes*, New York, Int. Univ. Press, 1957, p. 119.
72. *Ibid.*, p. 129.
73. *Ibid.*, p. 104.
74. Selye, Hans, *The Stress of Life*, New York, McGraw-Hill, 1956, p. 9.
75. Rosen, J., *Direct Analysis*, New York, Grune & Stratton, 1953, p. 8.
76. Honig, A. A., "Anxiety in Schizophrenia," *Psychoanalysis and The Psychoanalytic Rev.*, 1960, 47:30, p. 32.
77. Lowen, A., *Love and Orgasm*, New York, Macmillan, 1965, p. 295.

CHAPTER 14

78. Burrell, R. J. W., "The Possible Bearing of Voodoo on Myocardial Infarction," *Medical World News*, December 8, 1961, p. 33.
79. Neill, A. S., *Hearts, Not Heads in the School*, London, Herbert Jenkins, 1945.